The DevelopMentor Series

Don Box, Editor

Addison-Wesley has joined forces with DevelopMentor, a premiere developer resources company, to produce a series of technical books written by developers for developers. DevelopMentor boasts a prestigious technical staff that includes some of the world's best-known computer science professionals.

*"Works in **The DevelopMentor Series** are practical and informative sources on the tools and techniques for applying component-based technologies to real-world, large-scale distributed systems."*
—Don Box

Titles in the Series:

Don Box, *Essential COM*, 0-201-63446-5

Don Box, Aaron Skonnard, and John Lam, *Essential XML: Beyond Markup*, 0-201-70914-7

Keith Brown, *Programming Windows Security*, 0-201-60442-6

Matthew Curland, *Advanced Visual Basic 6: Power Techniques for Everyday Programs*, 0-201-70712-8

Doug Dunn, *Java™ Rules*, 0-201-70916-3

Tim Ewald, *Transactional COM+L: Building Scalable Applications*, 0-201-61594-0

Jon Flanders, *ASP Internals*, 0-201-61618-1

Richard Grimes, *Developing Applications with Visual Studio.NET*, 0-201-70852-3

Martin Gudgin, *Essential IDL: Interface Design for COM*, 0-201-61595-9

Stuart Halloway, *Component Development for the Java™ Platform*, 0-201-75306-5

Joe Hummel, Ted Pattison, Justin Gehtland, Doug Turnure, and Brian A. Randell, *Effective Visual Basic: How to Improve Your VB/COM+ Applications*, 0-201-70476-5

Stanley B. Lippman, *C# Primer: A Practical Approach*, 0-201-72955-5

Everett N. McKay and Mike Woodring, *Debugging Windows Programs: Strategies, Tools, and Techniques for Visual C++ Programmers*, 0-201-70238-X

Aaron Skonnard and Martin Gudgin, *Essential XML Quick Reference: A Programmer's Reference to XML, XPath, XSLT, XML Schema, SOAP, and More*, 0-201-74095-8

Watch for future titles in The DevelopMentor Series.

C# Primer
A Practical Approach

Stanley B. Lippman

✦ Addison-Wesley

Boston • San Francisco • New York • Toronto • Montreal
London • Munich • Paris • Madrid
Capetown • Sydney • Tokyo • Singapore • Mexico City

The publisher offers discounts on this book when ordered in quantity for special sales. For more information, please contact:

Pearson Education Corporate Sales Division
201 W. 103rd Street
Indianapolis, IN 46290
(800) 428-5331
corpsales@pearsoned.com

Visit AW on the Web: www.aw.com/cseng/

Library of Congress Cataloging-in-Publication Data

Lippman, Stanley B.
    C# Primer : a practical approach / Stanley B. Lippman.
        p. cm.—(DevelopMentor series)
    Includes bibliographical references and index.
    ISBN 0-201-72955-5
    1. C# (Computer program language) I. Title. II. Series.

    QA76.73.C154 L575 2001
    005.13'3—dc21   2002053659

Text printed on recycled and acid-free paper.

ISBN 0201729555

2 3 4 5 6 7   CRS   05 04 03 02

2nd Printing   February 2002

Beth

Imagine, we have shared a lifetime together.
Thanks for understanding
and being there

Danny

Hey, dude. Wassup?
So this is what I've been doing—
I know you thought I just didn't want to help with your algebra ...

Anna

Whoa. It's really done. I know, finally.
A slew of IOU's:
Legoland, the batting cage, Hogwarts ...

And in loving memory of
George and Ray Lippman

Contents

Preface

C# is a new language invented at Microsoft and introduced with Visual Studio.NET. More than a million lines of C# code already have gone into the implementation of the .NET class framework. This book covers the C# language and its use in programming the .NET class framework, illustrating application domains such as ASP.NET and XML.

My general strategy in presenting the material is to introduce a programming task and then walk through one or two implementations, introducing language features or aspects of the class framework as they prove useful. The goal is to demonstrate how to use the language and class framework to solve problems rather than simply to list language features and the class framework API.

Learning C# is a two-step process: learning the details of the C# language and then becoming familiar with the .NET class framework. This two-step process is reflected in the organization of this text.

In the first step we walk through the language—both its mechanisms, such as class and interface inheritance and delegates, and its underlying concepts, such as its unified type system, reference versus value types, *boxing*, and so on. This step is covered in the first four chapters.

The second step is to become familiar with the .NET class framework, in particular with Windows and Web programming and the support for XML. This is the focus of the second half of the book.

Working your way through the text should jump-start your C# programming skills. In addition, you'll become familiar with a good swatch of the .NET class framework. All the program code is available for download at my company's Web site www.objectwrite.com.

Mail can be sent to me directly at slippman@objectwrite.com.

Organization of the Book

The book is organized into eight relatively long chapters. The first four chapters focus on the C# language, looking at the built-in language features, the class mechanism, class inheritance, and interface inheritance. The second four chapters explore the various library domains supported within the .NET class framework.

Chapter 1 covers the basic language, as well as some of the fundamental classes provided within the class framework. The discussion is driven by the design of a small program. Concepts such as namespaces, exception handling, and the unified type system are introduced.

Chapter 2 covers the fundamentals of building classes. We look at access permission, distinguish between `const` and `readonly` members, and cover specialized methods such as indexers and properties. We walk through the different strategies of member initialization, as well as the rules for operator overloading and conversion operators. We look at the `delegate` type, which serves as a kind of universal pointer to a function.

Chapters 3 and 4 cover, in turn, class and interface inheritance. Class inheritance allows us to define a family of specialized types that override a generic interface, such as an abstract `WebRequest` base class and a protocol-specific `HttpWebRequest` subtype. Interface inheritance, on the other hand, allows us to provide a common service or shared attribute for otherwise unrelated types. For example, the `IDisposable` interface frees resources. Classes holding database connections or window handles are both likely to implement `IDisposable`, although they are otherwise unrelated.

Chapter 5 provides a wide-ranging tour of the .NET class library. We look at input and output, including file and directory manipulation, regular expressions, sockets and thread programming, the `WebRequest` and `WebResponse` class hierarchies, a brief introduction to ADO.NET and establishing database connections, and the use of XML.

Chapters 6 and 7 cover, in turn, drag-and-drop Windows Forms and Web Forms development. Chapter 7 focuses on ASP.NET, and the Web page life cycle. Both chapters provide lots of examples of using the prebuilt controls and attaching event handlers for user interaction.

The final chapter provides a programmer's introduction to the .NET Common Language Runtime. It focuses on assemblies, type reflection, and attributes, and concludes with a brief look at the underlying intermediate language that is the compilation target of all .NET languages.

Written for Programmers

The book does not assume that you know C++, Visual Basic, or Java. But it does assume that you have programmed in some language. So, for example, I don't assume that you know the exact syntax of the C# `foreach` loop statement, but I do assume that you know what a loop is. Although I will illustrate how to invoke a function in C#, I assume you know what I mean when I say we "invoke a function." This text does not require previous knowledge of object-oriented programming or of the earlier versions of ASP and ADO.

Some people—some very bright people—argue that under .NET, the programming language is secondary to the underlying Common Language Runtime (CLR) upon which the languages float like the continents on tectonic plates. I don't agree. Language is how we express ourselves, and the choice of one's language affects the design of our programs. The underlying assumption of this book is that C# is the preferred language for .NET programming.

The book is organized into eight relatively long chapters. The first set of four chapters focuses on the C# language, looking at the built-in language features, the class mechanism, class inheritance, and interface inheritance. The second set of four chapters explores the various library domains supported within the .NET class framework, such as regular expressions, threading, sockets, Windows Forms, ASP.NET, and the Common Language Runtime.

Lexical Conventions

Type names, objects, and keywords are set off in Courier font, as in `int`, a predefined language type; `Console`, a class defined in the framework; `maxCount`, an object defined either as a data member or as a local object within a function; and `foreach`, one of the predefined loop statements. Function names are followed by an empty pair of parentheses, as in `WriteLine()`. The first introduction of a concept, such as *garbage collection* or *data encapsulation*, is highlighted in italics. These conventions are intended to make the text more readable.

Acknowledgments

This book is the result of many invisible hands helping to keep its author on course. My most heartfelt thanks go to my wife, Beth, and my two children, Daniel and Anna. I have accumulated all too many IOUs in deferring this or that family outing in order to get this book done. Thank you all for being (mostly) patient and understanding and not too often asking if I was done yet.

I need to thank Caro Segal and Shimon Cohen of you-niversity.com, who provided me with a generous gift of time and encouragement. May the force be with you. I also owe a serious round of thanks to Eric Gunnerson, Peter Drayton, and Don Box, all of whom at one time or another fulfilled the role of white knight on horseback.

I would like to deeply thank Elena Driskill. Twice. First for the gift of those lovely drawings in Chapter 6. Second for her kind permission to reproduce them.

Deborah Lafferty has been my editor since the first edition of my *C++ Primer* back in 1986. She has been a constant source of good sense and understanding, and I deeply appreciate her encouragement (and prodding) in seeing this project through.

A pair of special production thanks go to Stephanie Hiebert and Steve Hall. Stephanie is the supreme copy editor of my nearly two decades of publishing. She made this a better book. Steve hoisted me back onto my typesetting saddle after having been thrown by wildly pernicious Framemaker problems. A tip of my virtual hat to the both of you.

The following reviewers offered numerous thoughtful comments and suggestions in reviewing various drafts of this manuscript: Indira Dhingra (special thanks for providing a final sanity check of the manuscript), Cay Horstmann, Eugene Kain, Jeff Kwak, Michael Lierheimer, Drew Nathanson, Clovis Tondo, and Damien Watkins.

Portions of this manuscript have been tried out in courses and talks held across the globe: Sydney, Amsterdam, Munich, Tel Aviv, Orlando, San Francisco, and San Jose. Thanks to everyone who provided feedback.

Resources

The richest documentation that you will be returning to time and again is the Visual Studio.NET documentation. The .NET framework reference is essential to doing any sort of C#/.NET programming.

Another rich source of information about .NET consists of the featured articles and columns in the *MSDN Magazine*. I'm always impressed by what I find in each issue. You can find it online at http://msdn.microsoft.com/msdnmag.

The DOTNET mailing list sponsored by DevelopMentor is a rich source of information. You can subscribe to it at http://discuss.develop.com.

Anything Jeffrey Richter, Don Box, Aaron Skonnard, or Jeff Prosise writes about .NET (or XML in Aaron's case) should be considered essential reading. Currently, most of their writing has appeared only as articles in *MSDN Magazine*.

Here is the collection of books that I have referenced or found helpful:

- *Active Server Pages+,* by Richard Anderson, Alex Homer, Rob Howard, and Dave Sussman, Wrox Press, Birmingham, England, 2000.
- *C# Essentials,* by Ben Albahari, Peter Drayton, and Brad Merrill, O'Reilly, Cambridge, MA, 2001.
- *C# Programming,* by Burton Harvey, Simon Robinson, Julian Templeman, and Karli Watson, Wrox Press, Birmingham, England, 2000.
- *Essential XML: Beyond Markup,* by Don Box, Aaron Skonnard, and John Lam, Addison-Wesley, Boston, 2000.
- *Microsoft C# Language Specifications,* Microsoft Press, Redmond, WA, 2001.
- *A Programmer's Introduction to C#,* 2nd Edition, by Eric Gunnerson, Apress, Berkeley, CA, 2001.

Stanley Lippman
Los Angeles
November 18, 2001
www.objectwrite.com

Chapter 1

Hello, C#

My daughter has cycled through a number of musical instruments. With each one she is anxious to begin playing the classics—no, not Schubert or Schoenberg, but the Backstreet Boys and Britney Spears. Her various teachers, keen to keep her interest while grounding her in the fundamentals, have tended to indulge her. In a sense this chapter attempts the same precarious balance in presenting C#. In this context the classics are represented by Web Forms and Type Inheritance. The fundamentals are the seemingly mundane predefined language elements and mechanisms, such as scoping rules, arithmetic types, and namespaces. My approach is to introduce the language elements as they become necessary to implement a small first program. For those more traditionally minded, the chapter ends with a summary listing of the predefined language elements.

C# supports both integral and floating-point numeric types, as well as a Boolean type, a Unicode character type, and a high-precision decimal type. These are referred to as the *simple types*. Associated with these types is a set of operators, including addition (+), subtraction (–), equality (==), and inequality (!=). C# provides a predefined set of statements as well, such as the conditional `if` and `switch` statements and the looping `for`, `while`, and `foreach` statements. All of these, as well as the namespace and exception-handling mechanisms, are covered in this chapter.

1.1   A First C# Program
The traditional first program in a new language is one that prints *Hello, World!* on the user's console. In C# this program is implemented as follows:

```
// our first C# program
using System;
class Hello
{
    public static void Main()
    {
        Console.WriteLine( "Hello, World!" );
    }
}
```

When compiled and executed, this code generates the canonical

```
Hello, World!
```

Our program consists of four elements: (1) a comment, introduced by the double slash (//), (2) a `using` directive, (3) a class definition, and (4) a class *member function* (alternatively called a class *method*) named `Main()`.

A C# program begins execution in the class member function `Main()`. This is called the program entry point. `Main()` must be defined as `static`. In our example, we declare it as both `public` and `static`.

`public` identifies the level of access granted to `Main()`. A member of a class declared as `public` can be accessed from anywhere within the program. A class member is generally either a member function, performing a particular operation associated with the behavior of the class, or a data member, containing a value associated with the state of the class. Typically, class member functions are declared as `public` and data members are declared as `private`. (We'll look at member access levels again as we begin designing classes.)

Generally, the member functions of a class support the behavior associated with the class. For example, `WriteLine()` is a public member function of the `Console` class. `WriteLine()` prints its output to the user's console, followed by a new-line character. The `Console` class provides a `Write()` function as well. `Write()` prints its output to the terminal, but without inserting a new-line character. Typically, we use `Write()` when we wish the user to respond to a query posted to the console, and `WriteLine()` when we are simply displaying information. We'll see a relevant example shortly.

As C# programmers, our primary activity is the design and implementation of classes. What are classes? Usually they represent the entities in our application domain. For example, if we are developing a library checkout system, we're likely to need classes such as `Book`, `Borrower`, and `DueDate` (an aspect of time).

Where do classes come from? Mostly from programmers like us, of course. Sometimes, it's our job to implement them. This book is designed primarily to make you an expert in doing just that. Sometimes the classes are already available. For example, the .NET System framework provides a `DateTime` class that is suitable for use in representing our `DueDate` abstraction. One of the challenges of becoming an expert C# programmer—and not a trivial one at that—is becoming familiar with the more than 1,000 classes defined within the .NET framework. I can't cover all of them here in this text, but we'll look at quite a number of classes, including support for regular expressions, threads, sockets, XML and Web programming, database support, and the new way of building a Windows application.

A challenging problem is how to logically organize a thousand or more classes so that users (that's us) can locate and make sense of them (and keep the names from colliding with one another). Physically, we can organize them within directories. For example, all the classes supporting Active Server Pages (ASP) can be stored in an `ASP.NET` directory under a root `System.NET` directory. This makes the organization reasonably clear to someone poking around the file directory structure.

What about within programs? As it turns out, there is an analogous organizing mechanism within C# itself. Rather than defining a physical directory, we identify a *namespace*. The most inclusive namespace for the .NET framework is called `System`. The `Console` class, for example, is defined within the `System` namespace.

Groups of classes that support a common abstraction are given their own namespace defined within the `System` namespace. For example, an `Xml` namespace is defined within the `System` namespace. (We say that the `Xml` namespace is nested within the `System` namespace.) Several namespaces in turn are nested within the `Xml` namespace. There is a `Serialization` namespace, for example, as well as `XPath`, `Xsl`, and `Schema` namespaces. These separate namespaces within the enclosing `Xml` namespace are factored out to encapsulate and localize shared functionality within the general scope of XML. This arrangement makes it easier to identify the support, for example, that .NET provides for the World Wide Web Consortium (W3C) XPath recommendation. Other namespaces nested within the System namespace include IO, containing file and directory classes, Collections, Threading, Web, and so on.

In a directory structure, we indicate the relationship of contained and containing directories with the backslash (\), at least under Windows—for example,

```
System\Xml\XPath
```

With namespaces, similar contained and containing relationships are indicated by the *scope operator* (.) in place of a backslash—for example,

```
System.Xml.XPath
```

In both cases we know that XPath is contained within Xml, which is contained within System.

Whenever we refer to a name in a C# program, the compiler must resolve that name to an actual declaration of something somewhere within our program. For example, when we write

```
Console.WriteLine( "Hello, World" );
```

the compiler must somehow discover that Console is a class name and that WriteLine() is a member function within the Console class—that is, within the scope of the Console class definition. Because we have defined only the Hello class in our file, without our help the compiler is unable to resolve what the name Console refers to. Whenever the compiler cannot resolve what a name refers to, it generates a compile-time error, which stops our program from building:

```
C:\C#Programs\hello\hello.cs(7):
```

```
    The type or namespace name 'Console' does
    not exist in the class or namespace
```

The using directive in our program,

```
    using System;
```

directs the compiler to look in the `System` namespace for any names that it cannot immediately resolve within the file it is processing—in this case, the file that contains the definition of our `Hello` class and its `Main()` member function.

Alternatively, we can explicitly tell the compiler where to look:

```
System.Console.WriteLine( "Hello, World" );
```

Some people—actually some very smart and otherwise quite decent people—believe that explicit listing of the *fully qualified name*—that is, the one that identifies the full set of namespaces in which a class is contained—is always preferable to a `using` directive. They point out that the fully qualified name clearly identifies where the class is found, and they believe that is useful information (even if it is repeated 14 times within 20 adjacent lines). I don't share that belief (and I really don't like all that typing). In my text—and this is one of the reasons we authors write books—the fully qualified name of a class is *never* used,[1] except to disambiguate the use of a type name (see Section 1.2 for an illustration of situations in which this is necessary).

Earlier I wrote that classes come mostly either from other programmers or from libraries provided by the development system. Where else do they come from? The C# language itself. C# predefines several heavily used data types, such as integers, single- and double-precision floating-point types, and strings. Each has an associated *type specifier* that identifies the type within C#: `int` represents the primitive integer type; `float`, the primitive single-precision type; `double`, the double-precision type; and `string`, the string type. (See Tables 1.2 and 1.3 in Section 1.18.2 for a list of the predefined numeric types.)

For example, an alternative implementation of our simple program defines a `string` object initialized with the `"Hello, World!"` string literal:

```
public static void Main() {
    string greeting = "Hello, World!"
    Console.WriteLine( greeting );
}
```

---

1. The Visual Studio wizards, such as Windows Forms and Web Forms, generate fully qualified names. However, because the names are machine generated, this does not really qualify as a counterexample.

`string` is a C# *keyword* — that is, a word reserved by the C# language and invested with special meaning. `public`, `static`, and `void` are also keywords in the language. `greeting` is referred to as an *identifier.* It provides a name for an object of type `string`. Identifiers in C# must begin with either an underscore (_) or an alphabet character. The names are case sensitive, so `greeting`, `Greeting`, and `Greeting1` each represent a unique identifier.

A common flash point among programmers centers on whether compound names should be separated by an underscore, as in `xml_text_reader`, or by capitalization of the first letter of each internal word, as in `xmlTextReader`. By convention, identifiers that represent class names usually begin with a capital letter, as in `XmlTextReader`.

Within a unit of program visibility referred to as a *declaration space*, or *scope*, identifiers must be unique. At *local scope*—that is, within a function body, such as within our definition of `Main()`—this is not a problem because we generally control the entire definition of any object within our function. As the extent of the scope widens—that is, as the number of programmers or organizations involved increases—the problem of unique identifiers becomes more difficult. This is where namespaces come into the picture.

1.2 Namespaces

Namespaces are a mechanism for controlling the visibility of names within a program. They are intended to help facilitate the combination of program components from various sources by minimizing name conflicts between identifiers. Before we look at the namespace mechanism, let's make sure we understand the problem that namespaces were invented to solve.

Names not placed within a namespace are automatically placed in a single unnamed global declaration space. These names are visible throughout the program, regardless of whether they occur in the same or a separate program file. Each name in the global declaration space must be unique for the program to build. Global names make it difficult to incorporate independent components into our programs.

For example, imagine that you develop a two-dimensional (2D) graphics component and name one of your global classes `Point`. You use your component, and everything works fine. You tell some of your friends about it, and they naturally want to use it as well.

Meanwhile, I develop a three-dimensional (3D) graphics component and in turn name one of my global classes `Point`. I use my component, and everything also works fine. I show it to some of my friends. They're excited about it and wish to use it as well. So far, everyone is happy—well, at least about our coding projects.

Now imagine that we have a friend in common. She's implementing a 2D/3D game engine and would like use our two components, both of which come highly praised. Unfortunately, when she includes both within her application, the two independent uses of the `Point` identifier result in a compile-time error. Her game engine fails to build. Because she does not own either component, there is no easy fix for the two components to work together.

Namespaces provide a general solution to the problem of global name collision. A namespace is given a name within which the classes and other types we define are encapsulated.[2] That is, the names placed within a namespace are not visible within the general program. We say that a namespace represents an independent declaration space or scope.

Let's help our mutual friend by providing separate namespaces for our two `Point` class instances:

```
namespace DisneyAnimation_2DGraphics
{
  public class Point { ... }

  // ...
}

namespace DreamWorksAnimation_3DGraphics
{
  public class Point { ... }

  // ...
}
```

---

2. Only namespaces and types can be declared within the global namespace. A function can be declared only as a class member. A data object can be either a class member or a local object within a function, such as our declaration of `greeting`.

The keyword `namespace` introduces the namespace definition. Following that is a name that uniquely identifies the namespace. (If we reuse the name of an existing namespace, the compiler assumes that we wish to add additional declarations to the existing namespace. The fact that the two uses of the namespace name do not collide allows us to spread the namespace declaration across files.)

The contents of each namespace are placed within a pair of curly braces. Our two `Point` classes are no longer visible to the general program; each is nested within its respective namespace. We say that each is a member of its respective namespace.

The `using` directive in this case is too much of a solution. If our friend opens both namespaces to the program—

```
using DisneyAnimation_2DGraphics;
using DreamWorksAnimation_3DGraphics;
```

the unqualified use of the `Point` identifier still results in a compile-time error. To unambiguously reference this or that `Point` class, we must use the fully qualified name—for example,

```
DreamWorksAnimation_3DGraphics.Point origin;
```

If we read it from right to left, this declares `origin` to be an instance of class `Point` defined within the `DreamWorksAnimation_3DGraphics` namespace.

The ambiguity within and between namespaces is handled differently depending on the perceived amount of control we have over the name conflict. In the simplest case, two uses of the same name occur within a single declaration space, triggering an immediate compile-time error when the second use of the name is encountered. The assumption is that the affected programmer has the ability to modify or rename identifiers within the working declaration space where the name conflict occurs.

It becomes less clear what should happen when the conflict occurs across namespaces. In one case, we open two independent namespaces, each of which contains a use of the same name, such as the two instances of `Point`. If we make explicit use of the multiply-defined `Point` identifier, an error is generated;

the compiler does not try to prioritize one use over the other or otherwise disambiguate the reference. One solution, as we did earlier, is to qualify each identifier's access. Alternatively, we can define an alias for either one or all of the multiply-defined instances. We do this with a variant of the `using` directive, as follows:

```
namespace GameApp
{
    // exposes the two instances of Point
    using DisneyAnimation_2DGraphics;
    using DreamWorksAnimation_3DGraphics;

    // OK: create unique identifiers for each instance
    using Point2D = DisneyAnimation_2DGraphics.Point;
    using Point3D = DreamWorksAnimation_3DGraphics.Point;

    class myClass
    {
        Point2D thisPoint;
        Point3D thatPoint;
    }
}
```

The alias is valid only within the current declaration space. That is, it doesn't introduce an additional permanent type name associated with the class. If we try to use it across namespaces, such as in the following:

```
namespace GameEngine
{
    class App
    {
        // error: not recognized
        private GameApp.Point2D origin;
    }
}
```

the compiler wants nothing to do with it, generating the following message:

```
The type or namespace name 'Point2D' does not exist in the class
or namespace 'GameApp'
```

When we use a namespace, we generally have no idea how many names are defined within it. It would be very disruptive if each time we added an additional namespace, we had to hold our breath while we recompiled to see if anything would now break. The language, therefore, minimizes the disruption that opening a namespace can cause to our program.

If two or more instances of an identifier, such as our two `Point` classes, are made visible within our working declaration space through multiple `using` directives, an error is triggered only with an unqualified use of the identifier. If we don't access the identifier, the ambiguity remains latent, and neither an error nor a warning is issued.

If an identifier is made visible through a `using` directive that duplicates an identifier we have defined, our identifier has precedence. An unqualified use of the identifier always resolves to our defined instance. In effect, our instance hides the visibility of the identifier contained within the namespace. The program continues to work exactly as it had prior to our use of the additional namespace.

What sorts of names should be given to our namespaces? Generic names such as `Drawing`, `Data`, `Math`, and so on are unlikely to be unique. A recommended strategy is to add a prefix that identifies your organization or project group.

Namespaces are a necessary element of component development. As we've seen, they facilitate the reuse of our software in other program environments. For less ambitious programs, however, such as the `Hello` program at the start of this chapter, the use of a namespace is unnecessary.

1.3 Alternative Forms of the `Main()` Function

In the rest of this chapter we'll explore the predefined elements of the C# language as we implement a small program called `WordCount`. `WordCount` opens a user-specified text file and calculates the number of occurrences of each word within the file. The results are sorted in dictionary order and written to an output file. In addition, the program supports two command-line options:

1. `-t` causes the program to turn a trace facility on; by default, tracing is off.

2. `-s` causes the program to calculate and report the amount of time it takes to read the file, process the words, and write the results; by default, timings are not reported.

Our first task in `Main()` is to access the command-line arguments passed in to our program, if any. We do that by using a second form of `Main()`, which defines a one-parameter function signature:

```
class EntryPoint
{
      public static void Main( string [] args ) {}
}
```

`args` is defined as an array of string elements. `args` is automatically filled with any command-line arguments specified by the user. For example, if the user invoked our program as follows:

```
WordCount -s mytext.txt
```

the first element of `args` would hold `-s` and the second element would hold `mytext.txt`.

In addition, either form of the `Main()` function may optionally return a value of type `int`:

```
public static int Main() {}
public static int Main( string [] args ) {}
```

The return value is treated as the exit status of the program. By convention, a return value of `0` indicates that the program completed successfully. A nonzero value indicates some form of program failure. A `void` return type, paradoxically, internally results in a return status of `0`; that is, the execution environment always interprets the program as having succeeded. In the next section we look at how we can use this second form of `Main()`.

1.4   Making a Statement

The first thing we need to do is determine if the user specified any arguments. We do this by asking `args` the number of elements it contains.[3] For our program I decided that if the user doesn't supply the necessary command-line arguments, the program shuts down. (As an exercise, you may wish to reimplement the pro-

---

3. In C#, we cannot write `if (!args.Length)` to test whether the array is empty because 0 is not interpreted as meaning false.

gram to allow the user to interactively enter the desired options. The program is certainly friendlier that way.)

In my implementation, if `args` is empty, the program prints an explanation of the correct way to invoke `WordCount`, then exits using a `return` statement. (The `return` statement causes the function in which it occurs to terminate—that is, to return to the location from which it was invoked.)

```
public static void Main( string [] args )
{
  if ( args.Length == 0 )
  {
      display_usage();
      return;
  }
}
```

`Length` is a *property* of an array. It holds a count of the number of elements currently stored in the array. The test of `Length` is placed within the conditional test of the C# `if` statement. If the test evaluates to true, the statement immediately following the test is executed; otherwise it is ignored. If multiple statements need be executed, as in our example, they must be enclosed in curly braces (the text within the braces is called a *statement block*).

A common mistake that beginners make is to forget the statement block when they wish to execute two or more statements: [4]

```
// this is an incorrect usage of the if statement
if ( args.Length == 0 )
    display_usage();
    return;
```

The indentation of `return` reflects the programmer's intention. It does not, however, reflect the program's behavior. Without the statement block, only the function is conditionally executed; the `return` statement is executed whether or not the array is empty.

The `return` statement can also return a value. This value becomes the return value of the function—for example,

---

4. These code fragments all occur within the `Main()` function. To save space, I do not show the enclosing declaration of `Main()`.

```
public static int Main( string [] args )
{

    if ( args.Length == 0 )
    {
        display_usage();
        return -1;     // indicate failure
    }
}
```

The rule is that the value following the `return` statement must be compatible with the return type of the function. *Compatible* can mean one of two things. In the simplest case, the value being returned is the same type as that indicated as the return type of the function. The value `-1`, for example, is of type `int`. The second meaning of compatible requires that an implicit conversion exist between the actual return value and the function's return type.

The `if-else` statement allows us to select between alternative statements on the basis of the truth of a particular condition. The `else` clause represents a statement or statement block to be executed if the tested condition evaluates to false. For example, if we chose not to immediately return on discovering an empty `args` array, we could provide the following `if-else` statement instead:

```
if ( args.Length == 0 )
    display_usage();
else { /* do everything else here ... */ }
```

To access the individual command-line options, we'll use a `foreach` loop to iterate across the array, reading each element in turn. For example, the following loop statement prints each option to the user's console:

```
foreach ( string option in args )
    Console.WriteLine( option );
```

`option` is a read-only `string` object. It is visible only within the body of the `foreach` statement. Within each iteration of the loop, `option` is set to refer to the next element of the `args` array.

For our program, we'll compare each `string` element against the set of supported options. If the string does not match any of the options, we'll check to see if the string represents a text file. Whenever we are testing a series of mutually exclusive conditions, as we are in this case, we typically combine the tests into a chain of `if-else-if` statements—for example,

```
bool traceOn = false,
bool spyOn   = false;

foreach ( string option in args )
{
    if ( option.Equals( "-t" ))
        traceOn = true;
    else
    if ( option.Equals( "-s" ))
        spyOn = true;
    else
    if ( option.Equals( "-h" ))
        { display_usage(); return; }
    else
        check_valid_file_type( option );
}
```

The `bool` keyword represents a Boolean data type that can be assigned the literal values `true` or `false`. In our example, `traceOn` and `spyOn` represent two Boolean objects initialized to `false`.

`Equals()` is a nonstatic member function of `string`. *Nonstatic* member functions (also referred to as *instance* member functions) are invoked through an instance of the class for which the function is a member—in this case, the `string` object `option`. The expression

```
option.Equals( "-t" )
```

instructs the compiler to invoke the `string` instance method `Equals()` to compare the string stored within `option` with the string literal `"-t"`. If the two are equal, `Equals()` returns `true`; otherwise, it returns `false`.

If the mutually exclusive conditions are constant expressions[5], we can turn our chain of `if-else-if` statements into the somewhat more readable `switch` statement—for example,

---

5. A constant expression represents a value that can be evaluated at compile time. Typically, this means that the expression cannot contain a data object. (The value associated with a data object cannot be evaluated until runtime execution of our program.)

```
foreach ( string option in args )
    switch ( option )
    {
      case "-t":
            traceOn = true;
            break;

      case "-s":
            spyOn = true;
            break;

      case "-h":
                display_usage();
                return;

            default:
                check_valid_file_type( option );
                break;
    }
```

The `switch` statement can be used to test a value of an integral type, a `char` type, an enumeration, or a `string` type. The `switch` keyword is followed by the expression enclosed in parentheses. A series of `case` labels follows the `switch` keyword, each specifying a constant expression. Each `case` label must specify a unique value.

The result of the expression is compared against each `case` label in turn. If there is a match, the statements following the `case` label are executed. If there is no match and the `default` label is present, the statements associated with the `default` label are executed. If there is no match and no `default` label, nothing happens. (There can be only one `default` label.)

Each nonempty `case` label must be followed either by a `break` statement or by another terminating statement, such as a `return` or a `throw`; otherwise a compiler error results. (`throw` passes program control out of the current function into the runtime exception-handling mechanism. We look at exception handling in Section 1.17. The `break` statement passes program control to the statement following the terminating curly brace of the `switch` statement.)

An empty `case` label is the one exception to this rule. It does need not have a `break` statement. We do this typically when multiple values require the same action—for example,

```
switch ( next_char )
{
  case 'a':
  case 'A':
      acnt++;
      break;

  // to illustrate an alternative syntax ...
  case 'e':  case 'E': ecnt++; break;

  // ... the other vowels

  case '\0': return; // OK

  default: non_vowel_cnt++; break;
}
```

If we wish to execute the body of two case labels—the first of which is not empty—we must use a special goto statement that targets either an explicit case label or the default label:

```
switch ( text_word )
{
  case "C#":
  case "c#":

      csharp_cnt++;
      goto default;

  case "C++":
  case "c++":

      cplus_cnt++;
      goto default;

  case "Java":
  case "java":  goto case "C#";

  default:

      word_cnt++;
      break;
}
```

1.5 Opening a Text File for Reading and Writing

Let's assume that the user has entered a valid text file name for the program. Our job, then, is to open the file, read its contents, and after processing those contents, write the results out to a second file, which we need to create. Let's see how we do this.

Support for file input/output is encapsulated in the `System.IO` namespace. So the first thing we need to do is open the namespace to the compiler:

```
using System.IO;
```

Text files are read and written through the `StreamReader` and `Stream-Writer` classes. There are various ways to create instances of these classes— for example,

```
string file_name = @"C:\fictions\gnome.txt";

StreamReader freader = File.OpenText( file_name );
StreamWriter fwriter =
        File.CreateText( @"C:\fictions\gnome.diag" );
```

`OpenText()` returns a `StreamReader` instance bound to the file repre-sented by the string argument passed to it. In this case, it opens a text file stored in the `fictions` directory on drive `C:`. The file represented by the string must exist, and the user must have permission to open it; otherwise `Open-Text()` throws an exception.

The @ character identifies the string literal that follows it as a *verbatim* string literal. In an ordinary string literal, a backslash is treated as a special character. For example, when we write `"\n"`, the backslash and the n are interpreted as an escape sequence representing the new-line character. When we wish an actual backslash to appear in a string literal, we must *escape* it by preceding it with an additional backslash—for example,

```
string fname1 = "C:\\programs\\primer\\basic\\hello.cs";
```

Within a verbatim string literal, special characters, such as the backslash, do not need to be escaped.

A second difference between an ordinary and a verbatim string literal is the ability of a verbatim string literal to span multiple lines. The nested white space within the multiple-line verbatim string literal, such as a new-line character or a tab, is preserved. This allows for the storage and generation of formatted text blocks. For example, here is how we might implement `display_usage()`:

```
public void display_usage()
{
    string usage =
        @"usage:  WordCount [-s] [-t] [-h] textfile.txt
            where [] indicates an optional argument
                -s prints a series of performance measurements
                -t prints a trace of the program
                -h prints this message";
      Console.WriteLine( usage );
}
```

`CreateText()` returns a `StreamWriter` instance. The file represented by the string argument passed to it, if it exists, is overwritten. To append to a file's existing text rather than overwriting it, we use `AppendText()`.

`StreamReader` provides a collection of read methods allowing us to read a single character, a block of characters, or, using `ReadLine()`, a line of text. (There is also a `Peek()` method to read one character ahead without extracting it from the file.) `StreamWriter` provides instances of both `WriteLine()` and `Write()`.

The following code segment reads each line of a text file in turn, assigning it to the string object `text_line`. `StreamReader` signals that it has reached the end of the file by returning a `null` string. The additional parentheses around the assignment of `text_line` are necessary because of what is called *operator precedence* (see Section 1.18.4 for a discussion):

```
string text_line;
while (( text_line = freader.ReadLine() ) != null )
{
    // write to output file
    fwriter.WriteLine( text_line );
}

// must explicitly close the readers
freader.Close();
fwriter.Close();
```

When we finish with the readers, we must invoke their associated `Close()` member functions in order to free the resources associated with them.[6]

1.6 Formatting Output

In addition to writing each line of text to the output file, let's extend the previous code segment to also write the line to the user's console. When writing to the console, however, we want to indicate the line number and the length of the line in characters, as well as the text itself. In addition, we don't want to echo an empty line. Here is the relevant portion of the modified code segment:

```
string text_line;
int    line_cnt = 1;

while (( text_line = freader.ReadLine() ) != null )
{
    // don't format empty lines
    if ( text_line.Length == 0 )
    {
        Console.WriteLine();
        continue;
    }


    // format output to console:
    // 1 (42): Master Timothy Gnome left home one morning

    Console.WriteLine( "{0} ({2}): {1}",
            line_cnt++, text_line, text_line.Length );
}
```

The `continue` statement allows us to short-circuit the remaining portion of the loop body. In this example, if the text line is empty, we write a new line to the console and then prematurely terminate this iteration of the loop body before writing the line of text to the console. The `continue` statement causes the next iteration of the loop to begin immediately.

---

6. If you are a C++ programmer, you are accustomed to having the class destructor automatically free resources. In a garbage-collected environment, however, destructors cannot provide that service. Rather we provide a `Dispose()` function, which is discussed in Section 4.8. `Close()` is an alternative form of `Dispose()`.

Similarly, a `break` statement causes the premature termination of the loop itself. For example, we might use the `break` statement when we are iterating through a collection searching for a value. Once the value has been found, we break out of the loop. An extreme example of this idiom is the nonterminating condition test for a loop—for example,

```
while ( true )
{
    // process until scme condition occurs

    // ...

    if ( condition_occurs )
        break;
}
```

The assumption is that an internal state of the class or application causes the eventual invocation of the `break` statement, terminating the loop.

`WriteLine()` allows us to pass positional arguments within a literal string—for example,

```
Console.WriteLine( "Hello, {0}! Welcome to C#", user_name );
```

When a number enclosed within curly braces, such as `{0}`, is encountered within the literal string, it's treated as a placeholder for the associated value in the list of parameters that follows the literal string. `0` represents the first value, `1` represents the second value, and so on. The numbered placeholders can appear in any order, as in this example:

```
Console.WriteLine( "{0} ({2}): {1}",
    line_cnt++, text_line, text_line.Length );
```

The same position value can appear multiple times as well—for example,

```
Console.WriteLine( "Hello, {0}! Everyone, please welcome {0}",
                user_name );
```

We can control numeric formatting of the built-in types through the addition of format characters. For example, a `c` interprets the value in terms of the local currency, `F` indicates a fixed-point format, `E` indicates an exponential (scientific)

format, and G leaves it to the system to pick the most compact form. Each may be followed by a value specifying the precision. For example, given the object

```
double d = 10850.795;
```

the `WriteLine()` statement

```
Console.WriteLine("{0} : {0:C2} : {0:F4} : {0:E2} : {0:G}",d);
```

generates the following output:

```
10850.795 : $10,850.80 : 10850.7950 : 1.09E+004 : 10850.795
```

We can use X or x to output the value n hexadecimal. X results in the upper-case values A through F; x results in lowercase a through f.

1.7 The `string` Type

Once we have read a line of text, we need to separate it into the individual words. The simplest method of doing that is to use the `Split()` method of `string`—for example,

```
string text_line;
string [] text_words;

while (( text_line = freader.ReadLine() ) != null )
{
        text_words = text_line.Split( null );
        // ...
}
```

`Split()` returns an array of string elements separated by a set of charac-ters indicated by the user. If `Split()` is passed `null`, as it is in our example, it separates the elements of the original string using white space, such as a blank character or a tab. For example, the string

```
A beautiful fiery bird, he tells her, magical but untamed.
```

is split into an array of 10 string elements. Three of them, however—bird, her, and untamed—retain their adjacent punctuation. One strategy for removing the punctuation is to provide `Split()` with an explicit array of characters with which to separate the string—for example,

```
char [] separators = {
    ' ', '\n', '\t', // white space
    '.', '\"', ';', ',', '?', '!', ')', '(', '<', '>', '[', ']'
};

text_words = text_line.Split( separators );
```

A character literal is placed within single quotation marks. The new-line and tab characters are represented by the two-character escape sequences \n and \t. Each sequence represents a single character. The double quotation mark must also be escaped (\") in order for it to be interpreted as a character rather than the beginning of a string literal.

The string type supports the subscript operator ([])—but for read operations only. Indexing begins at zero, and extends to Length-1 characters—for example,

```
for ( int ix = 0; ix < text_line.Length; ++ix )
    if ( text_line[ ix ] == '.' ) // OK: read access
       text_line[ ix ]  = '_';         // error: no write access
```

The string type does not support use of the foreach loop to iterate across the characters of its string.[7] The reason is the somewhat nonintuitive immutable aspect of a string object. Before we make sense of what that means, let me briefly make sense of the C# for loop statement.

The for loop consists of the following elements:

```
for ( init-statement; condition; expression )
    statement
```

init-statement is executed once before the loop is executed. In our example, ix is initialized to 0 before the loop begins executing.

condition serves as the loop control. It is evaluated before each iteration of the loop. For as many iterations as condition evaluates as true, statement is executed. statement can be either a single statement or a statement block. If condition evaluates to false on the first iteration, statement is

---

7. The technical reason is that the String class does not implement the IEnumerable interface. See Chapter 4 for a full discussion of the IEnumerable interface and interfaces in general.

never executed. In our example, `condition` tests whether `ix` is less than `text_line.Length`—that is, the count of the number of characters contained within the string. While `ix` continues to index a valid character element, the loop continues to execute.

`expression` is evaluated after each iteration of the loop. It is typically used to modify the objects initialized within `init-statement` and tested in `condition`. If `condition` evaluates to false on the first iteration, `expression` is never executed. In our example, `ix` is incremented following each loop iteration.

The reason we cannot write to the individual characters of the underlying string literal is that string objects are treated as immutable. Whenever it seems as if we are changing the value of a string object, what has actually happened is that a new string object containing those changes has been created.

For example, to do an accurate occurrence count of words within a text file, we'll want to recognize *A* and *a* as being the same word. One way to do that is to change each string to all lowercase before we store it:

```
while (( text_line = freader.ReadLine() ) != null )
{
        // oops: this doesn't work as we intended ...
        text_line.ToLower();
        text_words = text_line.Split( null );

        // ...
}
```

`ToLower()` correctly changes all uppercase characters within `text_line` to lowercase. (There is a `ToUpper()` member function as well.) The problem is that the new representation is stored in a new string object that is returned by the call to `ToLower()`. Because we do not assign the new string object to anything, it's just tossed away. `text_line` is not changed, and it won't change unless we reassign the return value to it, as shown here:

```
text_line = text_line.ToLower();
```

To minimize the number of new `string` objects generated when we are making multiple modifications to a `string`, we use the `StringBuilder` class. See Section 4.9 for an illustration.

1.8 Local Objects

A data object must be defined within either a function or a class; it cannot exist as an independent object either in a namespace or within the global declaration space. Objects that are defined within a function are called *local objects*. A local object comes into existence when its enclosing function begins execution. It ceases to exist when the function terminates. A local object is not provided with a default initial value.

Before a local object can be read or written to, the compiler must feel sure that the object has been assigned to. The simplest way to reassure the compiler is to initialize the local object when we define it—for example,

```
int ival = 1024;
```

This statement defines an integer object `ival` and initializes it with a value of `1024`.

iSometimes it doesn't make sense to initialize an object because we don't use it until after it has the target of an assignment. For example, consider `user_name` in the following program fragment:

```
static int Main()
{
        string      user_name;
        int         num_tries = 0;
        const int max_tries = 4;

        while ( num_tries < max_tries )
        {
                // generate user message ...

                ++num_tries;
                user_name = Console.ReadLine();

                // test whether entry is valid
        }

        // compiler error here!
        // use of unassigned local variable user_name
        Console.WriteLine( "Hello, {0}", user_name );
        return 0;
}
```

By inspection, we see that `user_name` must always be assigned to within the `while` loop. We know this because `num_tries` is initialized to `0`. The `while` loop is always evaluated at least once. The compiler, however, flags the use of `user_name` in the `WriteLine()` statement as the illegal use of an unassigned local object. What do we know that it doesn't?

Each time we access a local object, the compiler checks that the object has been *definitely assigned* to. It determines this through *static* flow analysis—that is, an analysis of what it can know at compile time. The compiler cannot know the value of a nonconstant object, such as `num_tries`, even if its value is painfully obvious to us. The static flow analysis carried out by the compiler assumes that a nonconstant object can potentially hold any value. Under that assumption, the `while` loop is not guaranteed to execute. Therefore, `user_name` is not guaranteed to be assigned to, and the compiler thus issues the error message.

The compiler can fully evaluate only constant expressions, such as the literal values `7` or `'c'`, and nonwritable constant objects, such as `max_tries`. Nonconstant objects and expressions can be definitely known only during runtime. This is why the compile treats all nonconstants as potentially holding any value. It's the most conservative and therefore safest approach.

One fix to our program, of course, is to provide a throwaway initial value:

```
string user_name = null;
```

An alternative solution is to use the fourth of our available loop statements in C#, the do-while loop statement. The do-while loop always executes its loop body at least once before evaluating a condition. If we rewrite our program to use the do-while loop, even the compiler can recognize that `user_name` is guaranteed to be assigned because its assignment is independent of the value of the nonconstant `num_tries`:

```
do
{
    // generate user message ...
    ++num_tries;
    user_name = Console.ReadLine();
    // test whether entry is valid
} while ( num_tries < max_tries );
```

Local objects are treated differently from other objects in that their use is order dependent. A local object cannot be used until it has been declared. There is also a subtle extension to the rule: Once a name has been used within a local scope, it is an error to change the meaning of that use by introducing a new declaration of that name. Let's look at an example.

```
public class EntryPoint
{
    private string str = "hello, field";
    public void local_member()
    {
            // OK: refers to the private member
            /* 1 */ str = "set locally";

            // error: This declaration changes the
            // meaning of the previous statement
            /* 2 */ string str = "hello, local";
    }
}
```

At 1, the assignment of str is resolved to the private member of the class EntryPoint. At 2, however, the meaning of str changes with the declaration of a local str string object. C# does not allow this sort of change in the meaning of a local identifier. The occurrence of the local definition of str triggers a compile-time error.

What if we move the declaration of the private str data member so that it occurs after the definition of the method? That doesn't change the behavior. The entire class definition is inspected before the body of each member function is evaluated. The name and type of each class member are recorded within the class declaration space for subsequent lookup. The order of member declarations is not significant—for example,

```
public class EntryPoint
{
    // OK: let's place this first
    public void local_member()
    {
            // still refers to the private class member
            /* 1 */ str = "set locally";
```

```
                // still the same error
                /* 2 */ string str = "hello, local";
        }

        // position of member does not change its visibility
        private string str = "hello, field";
}
```

Each local block maintains a declaration space. Names declared within the local block are not visible outside of it. The names are visible, however, within any blocks nested with the containing block—for example,

```
public void example()
{   // top-level local declaration space
    int ival = 1024;

    {
        // ival is still in scope here

        double ival = 3.14; // error: reuse of name
        string str = "hello";
    }

    {
        // ival still in scope, str is not!
        double str = 3.14159; // OK
    }

    // what would happen if we defined a str object here?
}
```

If we added a local declaration of str at the end of the function, what would happen? Because this declaration occurs at the top-level local declaration space, the two previous legal uses of the identifier str within the local nested blocks would be invalidated, and a compiler error would be generated.

Why is there such strict enforcement against multiple uses of a name within the local declaration spaces? In part because local declaration spaces are considered under the ownership of the programmer. That is, the enforcement of a strict policy is not considered onerous for the programmer. She can quickly go in and locally modify one or another of the dentifiers. And by doing so, the thinking goes, she is improving the clarity of her program.

1.9 Value and Reference Types

Types in C# are categorized as either value or reference types. The behavior when copying or modifying objects of these types is very different.

An object of a *value* type stores its associated data directly within itself. Any changes to that data does not affect any other object. For example, the predefined arithmetic types, such as `int` and `double`, are value types. When we write

```
double pi = 3.14159;
```

the value `3.14159` is directly stored within `pi`.

When we initialize or assign one value type with another, the data contained in the one is copied to the second. The two objects remain independent.

For example, when we write

```
double shortPi = pi;
```

although both `pi` and `shortPi` now hold the same value, the values are distinct instances contained in independent objects. We call this a *deep copy*.

If we change the value stored by `shortPi`,

```
shortPi = 3.14;
```

the value of `pi` remains unchanged. Although this may seem obvious—perhaps to the point of tedium—this is not what happens when we copy and modify reference types!

A *reference* type is separated into two parts:

1. A named *handle* that we manipulate directly.

2. An unnamed object of the handle's type stored on what is referred to as the *managed heap*. This object must be created with the `new` expression (see Section 1.11 for a discussion).

The handle either holds the address of an object on the heap or is set to `null`; that is, it currently refers to no object. When we initialize or assign one reference type to another, only the address stored within the handle is copied.

Both instances of the reference type now refer to the same object on the heap. Modifications made to the object through either instance are visible to both. We call this a *shallow copy*.

All class definitions are treated as reference types. For example, when we write

```
class Point
{
    float x, y;
    // ...
}

Point origin;
```

`Point` is a reference type, and `origin` reflects reference behavior.

A `struct` definition allows us to introduce a user-defined value type. For example, when we write

```
struct Point
{
    float x, y;
    // ...
}

Point origin;
```

`Point` is now a value type, and `origin` reflects value behavior. In terms of performance, a value type is generally more efficient, at least for small, heavily used objects. We look at this topic in more detail in Section 2.19.

The predefined C# array is a reference type. The discussion of the array in the next section should clarify reference type behavior.

1.10 The C# Array

The built-in array in C# is a fixed-size container holding elements of a single type. When we declare an array object, however, the actual size of the array is *not* part of its declaration. In fact, providing an explicit size generates a compile-time error—for example,

```
string []      text; // OK
string [ 10 ] text; // error
```

We declare a multidimensional array by marking each additional dimension with a comma, as follows:

```
string [,]     two_dimensions;
string [,,]    three_dimensions;
string [,,,]   four_dimensions;
```

When we write

```
string [] messages;
```

`messages` represents a handle to an array object of string elements, but it is not itself the array object. By default, `messages` is set to `null`. Before we can store elements within the array, we have to create the array object using the `new` expression. This is where we indicate the size of the array:

```
messages = new string[ 4 ];
```

`messages` now refers to an array of four string elements, accessed through index 0 for the first element, 1 for the second, and so on:

```
messages[ 0 ] = "Hi. Please enter your name: ";
messages[ 1 ] = "Oops. Invalid name. Please try again: ";
// ...
messages[ 3 ] = "Well, that's enough. Bailing out!";
```

An attempt to access an undefined element, such as the following indexing of an undefined fifth element for our `messages` array:

```
messages[ 4 ] = "Well, OK: one more try";;
```

results in a runtime exception being thrown rather than a compile-time error:

```
Exception occurred: System.IndexOutOfRangeException:
    An exception of type
    System.IndexOutOfRangeException was thrown.
```

1.11   The `new` Expression

We use the `new` expression to allocate either a single object:

```
Hello myProg = new Hello(); // () are necessary
```

or an array of objects:

```
messages = new string[ 4 ];
```

on the program's managed heap.

The name of a type follows the keyword `new`, which is followed by either a pair of parentheses (to indicate a single object) or a pair of brackets (to indicate an array object). We look at the allocation of a single reference object in Section 2.7 in the discussion of class constructors. For the rest of this section, we focus on the allocation of an array.

Unless we specify an initial value for each array element, each element of the array object is initialized to its default value. (The default value for numeric types is 0. For reference types, the default value is `null`.) To provide initial values for an array, we specify a comma-separated list of constant expressions within curly braces following the array dimension:

```
string[] m_message = new string[4]
{
    "Hi. Please enter your name: ",
    "Oops. Invalid name. Please try again: ",
    "Hmm. Wrong again! Is there a problem? Please retry: ",
    "Well, that's enough. Bailing out!",
};

int [] seq = new int[8]{ 1,1,2,3,5,8,13,21 };
```

The number of initial values must match the dimension length exactly. Too many or too few is flagged as an error:

```
int [] ia1;

ia1 = new int[128] { 1, 1 };   // error: too few
ia1 = new int[3]{ 1,1,2,3 };   // error: too many
```

We can leave the size of the dimension empty when providing an initialization list. The dimension is then calculated based on the number of actual values:

```
ia1 = new int[]{ 1,1,2,3,5,8 }; // OK: 6 elements
```

A shorthand notation for declaring local array objects allows us to leave out the explicit call to the `new` expression—for example,

```
string[] m_message =
{
    "Hi. Please enter your name: ',
    "Oops. Invalid name. Please try again: ",
```

```
      "Hmm. Wrong again! Is there a problem? Please retry: ",
      "Well, that's enough. Bailing out!",
};

int [] seq = { 1,1,2,3,5,8,13,21 };
```

Although `string` is a reference type, we don't allocate strings using the `new` expression. Rather, we initialize them using value type syntax—for example,

```
// a string object initialized to literal Pooh
string winnie = "Pooh";
```

1.12   Garbage Collection

We do not explicitly delete objects allocated through the `new` expression. Rather, these objects are cleaned up by garbage collection in the runtime environment. The garbage collection algorithm recognizes when an object on the managed heap is no longer referenced. That object is marked as available for collection.

When we allocate a reference type on the managed heap, such as the following array object:

```
int [] fib =
    new int[6]{ 1,1,2,3,5,8 };
```

the heap object is recognized as having an active reference. In this example, the array object is referred to by `fib`.

Now let's initialize a second array handle with the object referred to by `fib`:

```
int [] notfib = fib;
```

The result is a shallow copy. Rather than `notfib` addressing a separate array object with its own copy of the six integer elements, `notfib` refers to the array object addressed by `fib`.

If we modify an element of the array through `notfib`, as in

```
notfib [ 0 ] = 0;
```

that change is also visible through `fib`. If this sort of indirect modification (sometimes called *aliasing*) is not acceptable, we must program a deep copy:

```
// allocate a separate array object
notfib = new int [6];
```

```
// copy the elements of fib into notfib
// beginning at element 0 of notfib
fib.CopyTo( notfib, 0 );
```

`notfib` no longer addresses the same array object referred to by `fib`. If we now modify an element of the array through `notfib`, the array referred to by `fib` is unaffected. This is the semantic difference between a shallow copy and a deep copy.

If we now reassign `fib` to also address a new array object—for example, one that contains the first 12 values of the *Fibonacci sequence*:

```
fib = new int[12]{ 1,1,2,3,5,8,13,21,34,55,89,144 };
```

the array object previously referred to by `fib` no longer has an active reference. It may now be marked for deletion—when and if the garbage collector becomes active.

1.13   Dynamic Arrays: The `ArrayList` Collection Class

As the lines of text are read from the file, I prefer to store them rather than process them immediately. A string array would be the container of choice to do this, but the C# array is a fixed-size container. The required size varies with each text file that is opened, so the C# array is too inflexible.

The `System.Collections` namespace provides an `ArrayList` container class that grows dynamically as we either insert or delete elements. For example, here is our earlier read loop revised to add elements to the container:

```
using System.Collections;
private void readFile()
{
    ArrayList m_text = new ArrayList();
    string     text_line;

    while (( text_line = m_reader.ReadLine() ) != null )
    {
            if ( text_line.Length == 0 )
                   continue;

            // insert the line at the back of the container
            m_text.Add( text_line );
    }
```

```
        // let's see how many we actually added ...
        Console.WriteLine( "We inserted {0} lines", text.Count );
    }
```

The simplest and most efficient way to insert a single element is to use the `Add()` function. It inserts the new element at the back of the list:

```
text.Add( text_line );
```

`Count` returns the number of elements held in the `ArrayList` object:

```
Console.WriteLine( "We inserted {0} lines", text.Count );
```

Just as we do for all reference types, we create an `ArrayList` object on the managed heap using the `new` expression:

```
ArrayList text = new ArrayList();
```

The elements of an `ArrayList` are stored in a chunk of contiguous memory. When that memory becomes full, a larger chunk of contiguous memory has to be allocated (usually twice the size) and the existing elements are copied into this new chunk. We call this chunk the *capacity* of the `ArrayList` object.

The capacity of an `ArrayList` represents the total number of elements that can be added before a new memory chunk needs to be allocated. The count of an `ArrayList` represents the number of elements currently stored within the `ArrayList` object. By default, an empty `ArrayList` object begins life with a capacity of 16 elements.

To override the default capacity, we pass in an alternative capacity when we create the `ArrayList` object—for example,

```
ArrayList text = new ArrayList( newCapacity );
```

where `newCapacity` represents a reasoned integer value. `Capacity` returns the current capacity of the `ArrayList` object:

```
Console.WriteLine( "Count {0} Capacity {1}",
                   text.Count, text.Capacity );
```

Once we've completed our element insertion, we can trim the capacity of the `ArrayList` to the actual element count using the `TrimToSize()` method:

```
text.TrimToSize();
```

Trimming an `ArrayList` object does not restrict our ability to insert additional elements. If we do, however, we once again increase the capacity.

1.14   The Unified Type System

When we define an object, we must specify its type. The type determines the kind of values the object can hold and the permissible range of those values. For example, `byte` is an unsigned integral type with a size of 8 bits. The definition

```
byte b;
```

declares that b can hold integral values, but that those values must be within the range of 0 to 255. If we attempt to assign b a floating-point value:

```
b = 3.14159;   // compile-time error
```

a string value:

```
b = "no way"; // compile-time error
```

or an integer value outside its range:

```
b = 1024;      // compile-time error
```

each of those assignments is flagged as a type error by the compiler. This is true of the C# array type as well. So why is an `ArrayList` container able to hold objects of any type?

The reason is the *unified type system*. C# predefines a reference type named `object`. Every reference and value type—both those predefined by the language and those introduced by programmers like us—is a kind of `object`. This means that any type we work with can be assigned to an instance of type `object`. For example, given

```
object o;
```

each of the following assignments is legal:

```
o = 10;
o = "hello, object";
o = 3.14159;
```

```
o = new int[ 24 ];
o = new WordCount();
o = false;
```

We can assign any type to an `ArrayList` container because its elements are declared to be of type `object`.

`object` provides a fistful of public member functions. The most frequently used method is `ToString()`, which returns a string representation of the actual type—for example,

```
Console.WriteLine( o.ToString() );
```

1.14.1   Shadow Boxing

Although it may not be immediately apparent, there is something very strange about assigning an `object` type with an object of type `int`. The reason is that `object` is a reference type, while `int` is a value type.

In case you don't remember, a reference type consists of two parts: the named handle that we manipulate in our program, and an unnamed object allocated on the managed heap by the `new` expression. When we initialize or assign one reference type with another, the two handles now refer to the same unnamed object on the heap. This is the shallow copy that was introduced earlier.

A value type is not represented as a handle/object pair. Rather the declared object directly contains its data. A value type is not allocated on the managed heap. It is neither reference-counted nor garbage-collected. Rather its lifetime is equivalent to the extent of its containing environment. A local object's lifetime is the length of time that the function in which it is defined is executing. A class member's lifetime is equal to the lifetime of the class object to which it belongs.

The strangeness of assigning a value type to an `object` instance should seem a bit clearer now. The `object` instance is a reference type. It represents a handle/object pair. A value type just holds its value and is not stored on the heap. How can the handle of the object instance refer to a value type?

Through an *implicit* conversion process called *boxing*, the compiler allocates a heap address to assign to the `object` instance. When we assign a literal value or an object of a value type to an `object` instance, the following steps take place: (1) an `object` box is allocated on the heap to hold the value, (2) the value is copied into the box, and (3) the object instance is assigned the heap address of the box.

1.14.2 Unboxing Leaves Us Downcast

There is not much we can do with an `object` except invoke one of its public member functions. We cannot access any of the methods or properties of the original type. For example, when we assign a `string` object to an `object`:

```
string s = "cat";
object o = s;

// error: string property Length is not available
//        through the object instance ...
if ( o.Length != 3 )
```

all knowledge of its original type is unavailable to the compiler. If we wish to make use of the `Length` property, we must first return the `object` back to a `string`. However, an `object` is not automatically converted to another type:

```
// error: no implicit conversion of an object type
//        to any other type ...

string str = o;
```

A conversion is carried out automatically only if it can be guaranteed to be safe. For the compiler to determine that, it must know both the source and the target types. With an `object` instance, all type information is absent—at least for the compiler. (The type and environment information, however, is available both to the runtime environment and to us, the programmers, during program execution. We look at accessing that information in Chapter 8.)

For any conversion for which the compiler cannot guarantee safety, the user is required to do an explicit type cast—for example,

```
string str = ( string ) o;
```

The explicit cast directs the compiler to perform the type conversion even though a compile-time analysis suggests that it is potentially unsafe. What if the programmer is wrong? Does this mean we have a hard bug to dig out?

Actually, no.

The full type information is available to the runtime environment, and if it turns out that o really does not represent a `string` object, the type mismatch is recognized and a runtime exception is thrown. So if the programmer is incorrect with an explicit cast, we have a bug, but because of the automatic runtime check, not one that is difficult to track down.

Two operators can help us determine the correctness of our cast: `is` and `as`. We use the `is` operator to ask if a reference type is actually a particular type—for example,

```
string str;

if ( o is string )
    str = ( string ) c;
```

The `is` operator is evaluated at runtime and returns `true` if the actual object is of the particular type. This does not relieve us of the need for the explicit cast, however. The compiler does not evaluate our program's logic.

Alternatively, we can use the `as` operator to perform the cast at runtime if the actual object is of the particular type that interests us—for example,

```
string str = o as string;
```

If o is not of the appropriate type, the conversion is not applied and `str` is set to `null`. To discover whether the downcast has been carried out, we test the target of the conversion:

```
if ( str != null )
    // OK: o does reference a string ...
```

In converting an `object` instance to a particular reference type, the only work required is setting the handle to the `object`'s heap address. Converting an `object` instance to a particular value type requires a bit more work because an object of a value type directly contains its data.

This additional work in converting a reference type back to a value type is called *unboxing*. The data copied into the previously generated box is copied back into the object of the target value type. The reference count of the associated box on the managed heap is decremented by 1.

C# PRIMER

1.15 Jagged Arrays

Now that we've stored each line of text within an `ArrayList` container, we next want to iterate across the elements, separating each line into an array of the separate words. We'll need to store these arrays because they become fodder for the function implementing the word count. But this storage proves something of a problem—or at least a puzzle. Problem or puzzle, *jagged arrays* provide a solution.

If we are only reading the elements of the container, the `foreach` loop is the preferred iteration method. It spares us the explicit cast of the `object` element to an object of its actual type. Any other element assignment requires the cast:

```
for( int ix = 0; ix < text.Count; ++ix ){
    string str = ( string )text[ ix ];
    // ...
}

// read-only access ...
foreach ( string str in text ){ ... }
```

Splitting one line of text into an array of its individual words is simple:

```
string [] words = str.Split( null );
```

The next part is also simple, but it is sometimes initially confusing. What we want to do is store the collection of these arrays themselves in an array. That is, we want an array of arrays.

The outer array represents the actual text. The array at the first index represents the first line, at the second index the second line, and so on. An ordinary multidimensional array cannot support what we want because it requires that both dimensions be fixed.

In our case, the first dimension is fixed—it's the number of lines in the text file—but the second dimension varies with the number of words contained within each line of text. This is the situation a jagged array addresses. Each of its array elements can be an individual dimension. The syntax is an empty bracket pair for each dimension. For example, our array of arrays is two-dimensional, so its declaration looks like this:

```
string [][] sentences;
```

We initialize the array in two steps. In the first step we allocate the first dimension. This is the number of lines stored in the `ArrayList` object:

```
sentences = new string[ text.Count ][];
```

This statement says that `sentences` is an array of size `text.Count` that holds one-dimensional arrays of `string` elements. That is exactly what we want.

Next we need to individually initialize each of these elements with the actual string array. We'll do this by iterating across the `ArrayList` and assigning the resulting `Split()` of each of its strings:

```
string str;
for( int ix = 0; ix < text.Count; ++ix )
{
    str = ( string )text[ ix ];
    sentences[ ix ] = str.Split( null );
}
```

The individual string arrays are accessed through the first dimension. For example, to print out both the number of elements in the individual string arrays and the elements themselves, we could write the following:

```
// returns length of first dimension ...
int dim1_length = sentences.GetLength( 0 );
Console.WriteLine( "There are {0} arrays stored in sentences",
                        dim1_length );

for( int ix = 0; ix < dim1_length; ++ix )
{
    Console.WriteLine( "There are {0} words in array {1}",
                        sentences[ ix ].Length, ix+1 );

    foreach ( string s in sentences[ ix ])
            Console.Write( "{0} ", s );

    Console.WriteLine();
}
```

All the C# array types have access to the public members of the `Array` class defined in the `System` namespace. `GetLength()`, illustrated here, is one such member. The majority of the member functions, however, such as `Sort()`, `Reverse()`, and `BinarySearch()`, support arrays of only one dimension.

1.16 The `Hashtable` Container

The `System.Collections` namespace provides a `Hashtable` container. A `Hashtable` represents a key/value pair in which the key is used for fast lookup. In other languages, we might call our table `map` or `Dictionary`. We'll use the `Hashtable` object to hold the occurrence count of the individual words.

We'll use the word as the key. The occurrence count is the value. If the word is not yet entered in the table, we add the pair, setting the occurrence count to 1. Otherwise, we use the key to retrieve and increment the occurrence count. Here is what this looks like:

```
Hashtable words = new Hashtable();
int dim1_length = sentences.GetLength( 0 );

for( int ix = 0; ix < dim1_length; ++ix )
{
     foreach ( string st in sentences[ ix ] )
     {
        // normalize each word to lowercase
        string key = st.ToLower();

        // is the word currently in Hashtable?
        // if not, then we add it ...

          if ( ! words.Contains( key ))
               words.Add( key, 1 );

        // otherwise, we increment the count
          else
               words[ key ] = (int) words[ key ] + 1;
     }
}
```

To discover if a key is present in a `Hashtable`, we invoke its predicate `Contains()` method, which returns `true` if the entry is found. We add the key/value pair to a `Hashtable` either by an explicit assignment:

```
words[ key ] = 1;
```

or through the `Add()` method:

```
words.Add( key, 1 );
```

Typically, the key type is a `string` or one of the built-in numeric types. The value type, which holds the actual data to be retrieved, is generally more application specific—often a class implemented to support the problem domain. The `Hashtable` can support different key and value types because it declares both its key and value members to be of type `object`.

However, because `Hashtable` stores its value as an `object` type, we must explicitly cast it back to its original type. For a value type, recall, this requires unboxing. Any modification to the unboxed value is not automatically reflected in the stored instance, so we must reset it:

```
words[ key ] = (int) words[ key ] + 1;
```

Keeping track of trivial words, such as *a*, *an*, *if*, *but*, and so on, may or may not be useful. One strategy for eliminating these words from our occurrence count is to create a second `Hashtable` of common words—for example,

```
Hashtable common_words = new Hashtable();

common_words.Add( "the", 0 );
common_words.Add( "but", 0 );
// ...
common_words.Add( "and", 0  );
```

and to check each word against this table before entering it into our main table:

```
foreach ( string st in sentences[ ix ])
{
    string key = st.ToLower();
    if ( common_words.Contains( key ))
        continue;
}
```

All that's left for the completion of our program is to print out the occurrence count of the words to the output file in dictionary order. How do we do that?

Our first thought is to iterate across the `Hashtable` using a `foreach` loop. To do that, we access each key/value pair in turn through a `DictionaryEntry` object, which provides a `Key` and a `Value` pair of properties:

```
foreach ( DictionaryEntry de in word )
    fwriter.WriteLine( "{0} : {1}", de.Key, de.Value );
```

As with many programming solutions, this both works and doesn't work. The good news is that it prints out the word and occurrence count of each element. The bad news is that it doesn't do so in dictionary order. For example, here are the first few entries:

```
lime-tinted : 1
waist : 1
bold : 1
```

The problem is that the key is inserted within the `Hashtable` based on the key's hash value, and we cannot directly override that. One solution is to access the key values, place them in a sortable container, and then sort and iterate over that container. For each now sorted key, we retrieve the associated value:

```
ArrayList aKeys = new ArrayList( words.Keys );
aKeys.Sort();

foreach ( string key in aKeys )
    fwriter.WriteLine( "{0} :: {1}", key, words[ key ] );
```

This solves the final sticking point in our solution:

```
apron :: 1
around :: 1
blossoms :: 3
```

The `IDictionary` interface provides an abstract model for the storage and retrieval of key/value pairs. (We look at interfaces in detail in Chapter 4.) The `Hashtable` implements this interface, in which both the key and the value are defined to be of type object. Several strongly typed, specialized classes defined under `System.Collections.Specialized` are also available. These include

- `StringDictionary`: a hash table with the key strongly typed to be a string rather than an object. The key is treated as case insensitive.

- `ListDictionary`: an `IDictionary` implementation using a singly-linked list. If the number of elements is ten or less, it is smaller and faster than a `Hashtable`.

- `NameValueCollection`: a sorted collection of string keys and string values. These can be accessed through either a key hash or an index. `NameValueCollection` stores multiple string values under a single key.

1.17 Exception Handling

That pretty much wraps up the `WordCount` program—at least in terms of its functionality. The primary remaining issue is that of error detection. For example, what if the user has specified a file that doesn't exist? Or what if the file is in a format we don't currently support? Checking that is simple. To find out if a file exists, we can invoke the `Exists()` function of the `File` class, passing to it the string supplied to us by the user:

```
using System.IO;
if ( ! File. Exists( file_name ))
    // oops ...
```

The harder part is choosing how to handle and/or report the problem. In the .NET environment, the convention is to report all program anomalies through *exception handling.* And that is what we will do.

Exception handling consists of two primary components: (1) the recognition and raising of an exception through a `throw` expression and (2) the handling of the exception within a `catch` clause. Here is a `throw` expression:

```
public StreamReader openFile( string file_name )
{
    if ( file_name == null )
        throw new ArgumentNullException();

    // reach here only if no ArgumentNullException thrown
    if ( ! File.Exists( file_name ))
    {
        string msg = "Invalid file name: " + file_name;
        throw new ArgumentException( msg );
    }

    // reach here if file_name not null and file exists
    if ( ! file_name.EndsWith( ".txt" ))
    {
        string msg = "Sorry. ";
        string ext = Path.GetExtension( file_name );

        if ( ext != String.Empty )
            msg += "We currenly do not support " +
                            ext + " files."
```

```
            msg = "\nCurrenly we only support .txt files.";
            throw new Exception( msg );
    }

    // OK: here only if no exceptions thrown
    return File.OpenText( file_name );
}
```

The object of a `throw` expression is always an instance of the `Exception` class hierarchy. (We look at inheritance and class hierarchies in our discussion of object-oriented programming in Chapter 3.) The `Exception` class is defined in the `System` namespace. It is initialized with a string message identifying the nature of the exception. The `ArgumentException` class represents a subtype of the `Exception` class. It more precisely identifies the category of exception. The `ArgumentNullException` class is in turn a subtype of `ArgumentException`. It is the most specific of these three exception objects.

Once an exception has been thrown, normal program execution is suspended. The exception-handling facility searches the method *call chain* in reverse order for a catch clause capable of handling the exception.

We handle an exception by matching the type of the exception object using one or a series of `catch` clauses. A `catch` clause consists of three parts: the keyword `catch`, the declaration of the exception type within parentheses, and a set of statements within curly braces that actually handle the exception.

`catch` clauses are associated with `try` blocks. A `try` block begins with the `try` keyword, followed by a sequence of program statements enclosed within curly braces. The `catch` clauses are positioned at the end of the `try` block. For example, consider the following code sequence:

```
StreamReader freader = openFile( fname );
string textline;

while (( textline = freader.ReadLine() ) != null )
```

We know that `openFile()` throws three possible exceptions. `ReadLine()` throws one exception, that of the `IOException` class. As written, this code does not handle any of those four exceptions. To correct that, we place the code inside a `try` block and associate the relevant set of catch clauses:

```
try
{
    StreamReader freader = openFile( fname );
    string textline;

    while (( textline = freader.ReadLine() ) != null )
    {
        // do the work here ...
    }
    catch ( IOException ioe )
    { ... }

    catch ( ArgumentNullException ane )
    { ... }

    catch ( ArgumentException ae )
    { ... }

    catch ( Exception e )
    { ... }
```

What happens when an exception is thrown? The exception-handling mechanism looks at the site of the `throw` expression and asks, "Has this occurred
within a `try` block?" If it has, the type of the exception object is compared
against the exception type declaration of each associated `catch` clause in turn.
If the types match, the body of the catch clause is executed.

This represents a complete handling of the exception, and normal program
execution resumes. If the `catch` clause does not specify a `return` statement,
execution begins again at the first statement following the set of `catch` clauses.
Execution does *not* resume at the point where the exception was thrown.

What if the type of the exception object does not match one of the `catch`
clauses or if the code does not occur within a `try` block? The currently executing function is terminated, and the exception-handling mechanism resumes its
search within the function that invoked the function just terminated.

If one of the three `if` statements of `openFile()` throws an exception, the
assignment of `freader` and the remainder of the `try` block are not executed.
Rather the exception-handling mechanism assumes program control, examining
each associated `catch` clause in turn, trying to match the exception type.

What if the chain of function calls is unwound to the `Main()` program entry point, and still no appropriate `catch` clause is found? The program itself is then terminated. The unhandled exception is propagated to the runtime debugger. The user can either debug the program or let it prematurely terminate.

In addition to a set of `catch` clauses, we can place a `finally` block after the last `catch` clause. The code associated with the `finally` block is always executed before the function exits:

- If an exception is handled, first the `catch` clause and then the `finally` clause is executed before normal program execution resumes.

- If an exception occurs but there is no matching `catch` clause, the `finally` clause is executed; the remainder of the function is discarded.

- If no exception occurs, the function terminates normally. The `finally` clause is executed following the last non-`return` statement of the function.

The primary use of the `finally` block is to reduce code duplication due to differing exception/no-exception exit points that need to execute the same code.

1.18   A Basic Language Handbook for C#

The three things left undone for a complete implementation of our `WordCount` application are (1) to illustrate how to implement the timing diagnostics, (2) to show how to conditionally output tracing statements, and (3) to package our code into the `WordCount` class. This last item is so important that it deserves its own chapter—Chapter 2 to be exact.

We look at how to generate the tracing output in Section 5.5.2 in the discussion of the `TraceListener` class hierarchy. The timing support is presented in Section 8.6.3 in the discussion of interoperability with the Win32 API. The remainder of this section provides a brief handbook of the C# basic language in the form of a set of tables with brief commentary.

1.18.1   Keywords

Keywords are identifiers reserved by the language. They represent concepts or facilities of the basic C# language. `abstract`, `virtual`, and `override`, for example, specify different categories of dynamic functions that support object-oriented programming. `delegate`, `class`, `interface`, `enum`, `event`, and `struct` represent a variety of complex types that we can define. The full set of keywords is listed in Table 1.1.

Table 1.1   The C# Keywords

abstract	as	base	bool	break
byte	case	catch	char	checked
class	const	continue	decimal	default
delegate	do	double	else	enum
event	explicit	extern	false	finally
fixed	float	for	foreach	goto
if	implicit	in	int	interface
internal	is	lock	long	namespace
new	null	object	operator	out
override	params	private	protected	public
readonly	ref	return	sbyte	sealed
short	sizeof	stackalloc	static	string
struct	switch	this	throw	true
try	typeof	uint	ulong	unchecked
unsafe	ushort	using	virtual	void
while				

A name cannot begin with a number. For example, `1_name` is illegal but `name_1` is OK. A name must also not match a language keyword, with the one proverbial exception: We can reuse a C# keyword name by prefixing it with @— for example,

```
class @class
{
    static void @static(bool @bool)
    {
          if (@bool)
              Console.WriteLine( "true" );
          else Console.WriteLine( "false" );
    }
}
```

```
class Class1
{
    static void M { @class.@static( true ); }
}
```

This prefix option may prove useful in interfacing with other languages, in particular when a C# keyword is used as an identifier in the other programming language. (The @ character is not part of the identifier. Rather it provides a context for interpreting the keyword as an identifier.)

1.18.2   Built-in Numeric Types

Integral literals, such as `42` and `1024`, are of type `int`. To indicate an unsigned literal value, the lower- or uppercase letter `u` is added as a suffix—for example, `42u`, `1024U`. To indicate a literal value of type `long`, we add a lower- or uppercase `L` as a suffix—for example, `42L`, `1024l`. (For readability, the upper case `L` is the preferred usage.) To specify a literal value that is both unsigned and `long`, we combine the two suffixes—for example, `42UL`, `1024LU`.

The sizes (whether the value is signed or unsigned) determine the range of values a type can hold. A signed byte, for example, holds the range `-128` through `127`, an unsigned byte the range `0` through `255`, and so on.

However, using types smaller than `int` can be nonintuitive in some circumstances, and I find myself avoiding them except occasionally as class members. For example, the code sequence

```
sbyte s1 = 0;
s1 = s1 + 1; // error!
```

is flagged as an error with the following message:

```
Cannot implicitly convert type 'int' to 'byte'
```

The rule is that the built-in numeric types are implicitly converted to a type as large as or larger. So `int` is implicitly promoted to `double`. But any conversion from a larger to a smaller type requires an explicit user conversion. For example, the compiler does not implicitly allow the conversion of `double` to `int`. That conversion must be explicit:

```
s1 = (sbyte) ( s1 + 1 ); // OK
```

Why, though, you might ask, is a conversion necessary when `s1` is simply being incremented by 1? In C#, integral operations are carried out minimally through signed 32-bit precision values. This means that an arithmetic use of `s1` results in a promotion of its value to `int`. When we mix operands of different types, the two are promoted to the smallest common type. For example, the type of the result of `s1+1` is `int`.

When we assign a value to an object, as with our assignment of `s1` here, the type of the right-hand value must match the type of the object. If the two types do not match, the right-hand value must be converted to the object's type or the assignment is flagged as an error.

By default, a floating-point literal constant, such as `3.14`, is treated as type `double`. Adding a lower- or uppercase `F` as a suffix to the value turns it into a single-precision `float` value. Character literals, such as `'a'`, are placed within single quotes. Decimal literals are given a suffix of a lower- or uppercase M. (The decimal type is probably unfamiliar to most readers; Section 4.3.1 looks at it in more detail.) Table 1.2 lists the built-in numeric types.

Table 1.2   The C# Numeric Types

Keyword	Type	Usage
sbyte	Signed 8-bit int	`sbyte    sb = 42;`
short	Signed 16-bit int	`short    sv = 42;`
int	Signed 32-bit int	`int      iv = 42;`
long	Signed 64-bit int	`long     lv = 42, lv2 = 42L, lv3 = 42l;`
byte	Unsigned 8-bit int	`byte     bv = 42, bv2 = 42U, bv3 = 42u;`
ushort	Unsigned 16-bit int	`ushort   us = 42;`
uint	Unsigned 32-bit int	`uint     ui = 42;`
long	Unsigned 64-bit int	`ulong    ul = 42,  ul2 = 4ul,   ul3 = 4UL;`
float	Single-precision	`float    f1 = 3.14f, f3 = 3.14F;`
double	Double-precision	`double   d = 3.14;`
bool	Boolean	`bool     b1 = true, b2 = false;`
char	Unicode char	`char     c1 = 'e', c2 = '\0';`
decimal	Decimal	`decimal  d1 = 3.14M, d2 = 7m;`

The keywords for the C# predefined types are aliases for types defined within the `System` namespace. For example, `int` is represented under .NET by the `System.Int32` type, and `float` by the `System.Single` type.

This underlying representation of the prebuilt types within C# is the same set of programmed types as for all other .NET languages. This means that although the simple types can be manipulated simply as values, we can also program them as class types with a well-defined public set of methods. It also makes combining our code with other .NET languages considerably more direct. One benefit is that we do not have to translate or modify types in order to have them recognized in the other language. A second benefit is that we can directly reference or extend types built in a different .NET language. The underlying `System` types are listed in Table 1.3.

Table 1.3 The Underlying `System` Types

C# Type	System Type	C# Type	System Type
sbyte	System.SByte	byte	System.Byte
short	System.Int16	ushort	System.UInt16
int	System.Int32	uint	System.UInt32
long	System.Int64	ulong	System.UInt64
float	System.Single	double	System.Double
char	System.Char	bool	System.Boolean
decimal	System.Decimal		
object	System.Object	string	System.String

1.18.3 Arithmetic, Relational, and Conditional Operators

C# predefines a collection of arithmetic, relational, and conditional operators that can be applied to the built-in numeric types. The arithmetic operators are listed in Table 1.4, together with examples of their use; the relational operators are listed in Table 1.5, and the conditional operators in Table 1.6.

The binary numeric operators accept only operands of the same type. If an expression is made up of mixed operands, the types are implicitly promoted to the smallest common type. For example, the addition of a `double` and an `int` results in the promotion of the `int` to `double`. The `double` addition operator is then executed. The addition of an `int` and an unsigned `int` results in both operands being promoted to `long` and execution of the `long` addition operator.

Table 1.4   The C# Arithmetic Operators

Operator	Description	Usage
`*`	Multiplication	`expr1 * expr2;`
`/`	Division	`expr1 / expr2;`
`%`	Remainder	`expr1 % expr2;`
`+`	Addition	`expr1 + expr2;`
`–`	Subtraction	`expr1 - expr2;`
`++`	Increment by 1	`++expr1; expr2++;`
`– –`	Decrement by 1	`--expr1; expr2--;`

The division of two integer values yields a whole number. Any remainder is truncated; there is no rounding. The remainder is accessed by the remainder operator (`%`):

```
5 / 3 evaluates to 1, while 5 % 3 evaluates to 2
5 / 4 evaluates to 1, while 5 % 4 evaluates to 1
5 / 5 evaluates to 1, while 5 % 5 evaluates to 0
```

Integral arithmetic can occur in either a checked or unchecked context. In a *checked* context, if the result of an operation is outside the range of the target type, an `OverflowException` is thrown. In an *unchecked* context, no error is reported.

Floating-point operations never throw exceptions. A division by zero, for example, results in either negative or positive infinity. Other invalid floating-point operations result in NAN (not a number).

The relational operators evaluate to the Boolean values `false` or `true`. We cannot mix operands of type `bool` and the arithmetic types, so relational operators do not support concatenation. For example, given three variables—a, b, and c—that are of type `int`, the compound inequality expression

```
// illegal
a != b != c;
```

is illegal because the `int` value of `c` is compared for inequality with the Boolean result of `a != b`.

Table 1.5   The C# Relational Operators

Operator	Description	Usage
<	Less than	`expr1 < expr2;`
>	Greater than	`expr1 > expr2;`
<=	Less than or equal to	`expr1 <= expr2;`
>=	Greater than or equal to	`expr1 >= expr2;`
==	Equality	`expr1 == expr2;`
!=	Inequality	`expr1 != expr2;`

Table 1.6   The C# Conditional Operators

Op	Description	Usage
!	Logical NOT	`! expr1`
||	Logical OR (short circuit)	`expr1 || expr2;`
&&	Logical AND (short circuit)	`expr1 && expr2;`
|	Logical OR (`bool`)—evaluate both sides	`bool1 | bool2;`
&	Logical AND (`bool`)—evaluate both sides	`bool1 & bool2;`
?:	Conditional	`cond_expr ? expr1 : expr2;`

The conditional operator takes the following general form:

```
expr
   ? execute_if_expr_is_true
   : execute_if_expr_is_false;
```

If `expr` evaluates to `true`, the expression following the question mark is evaluated. If `expr` evaluates to `false`, the expression following the colon is evaluated. Both branches must evaluate to the same type. Here is how we might use the conditional operator to print either a space or a comma followed by a space, depending on whether `last_elem` is true:

```
Console.Write( last_elem ? " " : ", " )
```

Because the result of an assignment operator (=) is the value assigned, we can concatenate multiple assignments. For example, the following assigns `1024` to both the `val1` and the `val2` objects:

```
// sets both to 1024
val1 = val2 = 1024;
```

Compound assignment operators provide a shorthand notation for applying arithmetic operations when the object to be assigned is also being operated upon. For example, rather than writing

```
cnt = cnt + 2;
```

we typically write

```
// add 2 to the current value of cnt
cnt += 2;
```

A compound assignment operator is associated with each arithmetic operator:

```
+=, -=, *=, /=, and %=.
```

When an object is being added to or subtracted from by `1`, the C# programmer uses the increment and decrement operators:

```
cnt++; // add 1 to the current value of cnt
cnt--; // subtract 1 from the current value of cnt
```

Both operators have prefix and postfix versions. The *prefix* version returns the value after the operation. The *postfix* version returns the value before the operation. The value of the object is the same with either the prefix or the postfix version. The return value, however, is different.

1.18.4 Operator Precedence

There is one "gotcha" to the use of the built-in operators: When multiple operators are combined in a single expression, the order in which the expressions are evaluated is determined by a predefined precedence level for each operator. For example, the result of `5+2*10` is always `25` and never `70` because the multiplication operator has a higher precedence level than that of addition; as a result, in this expression `2` is always multiplied by `10` before the addition of `5`.

We can override the built-in precedence level by placing parentheses around the operators we wish to be evaluated first. For example, `(5+2)*10` evaluates to `70`.

Here is the precedence order for the more common operators; each operator has a higher precedence than the operators under it. Operators on the same line have equal precedence. In the case of equal precedence, the order of evaluation is left to right:

```
Logical NOT (!)
Arithmetic *, /, and %
Arithmetic + and -
Relational <, >, <=, and >=
Relational == and !=
Logical AND (&& and &)
Logical OR (|| and |)
Assignment (=)
```

For example, consider the following statement:

```
if (textline = Console.ReadLine() != null) ... // error!
```

Our intention is to test whether `textline` is assigned an actual string or `null`. Unfortunately, the higher precedence of the inequality operator over that of the assignment operator causes a quite different evaluation. The subexpression

```
Console.ReadLine() != null
```

is evaluated first and results in either a `true` or `false` value. An attempt is then made to assign that Boolean value to `textline`. This is an error because there is no implicit conversion from `bool` to `string`.

To evaluate this expression correctly, we must make the evaluation order explicit by using parentheses:

```
if ((textline = Console.ReadLine()) != null) ... // OK!
```

1.18.5   Statements

C# supports four loop statements: `while`, `for`, `foreach`, and `do-while`. In addition, C# supports the conditional `if` and `switch` statements. These are all detailed in Tables 1.7, 1.8, and 1.9.

Table 1.7 The C# Loop Statements

Statement	Usage
| while | ```
while ( ix < size ){
        iarray[ ix ] = ix;
        ix++;
}
``` |
| for | ```
for (int ix = C; ix<size; ++ix)
        iarray[ ix ] = ix;
``` |
| foreach | ```
foreach ( int val in iarray )
        Console.WriteLine( val );
``` |
| do-while | ```
int ix = 0;
do
{
        iarray[ ix ] = ix;
        ++ix;
}
while ( ix < size );
``` |

Table 1.8 The C# Conditional if Statements

Statement	Usage
| if | ```
if (usr_rsp=='N' || usr_rsp=='n')
    go_for_it = false;

if ( usr_guess == next_elem )
{ // begins statement block
    num_right++;
    got_it = true;
} // ends statement block
``` |
| if-else | ```
if ( num_tries == 1 )
    Console.WriteLine( " ... " );
else
if ( num_tries == 2 )
    Console.WriteLine( " ... " );
else
if ( num_tries == 3 )
    Console.WriteLine( " ... " );
else Console.WriteLine( " ... " );
``` |

Table 1.9   The C# `switch` Statements

Statement	Usage
| switch | ```
// equivalent to if-else-if clauses above
switch ( num_tries )
{
    case 1:
        Console.WriteLine( " ... " );
        break;

    case 2:
        Console.WriteLine( " ... " );
        break;

    case 3:
        Console.WriteLine( " ... " );
        break;

    default:
        Console.WriteLine( " ... " );
        break;
}

// can use string as well
switch ( user_response )
{
    case "yes":
        // do something
        goto case "maybe";

    case "no":
        // do something
        goto case "maybe";

    case "maybe":
        // do something
        break;

    default:
        // do something;
        break;
}
``` |
```

Chapter 2

Class Design

A class represents an abstraction, usually of our application domain. In computer graphics, for example, we manipulate classes representing lights, a camera, geometric shapes such as a sphere, cone, or cube, as well as curves and surfaces, and math classes such as matrices and vectors. In the design of a Windows application, we manipulate classes representing text boxes, buttons, labels, message boxes, and so on. The primary goal of this chapter is to familiarize you with the C# language support for designing and implementing classes.

In general, a class consists of two parts: a public set of operations and properties—called the *public interface*—and a private implementation. As users of a class, we are consumers of its public interface. For example, as users we know that to retrieve the number of elements currently held within an `ArrayList` object, we access its `Count` property. That's the public interface. Whether that value is stored as a data member or calculated on demand and cached is an implementation detail that is hidden from us as users. A secondary goal of this chapter is to look at how we separate interface and implementation in the design of our classes.

2.1 Our First Independent Class

A class may represent an independent abstraction, or it may represent a specialization of a more general abstraction. For example, `FileStream` and `MemoryStream` are both specialized class definitions of the `System.IO` namespace `Stream` class. A stream represents a general flow of data either into or out of our program. It is an *abstract* class because although it defines the behavior of a stream (the public interface); it does not provide a complete implementation. The completion of the stream implementation is left to the more specialized file and memory stream classes, which define the input/output medium. Both the file and the memory stream classes are called *subtypes* of the stream class type. This type/subtype relationship is at the heart of *object-oriented programming* (*OOP*). We look at OOP in detail in Chapter 3.

Before we define relationships between classes, we first need to feel comfortable in building them. That's what we'll do in this chapter: look at how to make independent classes. An *independent* class is one that provides a complete implementation of its functionality. Examples of independent abstractions include the `DateTime` and `Buffer` classes in the `System` namespace.

In Chapter 1 we worked through the general implementation of a program to count the words in a file. In this section we need to turn that work into the design of a `WordCount` class.

Where do we start?

The first thing we need to do is identify the set of operations that the class performs. These become the class member functions. One can always argue whether two or more functions should be combined, or whether a function should be factored into multiple functions. In general, however, a function is best organized to perform a single task. For the `WordCount` class, I have identified the following four operations:

1. `openFiles()`, which confirms the validity of the text file supplied by the user and if valid, it opens it. In addition, it opens the output file to hold the word count. Optionally it opens a file to hold the trace output.

2. `readFile()`, which reads the text, tucking it away for subsequent manipulation.

3. `countWords()`, which separates the text into individual words and computes the occurrence count.

4. `writeWords()`, which outputs the occurrence count of the words into the designated file in dictionary order.

In addition, there is an initialization task when we first create a `WordCount` class object, and a deinitialization task when the object is no longer needed. We'll look at the issues surrounding these operations in separate sections.

Once we have decided on the set of member functions, we need to identify the interface for each. For a member function, an interface consists of (1) the return type of the function and (2) the function parameter list, or *signature.*

A parameter list allows us to pass objects into a function. These parameters either are operated on or provide information that is extracted from within the function. The return type specifies the kind of object being passed back from the function. This object usually represents the result of the internal computation, although it may also represent the success/failure status of the operation. (Remember that in C# (and .NET programming in general), the convention is to throw an exception rather than to return a status code such as HRESULT.)

In the design of class member functions, we can often dispense with both an explicit return value and the set of parameters. This is possible because a class object can maintain its own state through class data members. Rather than passing in or returning values, a member function can operate on the internal members of the class object through which it is invoked. This often makes for a simpler programming model.

Once we have decided on the name, return type, and signature of the member functions, we next have to decide on an access level for each. That is, should a function be declared public, making it accessible to the entire program, or should it be declared private, in which case only the other member functions of the class can invoke it? (Object-oriented programming introduces a protected access level; we look at that in Chapter 3.)

At first glance it seems that each of our member functions should be declared public, allowing the user to—in any order—open, read, count, and write through the WordCount object. To allow this flexibility, however, would complicate our implementation because the invocation order of the methods is dependent. For example, it is hardly useful for a user to request a count of the words if a file has not even been opened yet. An alternative strategy is to package an invocation of the entire sequence in a single public function, which for this example I've named processFile(). The four member functions that it invokes in turn are declared private.

Let's see what we have so far. Here is a first iteration of a WordCount class definition:

```csharp
using System;
public class WordCount
{
    public void processFile()
    {
        openFiles();
        readFile();
        countWords();
        writeWords();
    }

    private void countWords()
    {
        Console.WriteLine( "!!! WordCount.countWords()" );
    }

    private void readFile()
    {
        Console.WriteLine( "!!! WordCount.readFile()" );
    }

    private void openFiles()
    {
        Console.WriteLine( "!!! WordCount.openFiles()" );
    }

    private void writeWords()
    {
        Console.WriteLine( "!!! WordCount.writeWords()" );
    }
}
```

Member functions must be defined inside the class definition. The order of their declaration is not significant. The compiler does not need to have seen the declaration of the member function before it can be invoked. Each member function is provided with an explicit access level. By default, if a member function (or class data member) does not have an explicit access level, it is treated as a private member.

A class that is defined either within a namespace or within the global declaration space can be declared as either private or internal. (Internal access means that the class is visible only within the *assembly* in which it occurs. We look at assemblies in more detail in Chapter 8.) A class without an explicit access level is treated as having internal access.

Although this implementation of our class is not very functional, it is complete. Before we proceed further with the implementation, it is probably useful to see that it compiles and that we can invoke the public `processFile()` method successfully. I've always found myself more productive when I incrementally add functionality to a working program rather than when I wait until I have coded everything before seeing if any of it works.

To execute the program, we need to provide a program entry point. Here's a stripped-down version that creates a `WordCount` object and invokes `process-File()`:

```
using System;
public class WordCountEntry
{
    static public void Main()
    {
        Console.WriteLine( "Beginning WordCount program ... " );

        WordCount theObj = new WordCount();
        theObj.processFile();

        Console.WriteLine( "Ending WordCount program ... " );
    }
}
```

This class, together with the `WordCount` class, constitutes a complete C# program.

Before continuing with our exploration of the C# class mechanism, let's open a Visual Studio project and execute the program.

2.2 Opening a New Visual Studio Project

For this program we want to create a C# project in Visual Studio using the Console Application template. Assuming that you have brought the Visual Studio **Start Page** to your screen (see Figure 2.1), click the **New Project** button. Under **Project Types,** click **Visual C# Projects.** Under **Templates,** click **Console Application.** Change the name of the project to *WordCount.* You can either leave the location at the default or choose another directory in which to store your project. When done, click **OK.**

Figure 2.1   Visual Studio

By default the program file is named `Class1.cs`. It's probably better to rename it something mnemonic, like `word_count.cs`. You will always want to rename a project file within Visual Studio. We do this within the **Solution Explorer** window. The lower right-hand window in Figure 2.1, labeled 4, is the **Solution Explorer** window. It lists all the project files. (In Figure 2.1 our file has already been renamed.) One way to navigate between the different source files is to click on the file name within this window.

If you don't have the **Solution Explorer** window open, do that now by clicking on the **Solution Explorer** icon identified by the tricolor Mobius strip. It's on the first toolbar on the upper right portion of the screen (labeled 1 in Figure 2.1). Once the **Solution Explorer** window is open, right-click on `Class1.cs` and select **Rename.**

Visual Studio generates a default namespace declaration and class skeleton. I always delete those and start with an empty file. Type in the `WordCount` class defined in the previous section. Notice that the compiler parses your code as you enter it, alerting you to potential errors before you even build.

We also need to enter the `WordCountEntry` class. We'll place this part of our program in a separate file. To add a new C# file, click on the **Add New Item** icon. (In Figure 2.1, it is at the top left of the window, labeled 5.) Under **Local Project Items,** select **C# Code File.** Give it the name `EntryPoint.cs`. When done, click **Open.**

To build our program and fix any errors reported by the compiler, we typically use the **Build** command. (In Figure 2.1, it is the left-hand icon of the two that are labeled 6.) Errors and warnings are reported in the bottom Visual Studio window. If you double-click on a compiler error, the program text window displays the line on which the error occurs.

The open files are listed at the top of the program text window. Displayed on the line below the open file names are the class currently being examined and the member of that class upon which the curser is active. (In Figure 2.1, the open class is `WordCount,` and the active member is `m_reader.`)

To hop around between classes or class members independently of the file in which they are stored, we use the **Class View** window (labeled 3 in Figure 2.1). This window shows all the classes in our project. Each class has its members listed below it. Clicking on a class or class member brings the corresponding program text into view.

Now that the project builds without error, we'll want to execute it. Press **Ctrl+F5** to execute it without starting the debugger. (The icon is the exclamation point, the right-hand icon of the two that are labeled 6 in Figure 2.1.) A console window should pop up, and the `WriteLine()` output of the various functions should display.

2.3 Declaring Data Members

A data member represents state information associated with an instance of a class, such as the name of a file or the capacity of an `ArrayList`. A class data member can be of any type. How do we discover the data members that we need to associate with a class?

One category of data members is the set that users provide when they create a class instance. For example, for our `WordCount` class, we require users to provide the name of a text file and optionally to indicate whether they wish a program trace or performance timings. It is likely that we'll need to store these values in associated class data members.

A second category of data members is the set of objects that are used across multiple member functions. If an object is necessary within a single member function only, we declare it as a local object to that function. However, if that object needs to be accessed subsequently by another member function, it is likely that we'll want to store it as a class data member.

For example, consider the following partial implementation of the `readFile()` member function. It makes use of one local object and two class data members:

```
private void readFile()
{
     m_text = new ArrayList();
     string    text_line;

     while (( text_line = m_reader.ReadLine() )
                      != null )
     {
          if ( text_line.Length == 0 )
              continue;

          m_text.Add( text_line );
     }

}
```

`text_line` is declared as a local object. It is used to temporarily store each line of text as it is read from the text file specified by the user. Once the file has been read, we have no further use for the object.

m_reader and m_text are declared as private data members. m_reader refers to the StreamReader object created in openFile(). m_text is an ArrayList object holding the nonempty lines of text. It is subsequently accessed within countWords().

Here is a partial declaration of the WordCount data members:

```
public class WordCount
{
        private bool            m_spy;
        private bool            m_trace;

        private string          m_file_name;
        private string          m_file_output;

        private StreamReader    m_reader;
        private StreamWriter    m_writer;

        private ArrayList       m_text;
        private Hashtable       m_words;

        private string [][]     m_sentences;
        // ...
}
```

Each data member must specify its own access level. A data member without an explicit access level by default is treated as private. A private member, recall, can be accessed only within the class for which it is a member. As a general design rule, our data members are always declared as private.

2.4   Properties

Often the internal representation of a class is modified after its initial release to users. For example, in this first version of WordCount, m_trace is declared as a bool data member; that is, it is able to be set either to true or to false. For large text files, however, users have found the generated trace text overwhelming—at least when generated to the console. They have requested that we allow them to specify whether to direct the trace to the console or to a file. Supporting this flexibility requires a change to the type representation of m_trace. It must now be able to represent three states: traceOff, toConsole, and toFile.

If `m_trace` is declared as public, users are free to access it directly within their code. The result is a *tight coupling* of the user's code with the class implementation—a tight coupling that the class designer is unaware of, at least until she changes the class implementation and the user discovers that his program is now broken.

Information hiding is the process of making the implementation details of a class inaccessible to users. This mechanism provides a *loose coupling* between the user's code and the class implementation, thereby enhancing the ability of the designer to modify the class implementation without disrupting the user's program. We enforce information hiding for class data members by declaring them as `private`.

Information hiding solves the problem of tight coupling. It also creates the problem of how to allow users read or write access to a private data member. In C#, the solution is to provide `get` and `set` *accessors* within a named class property—for example,

```
public class WordCount
{
    // private data member declaration
    private string m_file_output;

    // associated public property
    public string OutFile
    {
        get{ return m_file_output; }    // Read   access
        set
        { // Write access
            if ( value.Length != 0 )
                m_file_output = value;
        }
    }

    // ...
}
```

A *property* typically is a public class member providing read and possibly write access to a private data member of the class. We define a property by specifying an access level, type, and property name. `OutFile`, for example, is a public property of type `string`.

If we wish the property to support read access, we provide a `get` accessor. It must return a value of the property's type. The associated code is placed within a statement block. It does not specify a return type or signature. At its simplest, a `get` accessor returns the data member it encapsulates.

If we wish the property to support write access, we provide a `set` accessor. Within the `set` accessor, the identifier `value` is always an object of the same type as its containing property. At runtime, `value` is bound to the right-hand side of the assignment. At its simplest, a `set` accessor assigns `value` to the data member it encapsulates.

The user accesses a property as if it were a data member rather than a function. For example, in the code fragment

```
string defaultFile = @"c:\text\wordCount.txt";

if ( theObj.OutFile == null )
    theObj.OutFile = defaultFile;
```

the occurrence of `OutFile` within the condition of the `if` statement is replaced by the body of the `get` accessor. The second occurrence of `OutFile` that is the target of the assignment is replaced by the body of the `set` accessor. `value` is bound to the string object `defaultFile`.

If we wish to restrict a property to read-only access, we simply don't provide a `set` accessor.

2.5   Indexers

An indexer provides support for arraylike indexing of a class object. An indexer looks like a property. Like a property, an indexer provides a `get` and `set` pair of accessors. Unlike a property, however, an indexer is identified using the `this` keyword rather than a name. Indexers require *at least* one index parameter. The index can be of any type.

For example, imagine that users have requested the ability to retrieve the occurrence count of a word using the following subscript syntax:

```
int count = theObj[ "fiery" ];
```

How can we support that? The following indexer definition does the trick:

```
public class WordCount
{
    private Hashtable m_words;

    // our indexer; it supports only read ...
    public int this[ string index ]
    {
        get
        {
            if ( index.Length == 0 )
                throw new ArgumentException(
                    "WordCount: Empty string as index" );

            if ( m_words == null )
                throw new Exception(
                    "WordCount: No associated file" );

            return (int) m_words[ index ];
        }
    }

    // ...
}
```

We use the indexer by directly applying the subscript operator to an instance of the class. In this example we do not provide a `set` accessor. The use of the subscript operator to write to a `WordCount` object is flagged as a compile-time error—for example,

```
theObj[ "fiery" ] = 1; // error: set not supported
```

The following indexer supports both read and write. It encapsulates a private array data member:

```
public class Fibonacci
{
    public  decimal this[ int index ]
    {
        get
        {
            check_index( index );
            return ms_elems[ index ];
        }
```

```
            set
            {
                    check_index( index );
                    ms_elems[ index ] = value;
            }
        }

        private decimal [] ms_elems;
        private void check_index( int index ) { ... }
}
```

The following example shows a two-dimensional indexer for a `Matrix` class. Although this indexer takes two integer indices, multiple indices for an indexer do not need to be of the same type:

```
public class Matrix
{
    // not shown: constructors, methods ...

    public int rows{ get{ return m_row; }}
    public int cols{ get{ return m_col; }}

    public double this[ int row, int col ]
    {
            get
            {
                    check_bounds(row,col);
                    return m_mat[row,col];
            }

            set
            {
                    check_bounds(row,col);
                    m_mat[row,col] = value;
            }
    }

    private int m_row;
    private int m_col;

    private double [,] m_mat;
    private void check_bounds( int r, int c ) { ... }
}
```

This indexer can be used as follows:

```
Matrix mat = new Matrix( 4, 4 );
for ( int ix = 0; ix < mat.rows; ++ix )
    for ( int iy = 0; iy < mat.cols; ++iy );
        if ( mat[ix,iy] == 0 )
            mat[ix,iy] = ix+iy;
}
```

2.6 Member Initialization

Each class data member is automatically initialized to the default value of its type. Numeric types, such as `int` and `double`, have a default value of `0`. `false` is the default value of type `bool`. `null` serves as the default value of all reference types. This default initialization is carried out as part of the invocation of operator `new`.

If the default values are the appropriate initial member values, there is nothing additional for us to program—at least in terms of initialization. Otherwise, how we assign an alternative initial value depends on whether the class designer or class user designates what that value should be.

If the class designer is the one determining the alternative initial value, she can explicitly specify that value in the declaration of the class member—for example,

```
class Login
{
    private string m_password = "ChangeMe";
    private int    m_max_dirs = 20;
    private bool   m_save_all = true;
    private string m_login;
    // ...
}
```

When we declare an instance of `Login`, only `m_login` retains its default value of `null`. The other three members have their default values reassigned to the explicit values indicated in their definitions. These reassignments are carried out in the member declaration order. `m_password`, for example, is initialized before `m_max_dirs`, and `m_save_all` is initialized last. The explicit value is not limited to a constant expression—for example,

```
class Login
{
    private ArrayList m_history = new ArrayList();
    private string [] m_lib_dirs = new string []
    {
            @"C:\ProgramFiles\Microsoft.Net\FrameworkSDK\Lib\",
            @"C:\Platform SDK\Lib\".
            @"C:\MSSDK\DXF\LIB"
    };
    // ...
}
```

The *explicit-value* declaration syntax allows the designer of the class to specify an explicit value with which to assign a member. This is in addition to, not in place of, the initialization of each class member with the default value of its type. The missing piece of the initialization puzzle is the ability to let the user specify an initial value for a member at the creation point of the class object. This is the service provided by the class constructor, which we explore in the next section.

2.7   The Class Constructor

Our `WordCount` program requires that the user provide a file name. Optionally, the user can turn on several options, such as generating trace output and timing diagnostics. The `Main()` entry point processes the command-line options. That done, it must create a `WordCount` object and pass the file name and possible options to that object before asking the object to process the file.

One solution, of course, is to create a `WordCount` object with the default values and then reset the values the user passed in through the command-line options. The problem with this strategy is that it requires two steps, and the crucial second one is something that the user might overlook.

The *class constructor* is a mechanism by which the user can provide values to assign to data members during construction of the class object. For example, here is how we would like to create a `WordCount` object:

```
WordCount theObj = new WordCount( file_name, spyOn, traceOn );
theObj.processFile();
```

where `file_name`, `spyOn`, and `traceOn` are set during the processing of the command-line options.

The constructor associated with this invocation looks like this:

```
public WordCount( string file_name, bool spy, traceFlags trace )
{
       m_file_name = file_name;
       m_spy = spy;
       m_trace = trace;

       if ( m_spy )
            m_times = new ArrayList();
}
```

A constructor is a special member function of the class. We identify it as a constructor by giving it the same name as its class. It cannot return a value, nor can it declare a return type—not even a return type of `void`.

When the user creates a `WordCount` object through the operator `new`, the process is broken down into two steps. In the first step, `new` allocates the heap memory to contain the object. In the second step, the constructor initializes the object. The constructor is automatically invoked by the compiler.

If the class provides only one constructor definition, all invocations of operator `new` must provide the correct number and type of arguments to pass to that constructor. For the `WordCount` class, we must now always supply three arguments when invoking operator `new`. In particular, we can no longer create a class object with no arguments. The following invocation, for example, results in a compile-time error:

```
WordCount theObj = new WordCount(); // error
```

because the only constructor we've provided expects three arguments.

One of the decisions we must make as class designers is whether to provide constructors and, if so, how many to provide. That is, how many ways do we wish to support constructing an object of our class?

We can define multiple constructors, provided that the parameter list of each constructor is unique in either the number or type of its parameters. (When we provide multiple instances of a function with the same name, we say that we have *overloaded* the function.) For example, a second `WordCount` constructor requires only that the user provide a file name:

```
public WordCount( string file_name )
    : this( file_name, false, traceFlags.turnOff ) {}
```

A class constructor can invoke a second constructor of its class. The syntax requires three elements:

1. A *colon* (:) following the signature of the constructor, which alerts both the compiler and reader of the code that there will be an additional constructor invocation.
2. The `this` *keyword*, which alerts both the compiler and the reader of the code that the constructor being invoked is a member of this class.
3. The *arguments* to be passed to the other constructor, whose type and number determine exactly which other constructor is invoked.

The constructor represented by the `this` keyword is invoked first. In our case, this is the three-parameter constructor. When this constructor terminates, the body of the original constructor is invoked. In our case, there is nothing for it to do. This is why we've provided an empty constructor body.

The following `Point3D` class is another example of the *dispatch-to-another-instance* constructor idiom. Its purpose is to allow the user to create a `Point3D` object with three, two, one, or no initial values. Each absent coordinate value is assigned a default value of 0:

```
Point3D origin = new Point3D(); // Point3D(0,0,0)
Point3D x_offset = new Point3D(1.0)  // Point3D(1.0,0,0)
Point3D translate = new Point3D(1.0,1.0);// Point3D(1.0,1.0,0)
Point3D mumble = new Point3D(1.0,1.0,1.0);
```

The `Point3D` constructor set to support this would look like this. (Note that the declaration order is not significant.)

```
class Point3D
{
    public Point3D( double v1, double v2, double v3 )
                { x = v1; y = v2; z = v3; }

    public Point3D(double v1,double v2): this(v1,v2,0.0) {}
    public Point3D( double v1) : this( v1, 0.0, 0.0 ){}
    public Point3D() : this( 0.0, 0.0, 0.0 ){}

    // ...
}
```

It is possible to declare a nonpublic constructor —that is, as either `private` or `protected`. A nonpublic constructor is unavailable to users of the class. However, it can be invoked within the class member functions, allowing the class to create specialized objects for internal use.

C# provides the class designer with three initialization options, only one of which requires the introduction of a class constructor. A side effect of the `new` expression is the automatic initialization of each data member to its type's default value. We never need to explicitly set a data member to its default value.

If a value other than the default value needs to be set, we have two choices for how to set it. If the initialization is based on user input, we'll need to solicit that input through a constructor. Otherwise we can specify it as part of the member declaration.

2.8   The Implicit `this` Reference

Up to this point, all our data members and member functions have been *instance members.* An instance data member has a copy of itself stored within each class object that we create. To call a member function an instance member means that the function must be invoked through an object of its class.

When an instance data member is accessed within a member function, the name of the data member serves as a placeholder. A member function does not maintain a copy of each class data member it accesses. Rather, when the member function is invoked through an actual class object, the name of the data member within the function is bound to the instance associated with the class object. This binding is accomplished through the implicit `this` *reference.*

Within an instance member function, the `this` reference refers to the class object through which the member function is invoked. The `this` reference is used internally to bind a use of a data member to the instance of that member within the class object. For example, consider the following code fragment:

```
private void countWords()
{
    m_sentences = new string[ m_text.Count ][];
    m_words    = new Hashtable();

    string str;
```

```
        for( int ix = 0; ix < m_text.Count; ++ix ) { ... }
}
```

Internally, each unqualified access of an instance data member is augmented to refer to the member through the `this` reference—for example,

```
this.m_sentences = new string[ this.m_text.Count ][];
this.m_words     = new Hashtable();

for( int ix = 0; ix < this.m_text.Count; ++ix ) { ... }
```

We pass the `this` reference to each instance member function by augment-
ing the function's parameter list with an additional class parameter:

```
private void countWords( WordCount this ){ ... }
```

This means that the invocation of the member function must also be rewritten internally by the compiler to reflect the internal signature. For example, when
we internally write

```
theObj.processFile();
```

it is turned into

```
processFile( theObj );
```

An unqualified invocation of an instance member function, such as

```
public void processFile(){ countWords(); }
```

first has its invocation augmented by the addition of the `this` reference:

```
public void processFile( WordCount this )
        { this.countWords(); }
```

which is then rewritten to reflect the augmented parameter list of each function:

```
public void processFile( WordCount this )
        { countWords( this ); }
```

In some instances within a program, having access to the `this` reference
solves an otherwise intractable problem. For example, let's say that we need to
implement a doubly-linked list of strings. We'll call the class `StringNode`. It contains three data members:

```
class StringNode
{
    private StringNode back_link;
    private StringNode front_link;
    private string      text;

    public StringNode( string str ){ text = str; }
    // ...
}
```

We need to provide an `Append()` operation supporting the following usage:

```
StringNode node = new Node( "a node" );
// ...
node.Append( new StringNode( "also a node" ));
```

There are three steps to appending a `StringNode` object: (1) The `front_link` of the new node is set to the `front_link` of the existing node; (2) the `front_link` of the existing node is set to the new node; and (3) the `back_link` of the new node is set to the existing node:

```
public void Append( StringNode new_node )
{
    new_node.front_link = front_link;   // (1)
    front_link = new_node;              // (2)
    new_node.back_link = ?????          // (3)
}
```

Without the `this` reference, we have no way to directly reference the object through which `Append()` is invoked. We complete the implementation by assigning `back_link` to refer to `this`:

```
new_node.back_link = this; // (3)
```

If we wish, we can explicitly prefix the access of an instance member with the `this` reference. Some people claim that this prefix makes the code more readable; the idea is that it clearly identifies instance members within the function. Personally, I find that the presence of the `this` reference within a function gives the code a cluttered feel.[1]

---

1. The Visual Studio code generation wizards, for example, mechanically insert an explicit instance of `this`.

2.9 `static` Class Members

Not all members of a class make sense as instance members. Some members provide a service or contain information that is independent of an individual class object. The current value of an integer, for example, is an instance member. The maximum value an integer can hold is not. It holds true for all integer objects.

We would not want each integer object to hold a copy of the maximum value an integer can hold. However, it is information that users of the integer type would like to retrieve and to compare individual instances against.

That is, the maximum integer value makes sense as a member of the class representing the integer type. It does not make sense as an instance member of that class. This is why we declare certain class members as `static` or `const`.

A static member represents a *class member* rather than an instance member. `Today` and `Now`, for example, are `static` properties of the `DateTime` class. `Today` represents the current date, with the time set to 0. `Now` represents the current date and time. The member functions `WriteLine()` and `Read-Line()` are `static` member functions of the `Console` class. `MaxValue` is a `static` data member of the `Int32` class.

In our `WordCount` class, the character array of separators with which to split a line of text into individual words makes sense as a `static` member. Here is how we declare that:

```
public class WordCount
{
    static public char [] ms_separators;
```

Only a single instance of a `static` data member exists in a program. It exists independently of the individual class instances. Within a class member function, we can syntactically access a `static` member just as we do an instance member—for example,

```
private void countWords()
{
    // ...
    for( int ix = 0; ix < m_text.Count; ++ix )
    {
        str = ( string )m_text[ ix ];
        m_sentences[ ix ] = str.Split( ms_separators );
```

Outside the class, we access a `static` member through the name of the class to which it belongs—for example,

```
static void Main()
{
    char bang = '!';
    int ix = 0;

    for( ;  ix < WordCount.ms_separators.Length; ++ix )
        if ( WordCount.ms_separators[ ix ] == bang )
            break;

    if ( ix == WordCount.ms_separators.Length )
        throw new Exception( "Insufficient separators" );
```

A `static` member may not be accessed through an object of the class. Doing so triggers an error—for example,

```
int len = theObj.ms_separators.Length; // error
```

A `static` member is also initialized to the default value of its type—in our example, `ms_separators` is set to `null` because an array is a reference type. We can provide an explicit initial value with its declaration —for example,

```
public class WordCount
{
    static public char [] ms_separators = new char []
            { ' ', '\n', '\t', '.', '\"', ';', ',',
                '?', '!',')', '(', '<', '>', '[', ']' };
```

Alternatively, we can initialize the `static` members of a class within a *static constructor*—for example,

```
public struct WordCount
{
    static public char [] ms_separators;
    static WordCount() // static constructor
    {
        ms_separators = new char []
            { ' ', '\n', '\t', '.', '\"', ';', ',',
                '?', '!',')', '(', '<', '>', '[', ']' };
    }

    // ...
}
```

Only one static constructor can be defined for a class. We identify a *static* constructor by prefixing its name with the `static` keyword. By default, the static constructor is public; however, it is an error to explicitly provide an access level—even that of `public`. The static constructor must be declared to have an empty parameter list. (This is why we can define only one static constructor. If we want to overload a function, each overloaded instance must have a unique signature.)

The static constructor is invoked only once, and only if an instance of the class is created or a static member of the class is accessed. The exact ordering of static-constructor invocations within the program is undefined.

We can initialize or invoke static members only within the static constructor. An attempt to access an instance member results in an error. A static constructor, however, is not limited to initializing static class members. We can use it to perform any action before we create an initial class object or access a class static member. An interesting example of using static constructors is presented in Section 8.5.

Typically we declare static data members as `private,` and we provide read and write access through a static property. We can also declare member functions as static. A static member function lacks a `this` reference and cannot directly access any instance members of its class.

2.10 `const` and `readonly` Data Members

The declaration of a `const` data member *must* include an initial value. Moreover, that initial value *must* be a constant expression—that is, an expression that can be fully evaluated at compile time. For example, the code fragment

```
class Matrix {
    private const int ms_default_row_size = 4,
                      ms_default_col_size = 4;
```

declares two `const int` members initialized with a value of 4. An attempt to modify a `const` member generates a compile-time error.

A `const` member can always be initialized with another `const` member, provided there is no circular dependency. For example, the three `const` declarations below compile without error, setting x to 10, y to 8, and z to 4:

```
class Illustrate
{
    // OK: no circular dependency

    private const int x = y + z/2;
    private const int y = z * 2;
    private const int z = 4;
}
```

The next example, however, results in a compile-time error because of the circular dependency between the definitions of x and z:

```
class Illustrate
{
    // error: circular dependency

    private const int x = y + z/2;
    private const int y = z * 2;
    private const int z = x;
}
```

A const data member is not an instance member. Only a single instance of the const member exists. A const member is essentially a read-only static member: Qualified access must be through the class name and not through an object of the class.

A const member cannot be a reference type. Take a moment to think why. A reference type requires an invocation of operator new. Operator new cannot be evaluated until runtime. We must initialize a const member with an expression that can be evaluated at compile time. For example, the following declaration is illegal and generates a compile-time error:

```
// illegal: cannot be evaluated at compile time
public const Matrix identity =
    new Matrix( 1,0,0,0,0,1,0,0,0,0,1,0,0,0,0,1 );
```

readonly allows us to initialize an object at runtime but enforce read-only access. An attempt to modify a readonly member generates a compile-time error. To simulate a const member, we can declare the readonly member as static—for example,

```
public static readonly Matrix identity =
    new Matrix( 1,0,0,0,0,1,0,0,0,0,1,0,0,0,0,1 );
```

The only reference type that can be declared `const` is the `string` type, which, if you recall, is initialized without use of the `new` expression—for example,

```
class Illustrate {
        // OK: string reference type is an exception
        private const string default_login = "Guest";
        private const string default_pswrd = "ChangeMe";
}
```

The primary difference between a `const` and a `readonly` member is the different initialization time (compile time versus runtime). Because the value of a `const` is available at compile time, it can be *constant-folded* (i.e., substituted) at each occurrence of its name. This is not possible for a `readonly` member.

2.11   The `enum` Value Type

Often when we program we need to define a set of alternative attributes to associate with an object. A file, for example, might be open in one of three states: `input`, `output`, and `append`. One strategy to keep track of these state values is to associate a unique constant number with each one. Thus we might write

```
public class fileMode
{
        public const int input  = 1;
        public const int output = 2;
        public const int append = 3;
        // ...
}
```

and use these constants as follows:

```
bool open_file( string file_name, int open_mode);
// ...
open_file( "Phoenix_and_the_Crane", fileMode.append );
```

The benefit is that it is much easier to use a set of mnemonic constant objects than to remember and make sense of the associated literal values. The drawback is that there is no way to constrain the input values to only those of `input`, `output`, and `append`. The compiler, for example, happily accepts an input value of `1024` to `open_file()`; the burden of constraining the accepted values falls to the programmer.

An `enum` type defines a group of related named integral constants. An object of `enum` type can be assigned only one of those named constants. We define an `enum` type with the `enum` keyword, followed by the `enum` type identifier. Individual values are identified within a comma-separated list of named *enumerators* placed within curly braces. Each enumerator must have a unique name; however, multiple enumerators can be associated with the same value.

By default, the first enumerator is assigned `0`. Each subsequent enumerator is incremented by one. To override the default assignment, we simply assign the enumerator a constant integral expression—for example,

```
enum open_modes{
    input = 1, output, append,
    last_input_mode = input, last_output_mode = append };
```

Within the `enum`, the enumerators can be referenced without qualification. Outside the `enum`, however, an enumerator must be qualified with the type of its `enum`: `open_modes.input`. A nested `enum` must be qualified with the name of the class as well: `MyFileClass.open_modes.input`.

If we insist on assigning an integral constant expression to an `enum` object, we must explicitly cast it to the `enum` type:

```
void open_file( string file_name, open_modes om );

open_modes om;
string     fname;
// ... set om and fname ...

open_file( fname, om );                 // OK
open_file( fname, open_modes.append ); // OK
open_file( fname, 1 );                   // error!
open_file( fname, (open_modes)1 );      // OK, but ...
```

This overrides any type checking of the value. It is not a recommended practice.

We can use an `enum` type to represent the possible trace modes of our `WordCount` class—for example,

```
public class WordCount
{
    public enum traceFlags { turnOff, toConsole, toFile };
    private traceFlags m_trace;
```

On the basis of the command-line options, the `Main()` entry point determines which of the three values to use for initializing `m_trace`:

```
static public void Main( string [] args )
{
    WordCount.traceFlags traceOn =
            WordCount.traceFlags.turnOff;
    // ...

    foreach ( string option in args )
          switch ( option )
        {
                case "-t":
                        traceOn = WordCount.traceFlags.toConsole;
                break;

                case "-tf":
                        traceOn = WordCount.traceFlags.toFile;
                break;

                // ...
```

Enumerators are natural targets of `switch` statement `case` labels. For example, in the `openFile()` method of `WordCount`, we create a trace object that is bound either to the console or to a file based on `m_trace`:

```
if( m_trace != traceFlags.turnOff )
      switch ( m_trace )
    {
        case traceFlags.toConsole:
                cout = new TextWriterTraceListener(Console.Out);
            Trace.Listeners.Add( cout );
        break;

        case traceFlags.toFile:
            m_tracer = File.CreateText(m_diag_file);
            cout = new TextWriterTraceListener(m_tracer);
            Trace.Listeners.Add( cout );
        break;
    }
```

By default, the type representation of each enumerator is `int`. We can override that type by specifying an alternative integral type, provided that the type we specify can represent all the enumerator values—for example,

```
public enum weekdays : byte
{
    sunday, monday, tuesday, wednesday,
    thursday, friday, saturday
};
```

We can iterate across the enumerators using the increment (or decrement) operator, as in the following example:

```
public static void translator( string [] foreign )
{
    weekdays wd = weekdays.sunday;

    for ( ; wd <= weekdays.saturday; ++wd )
        Console.WriteLine( wd + " : " + foreign[(int)wd] );
}
```

`foreign` represents a `string` array of the days of the week in a foreign (i.e., non-English) language. `translator()` prints out the days of the week in both English and the foreign language represented by the array. Notice that the indexing of the array requires an explicit cast of the `wd` enum object. After the code has been compiled and executed, the following output is generated:

```
sunday : dimanche
monday : lundi
tuesday : mardi
wednesday : mercredi
thursday : jeudi
friday : vendredi
saturday : samedi
```

The .NET class framework uses `enum` types extensively to encapsulate alternative modes or attributes of class properties, such as `BorderStyle`, `TextBoxMode`, `FontSize`, and so on.

2.12 The `delegate` Type

A `delegate` type creates a kind of function object. The `delegate` type looks like a function declaration, but instead it defines a type that can refer to one or multiple functions of a particular signature and return type. A `delegate` type has three primary characteristics:

1. A delegate *object* can address multiple methods rather than only one method at a time. When we invoke a delegate that addresses multiple methods, the methods are invoked in the order in which they are assigned to the delegate object. We'll see how to do that shortly.

2. The *methods* addressed by a delegate object do not need to be members of the same class. All the methods addressed by a delegate object must share the same prototype and signature. Those methods, however, can be a combination of both static and nonstatic methods, and they may be members of one or more different classes.

3. A *declaration* of a `delegate` type internally creates a new subtype instance of either the `Delegate` or the `MulticastDelegate` abstract base class of the .NET library framework, supporting a collection of public methods to query the delegate object and the method(s) to which it refers.

The declaration of a `delegate` type generally consists of four components: (1) an access level, (2) the keyword `delegate`, (3) the return type and signature of the method that the `delegate` type addresses, and (4) the name of the `delegate` type, which is placed between the return type and the signature of the method.

The following, for example, declares `Action` to be a `public delegate` type that addresses methods taking no parameters and with a return type of `void`:

```
public delegate void Action();
```

If a `delegate` type is used to address only a single method at any one time, it may address a member function of any return type and signature. If, however, the `delegate` type addresses two or more methods simultaneously, the return type *must* be `void`. `Action`, for example, can be used to address either a single or multiple methods.

For example, consider the design of a `testHarness` class. It must permit any class to register one or more either static or nonstatic class methods for subsequent execution. The `delegate` type is at the center of this implementation.

Let's declare the delegate object as a `private static` member of our `testHarness` class—for example,

```
public delegate void Action();
public class testHarness
{
    static private Action theAction;
    static public Action Tester
    {
        get{ return theAction;   }
        set{ theAction = value;  }
    }

    // ...
}
```

A `delegate` type in C# is a reference type. Therefore its declaration—for example,

```
Action theAction;
```

represents a handle to a delegate object of the `Action delegate` type, but is not itself a delegate object. By default this handle is set to `null`. If we attempt to use it before it is assigned a value, a compile-time error is generated. For example, the statement

```
theAction();
```

causes invocation of the method(s) addressed by `theAction`. However, unless it has been unconditionally assigned to between being defined and this use, the invocation triggers a compile-time error message.

To set `theAction` to address a class member function, we must create an `Action delegate` type using the `new` expression. For a static method, the argument to the constructor is the name of the class to which the method belongs and the name of the method itself, joined by the dot operator (`.`):

```
theAction = new Action( Announce.announceDate );
```

For a nonstatic method, the argument to the constructor is the class object through which we wish to invoke the method joined to the method name—again joined by the dot operator:

```
Announce an = new Announce();
theAction   = new Action( an.announceTime );
```

The static `announceDate()` member function of the `Announce` class prints the current date to standard output in the *long* form,

```
Monday, February 26, 2001
```

while the nonstatic `announceTime()` member function prints the current time to standard output in the *short* form, `00:53`, where the first two digits represent the hour, beginning at `00` for midnight, and the second two digits represent the minute. The class definition makes use of the `DateTime` class provided within the .NET class framework. We look at it in more detail in Section 5.5.4.

```
public class Announce
{
    public static void announceDate()
    {
        DateTime dt = DateTime.Now;
        Console.WriteLine( "Today's date is {0}",
                                dt.ToLongDateString() );
    }

    public void announceTime()
    {
        DateTime dt = DateTime.Now;
        Console.WriteLine( "The current time is {0}",
                                dt.ToShortTimeString() );
    }
}
```

As we saw earlier, we invoke the method addressed by the delegate object by applying the call operator to the delegate

```
testHarness.Tester();
```

First the `get` accessor of the `Tester` property is invoked. This returns the `theAction` delegate handle. The call operator (`()`) is then applied to the handle, resulting in the invocation of the method addressed by the delegate object. However, if `theAction` is not currently addressing a delegate object when the call operator is applied, an exception is thrown. To safeguard against this, we use the canonical *delegate-test-and-execute* sequence. From outside the class, this sequence looks like this:

```
if ( testHarness.Tester != null )
    testHarness.Tester();
```

From within the class, it looks like this:

```
static public void run()
{
    if ( theAction != null )
        Action();
}
```

To assign a delegate address more than a single method, we use primarily the `+=` and `-=` operators. For example, imagine that we have defined a `testHashtable` class. Within its static constructor, we add each associated test to the `testHarness` object:

```
public class testHashtable
{
    public void test0();
    public void test1();
    static testHashtable()
    {
        testHarness.Tester += new testHarness.Action( test0 );
        testHarness.Tester += new testHarness.Action( test1 );
    }
    // ...
}
```

Similarly, when we define a `testArrayList` class, we add each associated test within its static constructor. Notice that these methods are static:

```
public class testArrayList
{
    static public void testCapacity();
    static public void testSearch();
    static public void testSort();

    static testArrayList()
    {
        testHarness.Tester += new testHarness.Action(testCapacity);
        testHarness.Tester += new testHarness.Action(testSearch);
        testHarness.Tester += new testHarness.Action(testSort);
    }
    // ...
}
```

What is the order of invocation? The multiple methods are invoked in the order in which they are added to the delegate. So, for example, `test0` is always invoked before `test1` for the `testHashtable` class. Because we cannot know in general when a static constructor is invoked—only that it is invoked prior to a use of the class—we cannot say with certainty whether the `testArrayList` member functions or the `testHashtable` member functions are added to `Tester` first.

Consider the following code sequence within a local block:

```
{
    Announce annc = new Announce();
    testHarness.Tester +=
            new testHarness.Action( annc.announceTime );

}
```

When we initialize a delegate object to a nonstatic method, both the address of the method and a handle to the class object through which to invoke the method are stored. The result is that the class object's associated reference count is incremented.

When `annc` is initialized with the `new` expression, the associated reference count of the object on the managed heap is initialized to 1. When `annc` is passed to the constructor of the delegate object, the `Announce` object's reference count is incremented to 2. With the termination of the local block, the lifetime of `annc` terminates, and the reference count is decremented back to 1.

The good news is that the object associated with an invocation of a method referred to by a delegate object is guaranteed not to be garbage-collected until the delegate object no longer references the method. We don't have to worry about the object being cleaned up out from under us. The bad news is that the object persists until the delegate object no longer references the method.

The method can be removed with the `-=` operator. For example, the following revised local block first sets, then executes, and then removes `announceTime()` from the delegate object:

```
{
    Announce an = new Announce();
    Action act  = new testHarness.Action( an.announceTime );
```

```
        testHarness.Tester -= act;
        testHarness.run();
        testHarness.Tester -= act;
    }
```

An alternative implementation might first check if `Tester` already addresses one or several other methods. If so, it would save the currently set delegation list, reset `Tester` to `act`, invoke `run()`, and then reset `Tester` to the original delegation list.

To discover the number of methods a delegate addresses, we can make use of the underlying `Delegate` class interface—for example,

```
    if ( testHarness.Tester != null &&
         testHarness.Tester.GetInvocationList().Length != 0 )
    {
        Action oldAct = testHarness.Tester;

        testHarness.Tester = act;
        testHarness.run();
        testHarness.Tester = oldAct;
    }
    else { ... }
```

`GetInvocationList()` returns an array of `Delegate` class objects, each element of which represents a method currently addressed by the delegate object. `Length` is a property of the underlying `Array` class that implements the built-in C# array type.

2.13   Function Parameter Semantics

The parameters of a function serve as placeholders within the function body. With each invocation, the parameters are bound to the actual *arguments* passed to the function. By default, this binding is carried out by value. We can override the default by modifying the parameter with either the `ref` or the `out` keyword. These kinds of parameters are bound by reference.

Each parameter minimally consists of a type specifier, such as `int`, `string`, or `Matrix`, and a name. The parameter name is visible only within the function, so the name can be reused outside the function without conflict. A comma separates multiple parameters. We write

```
f( int i, int j ){ ... }
```

not

```
// error!
f( int i, j ){ ... }
```

An empty parameter list indicates that the function takes no parameters.

Consider the following static method. It accepts two parameters: a `Matrix` object, and a value of type `double`. It multiplies each matrix element of the first parameter by the second parameter, storing the result in a new `Matrix` object. It then returns the new `Matrix` object:

```
public static
Matrix multiplyByDouble( Matrix mat, double dval )
{
    Matrix result = new Matrix( mat.rows, mat.cols );

    for ( int ix = 0; ix < mat.rows; ix++ )
        for ( int iy = 0; iy < nat.cols; iy++ )
            result[ ix, iy ] = mat[ ix, iy ] * dval;

    return result;
}
```

This function can be invoked as follows:

```
Matrix mat = Matrix.multiplyByDouble( location, modval );
```

where `location` represents a `Matrix` object and `modval` represents an object of type `double`—both of which have been defined earlier in the program.

What is the relationship between the formal parameters (`mat` and `dval`) and the actual arguments (`location` and `mocval`)? Each formal parameter represents a local object within the function, the same as with objects defined within the function body. Five local objects are defined within `multiplyByDouble()`: the two local `Matrix` objects (`mat` and `result`), the second parameter (`dval`), and the two integer objects (`ix` and `iy`) used as indices into the matrix.

Each local object needs to be initialized (or at least assigned to) before it is used. In the case of `result`, `ix`, and `iy`, the initializations are explicit. What about the parameters? When and how are they initialized?

2.13.1 Pass by Value

The parameters are initialized at each call point of the function. By default, they are initialized through a mechanism called *pass by value*. This means that each parameter is initialized with a copy of the value of the actual argument. `dval`, for example, is initialized with a copy of the value that `modval` holds when the function is invoked. Because `dval` and `modval` represent separate objects, any changes made to `dval` from within the function have no effect on `modval`. This is both good and not so good.

The good part is that we don't have to protect the actual argument from being unintentionally modified. Within the function, we are manipulating a local copy of the argument. Any changes made to the local object disappear with the disappearance of the function. The actual argument is not changed.

It is not so good if we need the changes that we make to the local object to be reflected in the actual argument of the call. In this case, we have to override the pass-by-value mechanism. We'll see how to do that in the next subsection.

Pass by value becomes slightly more confusing when the formal parameter is a reference type. When we pass a reference type by value, a separate local instance is created just as for a value type. The difference is that both the argument and the local instances refer to the same object on the heap.

Recall that a reference type consists of a handle/object pair. The handle of a reference type contains the address of the object to which the handle refers. The object itself resides on the managed heap. When the reference type is passed by value, its handle part is copied into the local instance. The object on the heap is now referenced by both the handle and the object. In our example, both `location` and `mat` refer to the same `Matrix` object on the heap.

This means that any modification made to the heap object through the local instance permanently changes the object. This is not true of any changes made to the handle portion of the reference type, which affect only the local instance and are discarded with completion of the function.

To make sure this is clear, let's look at an example.

`byValue()` takes a single string parameter by value. Inside the function, its characters are turned to all uppercase using `ToUpper()`. Because strings are immutable, `ToUpper()` returns a `string` object. The parameter is modified to address this new object. At this point, the parameter and the local object refer to different `string` objects:

```
static public void byValue( string s )
{
    Console.Write( "\nInside byValue: " );
    Console.WriteLine( "original parameter: \n\t" + s );

    // now refers to a different string object!
    s = s.ToUpper();

    Console.Write( "\nInside byValue: " );
    Console.WriteLine("modified parameter: \n\t" + s );
}
```

The local instance refers to the new `string` object, in which the letters have been changed to uppercase. Because we have modified the handle of a value parameter, this change is not reflected in the actual argument. This is illustrated in the program's output:

```
string to be passed by value:
        A fine and private place

Inside byValue: original parameter:
        A fine and private place

Inside byValue: modified parameter:
        A FINE AND PRIVATE PLACE

back from call -- string:
        A fine and private place
```

As you can see, the `string` object appears the same both before and after the invocation of `byValue()`. In such cases our first thought is that we somehow fouled up the string transformation. However, when we display the `string` object from within `byValue()`, we see that the method actually works fine. The problem isn't with our method, but with how we pass parameters in and out of the function. We'll override the default pass-by-value behavior in the next section.

Before we do that, however, I'd like to review again briefly the impact of shallow copy on reference types. Consider the following code:

```
public static
Matrix multiplyByDouble( Matrix mat, double dval )
{
    Matrix result = new matrix( mat.rows, mat.cols );
    for ( int ix = 0; ix < mat.rows; ix++ )
         for ( int iy = 0; iy < mat.cols; iy++ )
                result[ ix, iy ] = mat[ ix, iy ] * dval;

    return result;
}
```

Why does this code create a new `Matrix` object on the heap rather than just copying `mat` into `result`? After all, just copying `mat` into `result` simplifies the multiplication:

```
public static
Matrix multiplyByDouble( Matrix mat, double dval )
{
    Matrix result = mat;
    for ( int ix = 0; ix < mat.rows; ix++ )
         for ( int iy = 0; iy < mat.cols; iy++ )
                result[ ix, iy ] *= dval;

    return result;
}
```

If we initialize `result` with `mat`, we get a shallow copy. `result` is simply a second handle to the actual `Matrix` object. Later, when we multiply each element by `dval`, we are directly modifying the original `Matrix` object, which is not what we want. To create a modified copy of the `Matrix` object, we simulate a deep copy by invoking the `new` expression.

Whenever we pass around or copy a reference type, we need to be sure whether a shared or independent instance is appropriate.

2.13.2 Pass by Reference: The `ref` Parameter

The negative aspect of pass by value is the same as its positive aspect: We lose all the changes made to the local instance of the argument. When we need to have these local changes persist, we must tell the compiler to pass the actual argument by reference rather than by value. We do this by prefixing the parameter declaration with the `ref` keyword:

```
static public void byRef( ref string s )
    { /* the body of the function is the same ... */ }
```

A reference parameter serves as an alias to the actual argument passed in.[2] The reference parameter does *not* represent an independent local entity. This form of parameter binding is called *pass by reference*. A change to the reference parameter directly changes the associated argument. For example, when we run `byRef()`, modifying the string internally as before, we see that the modification of the parameter within the function has caused the actual argument that we passed in to be modified:

```
string to be passed by ref:
        A fine and private place

Inside byRef: original parameter:
        A fine and private place

Inside byRef: modified parameter:
        A FINE AND PRIVATE PLACE

back from call -- string:
        A FINE AND PRIVATE PLACE
```

The `ref` keyword must also prefix the actual argument in the invocation of the function:

```
string str = "A text string";
byRef( ref str );
```

If we forget to include the `ref` keyword when we invoke the function, its absence is flagged as a compile-time error. Although this may initially seem overly fussy, it allows us to overload and resolve methods solely on the presence (or absence) of the `ref` keyword. (We look at function overloading in Section 2.14.)

2.13.3 Pass by Reference: The `out` Parameter

The actual argument we pass to either a value parameter or a `ref` parameter must be recognized by the compiler as having a value assigned to it prior to invocation of the function. Otherwise, a compile-time error is triggered.

---

2. It does not result in the boxing of value types, however! (Boxing was discussed in Section 1.14.1.)

Sometimes, however, we implement a function such that a parameter is assigned a value within the function body. In effect, this allows us multiple return values. We still need to pass the argument in by reference; otherwise the change made to the parameter would be discarded at the completion of the function. But we don't really want to initialize the argument to a dummy value just to satisfy the compiler; after all, that value is overwritten when we invoke the function.

We accomplish this by prefixing a parameter with the `out` keyword, thereby alerting the complier that this parameter will be assigned to within the function body. In fact, the compiler requires that an `out` parameter be assigned to at every exit point of the function. Otherwise, a compile-time error is triggered. In the following example, `multiplyByDouble()` is reimplemented to accept an `out` parameter:

```
public static
void multiplyByDouble( out Matrix mat, double dval )
{
    for ( int ix = 0; ix < mat.rows; ix++ )
        for ( int iy = 0; iy < mat.cols; iy++ )
            mat[ ix, iy ] *= dval;
}
```

As with the `ref` keyword, the `out` keyword must be specified both in the signature of the function and in the call of the function:

```
MultiplyByDouble( out scaleMat, factor );
```

The argument passed to an `out` parameter may or may not already have had a value assigned. Within the function declaring an `out` parameter, however, the assumption is that the parameter is *uninitialized*. An `out` parameter cannot be used within its function until the parameter is explicitly assigned a value. For example, the reimplementation of `byValue()` using an `out` parameter is *illegal:*

```
static public void byValue( out string s )
{
    Console.Write( "\nInside byValue: " );

    // error: s is treated as being uninitialized
    Console.WriteLine( "original parameter: \n\t" + s );

    // ... rest of the function
}
```

As an example of a situation in which we might wish to use an `out` parameter, consider the scenario of entering a word into a lookup table. We would want to "normalize" the word's case and suffixing—*Fly, flies,* and *fly* should all match, for example—but without modifying the original text word.

We could easily do this by passing in the original word by value, and passing in a second string as an `out` parameter assigned the modified word. Why would we do this rather than simply return the new string? Perhaps we want the formal return value of the function to indicate whether we were able to suffix it, or attempt to indicate its part of speech.

An `out` parameter provides us with an alternative way of returning a value from a function—of allowing us in effect to have multiple return values.

2.14 Function Overloading

Two or more functions can be given the same name if the parameter list of each function is unique either by the type or by the number of parameters. For example, the following five declarations represent overloaded instances of a method called `message()`:

```
class MessageHandler
{
    public void message(){ ... }
    public void message( char ch ){ ... }
    public void message( string msg ){ ... }
    public void message( string msg,int val ){ ... }
    public void message( string msg,int v1,int v2 ){ ... }

}
```

How does the compiler know which instance of an overloaded function to invoke? It compares the actual arguments supplied to the function invocation against the parameters of each overloaded instance, choosing the *best* match.

The return type of a function by itself cannot be used to distinguish two overloaded instances of that function. The reason is that the return type cannot guarantee a sufficient context for distinguishing between the overloaded instances. For example, imagine multiple instances of `message()` distinguished only by the return type. The following call provides no context to determine which instance the user wished to have invoked:

```
// which one?
message( '\t' );
```

Overloading a set of functions that have unique implementations but perform similar tasks simplifies the use of these functions for our users. Without overloading, we would have to provide each function with a unique name.

2.14.1 Resolving Overloaded Functions

Resolving the selection of an overloaded function requires finding the best match between the actual arguments passed to the call and the formal parameters of an overloaded instance. The first step involves identifying the *candidate* functions that can be considered for resolving the call. The next step is to select the *viable* functions—those that can be invoked given the number and type of the actual arguments. Finally, from the list of viable functions, the final step is to select the function that *best matches* the call.

As illustration, consider the following set of overloaded functions:

```
public static void f( int    i1, int i2 )  { ... }
public static void f( float f1, float f2 ){ ... }
public static void f( string s ){ ... }
```

Now assume that we invoke `f()` with two integer arguments:

```
f( 1024, 2048 );
```

The set of candidate functions consists of the three instances listed above. The viable candidates, however, include only the first two. Both of the viable candidates accept two parameters, and two integer arguments can be passed to either one. The final step is deciding which of the two viable instances is the best match. The two integer arguments *exactly match* the formal parameters of the first instance. In order for them to match the two `float` parameters of the second instance, each argument must be *implicitly converted* from `int` to `float`. An exact match is always better than a match requiring conversion, so `f(int,int)` is selected.

Do things always go correctly? No. In the first step, it may be that *no candidate functions* are found. The result is a compile-time error: The name of the function is unknown. For example, if we mistype `f()` as `F()`, the call cannot be resolved. Similarly, in the second step, there may be *no viable functions,* because of either a type mismatch or a mismatch of the number of arguments. For example, if we invoke `f()` with three arguments, there are no viable instances, and the call results in a compile-time error.

2.14.2 Determining a Best Match

A viable function has the same number of formal parameters as the number of actual arguments passed to the call. In addition, either the argument type must exactly match the type of its corresponding parameter, or an implicit conversion from the argument type to the type of its corresponding parameter must exist. For `ref` and `out` parameters, the argument type must match exactly; *no conversions are considered.*

In C#, conversions are either *implicit* or *explicit.* Only implicit conversions—that is, conversions carried out automatically by the compiler—are considered in attempts to resolve an overloaded function call.

C# defines a set of standard implicit conversions among the built-in numeric types. The rule is that a numeric type only implicitly converts to a type the same size or larger. So, for example, `long` implicitly converts to `float`, `double`, or `decimal`. It does not implicitly convert to `int`. For instance, the invocation

```
int ival;
long lval;
// ...
f( ival, lval ); // which one?
```

results in a single viable function. Because `long` does not implicitly convert to the smaller `int` type, it is not possible to invoke `f(int,int)`; therefore, the only viable function is `f(float,float)`.

Let's modify the invocation of `f()` to give us two viable functions:

```
int ival;
short sval;
// ...
f( ival, sval ); // which one?
```

How do we decide the *best viable function?* The decision involves ranking the necessary conversions between each parameter and actual argument. How is one conversion better than another? The reference manual describes the criteria as follows:

> If an implicit conversion from T1 to T2 exists, and no implicit conversion from T2 to T1 exists, then the conversion of S to T1 is better.

where S represents the actual argument type, and T1 and T2 represent the formal parameter types of two viable functions. Let's see if we can make sense of this statement.

Our second argument, sval, a short, does not exactly match either the formal int parameter of the first viable function or the formal float parameter of the second. An implicit conversion is required for both matches. For the first, short is promoted to int. For the second, short is promoted to float. Which is better?

To apply the rule stated in the reference manual, we have to map the actual types to S, T1, and T2. The actual type of the argument, short, maps to S; int maps to T1; and float maps to T2.

Does an implicit conversion from T1 to T2 (i.e., from int to float) exist? Yes. Then does an implicit conversion from T2 to T1 (i.e., from float to int) also exist? No. Therefore, the conversion of short to int is better than the conversion of short to float.

In general, this rule means that the conversion requiring the smallest effort is always the preferred conversion. A conversion of long to float, for example, is *always* preferred to a conversion of long to double, although they are both viable. This rule parallels our intuitive understanding of how conversions should work.

Sometimes there is no best viable function. (One function might be better for one parameter, another for a second.) In this case, the invocation is tagged as ambiguous, and a compile-time error results—for example,

```
public static void g( long l, float f  ){ ... }
public static void g( int i,  double d ){ ... }

g( 0, 0 ); // ambiguous
```

The first argument *exactly matches* the first parameter of the second function but requires an *implicit conversion* to match the first parameter of the first

C# PRIMER

function. Therefore, for the first parameter the second function has the best match.

The second argument requires a conversion for both parameters. However, the standard conversion of `int` to `float` is better than that of `int` to `double`. So for the second parameter, the first function has the best match.

The result is literally a draw: Each function has one best match. There is no best viable function, so the call results in an ambiguity error. To resolve it, we can explicitly convert one or the other argument—for example,

```
// OK: public static void g(int i, double d)
g( 0, (double)0 );
```

2.15 Variable-Length Parameter Lists

Our `message()` function of the preceding section is actually something of a problem. It represents the collection of values a user may wish to display. The problem is that the type and number of these values of interest to users are limitless. Trying to accommodate even a subset of all the requested variations soon begins to drive us crazy.

A more manageable solution is to declare a signature that can be passed an arbitrary number of arguments of possibly arbitrary types. We do this through the `params` variable-length parameter, which is characterized as follows:

- The `params` keyword identifies that we are passing a variable number of parameters.

- An array of the type of arguments we wish to accept follows the `params` keyword. This array holds the actual arguments that are being passed. If we wish to accept heterogeneous types, we declare the array to be of type `object`.

For example, here is a revised set of `message()` functions illustrating uses of the `params` keyword:

```
class MessageHandler
{
    // our fixed-length parameter instances
    public void message(){ ... }
    public void message( char ch )   { ... }
    public void message( string msg ){ ... }
```

```
// our variable-length parameter instances
public void message(string msg, params int[] args)    {...}
public void message(string msg, params double[] args){...}
public void message(string msg, params object[] args){...}
// ... rest of class
}
```

The first three instances take a fixed number of parameters: The first takes no parameters, the second a single parameter of type `char`, the third a single parameter of type `string`. Here are some examples of their invocation:

```
MessageHandler mh = new MessageHandler( file );

mh.message();
mh.message( 'a' );
mh.message( "hello" );
```

Each of these calls *exactly matches* the parameter list of one of the first three overloaded instances of `message()`. There is nothing surprising in these invocations. The next three instances are what become interesting.

For example, the following invocations all match the instance of `message()` that declares an integer `params` array:

```
int ival= 10, dval = 0;

// all match: message( string, params int[] )
mh.message( "mumble", 10, ival, dval, 1024 );
mh.message( "mumble", ival );
mh.message( "fib: ", 1,1,2,3,5,8,13,21,34,55 );
```

The same invocations, but with arguments of type `double` rather than `int`, match the instance of `message()` that declares a `double params` array. What happens if we mix the types of values? For example, the call

```
mh.message( "mix types", 10, 3.14159 );
```

mixes types of `int` and `double`. Which function best matches the call? In this case, the second value, `3.14159`, is of type `double`. A `double` is not implicitly converted to type `int`, so the integer `params` array instance is not a viable function. The `double params` array instance is selected, and the first numeric value, `10,` is implicitly promoted to `double`.

What if we introduce types for which no conversion to either `int` or `double` exists? For example, consider this call:

```
mh.message( "weird types", false, mh, 3.14, 2m );
```

None of the instances on the surface seem to match this call, yet it is handled successfully. The instance invoked is that of the `object params` array. The `bool` literal `false`, the `MessageHandler` object `mh`, a value of type `double`, and a value of type `decimal` are all implicitly converted to type `object`.

To find out the number of parameters passed in with each call, we query the array parameter about its length. If nonzero, we iterate across the array, accessing each argument in turn. (We would use *type reflection* to discover the actual type of each object. This is covered in Section 8.2.) For example, here is a possible implementation:

```csharp
public void message( string msg, params object[] args )
{
    Console.WriteLine( msg );

    if ( args.Length != 0 )
            foreach ( object o in args )
                    Console.WriteLine( "\t{0}", o.ToString() );
}
```

Alternatively, we can access each variable parameter through an explicit index into the array:

```csharp
public void message( string msg, params int[] args )
{
    Console.WriteLine( msg );

    for ( int ix = 0; ix < args.Length; ++ix )
        Console.Write( "{0} ", args[ix].ToString() );
    Console.WriteLine();
}
```

A function signature can have only one `params` array. It must be declared last. The `params` array must be one-dimensional, and we cannot modify it with either the `ref` or the `out` keyword.

Typically, the use of a `params` array augments an existing set of function instances that take one or more explicit parameters, such as the definition of `message()`. In our example, we handle three conditions explicitly—no parameters, a single `string` parameter, and a single `char` parameter. All other invocations must start with a `string`, followed by zero or more arguments of any type.

If the `params` array follows one or more explicit parameters, as it does with our three `message()` instances, each of those explicit parameters must have an actual argument provided by the user. The `params` array handles all additional arguments, if any.

If we want to accept zero or more arguments of a *particular* type, we make the `params` array the only parameter of the function. To accept zero or more arguments of *any* type, we declare the `params` array to be of type `object`:

```
// accepts zero or more arguments of type int
static void func( params int [] args )

// accepts zero or more arguments of type string
static void func( params string [] args )

// accepts zero or more arguments of any type
static void func( params object [] args )
```

How does overloading resolution work in the presence of a `params` keyword? Consider the following two functions:

```
static void display( string msg )
static void display( string msg, int ix, params object [] args )
```

and the following invocation:

```
display( "message", 42, arg1, arg2 );
```

The first instance of `display()` is not a viable candidate because it takes a single parameter. The second instance may match.

The compiler evaluates the signature as follows: It tries to match by first *not* considering the `params` array. The explicit parameters of the function, in this case `string` and `int`, must match—either exactly or through an implicit conversion. If a match is achieved, the remaining arguments, if any, are packed into an array by the compiler and passed to the function. In this example, `arg1` and `arg2` become the first and second elements of the array.

2.16   Operator Overloading

Operator overloading allows us to provide class-specific instances of the existing operators, such as addition, multiplication, equality, and so on. For example, rather than providing a named function, such as `multiplyByDouble()`, for a `Matrix` class, we can overload the multiply operator to perform the same task. That is, rather than writing

```
Matrix newMat = Matrix.multiplyByDouble( mat, dval );
```

the user can write the more intuitive

```
Matrix newMat = mat * dval;
```

Here is how we might implement this instance of the multiply operator:

```
public class Matrix
{
    public static Matrix operator*(Matrix mat, double dval)
    {
        Matrix result = new Matrix( mat.rows, mat.cols );

        for ( int ix = 0; ix < nat.rows; ix++ )
            for ( int iy = 0; iy < mat.cols; iy++ )
                result[ix,iy] = mat[ix,iy] * dval;

        return result;
    }

    // ... rest of the Matrix class
}
```

All operator functions must be declared `public` and `static`. The `operator` keyword is followed by the operator symbol we wish to overload. At least one of the parameters of the operator must be a class instance. In this case, we overload the multiplication operator to accept a `Matrix` object and a value of type `double`, and the operator returns a new object of type `Matrix`.

The operator is applied directly to the class object. The use of the operator looks no different from the use of the built-in operators. When the compiler encounters an expression, such as `mat*dval`, it resolves which instance of the multiplication operator to invoke on the basis of the types of the operands. In this case, it invokes our overloaded `Matrix` instance.

What happens if we write the following?

```
mat *= dval;
```

Since we have not explicitly provided an overloaded instance of the compound assignment operator for multiplication, does this statement result in a compile-time error? No. Support of the compound operator is automatic when we provide an overloaded instance of an operator for which there exists a compound assignment operator, such as addition, subtraction, multiplication, and so on. In fact, providing an explicit overloaded instance of a compound assignment operator results in a compile-time error.

What about when we reverse the operands, as in

```
Matrix newMat = dval * mat;
```

In this case, the compiler flags the expression as invalid. It doesn't know how to multiply a `double` by a `Matrix`; it knows only how to multiply a `Matrix` by a `double`. We have to provide an explicit second instance in order for this to work. In this case, the implementation simply invokes the first instance:

```
public static Matrix
operator*( double dval, Matrix m ){ return m*dval; }
```

What if we multiply a `Matrix` object by an `int` or a `float`? Since our operator expects an operand of type `double`, does an error result?

No. If a single implicit conversion can match the type of the formal parameter, everything is fine.

The parameters to the overloaded operator cannot be either `ref` or `out`. Nor can we change the predefined *arity* of an operator (i.e., the number of arguments that an operator can take). For example, we cannot define a division operator that accepts only one operand. Similarly, we cannot change the precedence of an operator. For example, the multiplication operator always has a higher precedence than that of the addition operator. (See Section 1.18.4 for a discussion of operator precedence.)

The language requires that at least one parameter of the operator be of the class type to which the operator belongs. This restriction prevents us from redefining existing operators such as the `int` addition operator.

Eight unary operators can be overloaded:

```
// the overloadable unary operators
+, -, !, ~, ++, --, true, false
```

The single parameter must be of the class type to which the operator is a member. Three unary operators are not permitted to be overloaded: the selection operator (.), the call operator (()), and new.

If we define a true operator, we must also define a false operator. Both must return a bool value. For example, our StringNode class might define true to mean that its string member is not null and false to mean that it is:

```
class StringNode
{
    private string text;
    public  string Text{ get{ return text; }};

    private StringNode front_link;
    public  StringNode Next{ get{ return front_link; }};

    public static bool
        operator true(StringNode sn) {return sn.text != null;}

    public static bool
        operator false(StringNode sn){return sn.text == null;}
}
```

A StringNode object might then be used as follows:

```
static public void display( StringNode sn )
{
    while ( sn != null )
    {
        // invokes: bool operator true( StringNode )
        if ( sn )
            Console.WriteLine( sn.Text );
        sn = sn.Next;
    }
}
```

The increment and decrement operators (++, --) must return an object of the class for which they are members. The language *does not* support prefix and postfix forms of the operator.

The following binary operators can be overloaded:

```
// the overloadable binary operators
+, -, *, /, %, &, |, ^, <, >, <<, >>, ==, |=, <=, >=
```

At least one of the two parameters must be of the type of the class to which the operator belongs. The following binary operators *cannot* be overloaded:

```
&&, ||, =, ?:, +=, -=, *=, /=, %=, &=, |=, ^=, <<=, >>=
```

In the following operator pairs, both members must be overloaded:

```
(==, |=); (<, >); (<=, >=)
```

If we overload the equality operator but not the inequality operator, for example, the compiler flags the absence of the inequality instance as an error.

2.17 Conversion Operators

C# provides a mechanism by which each class can define a set of both implicit and explicit conversions that can be applied to objects of its class type. Why might we wish to do that?

Imagine that we have designed a `BitVector` class. As a convenience to our users, we choose to convert its internal sequence of `0,1` bits into either an unsigned `long` or a `string` representation. Similarly, we may wish to allow a `string` or unsigned `long` to be used wherever a `BitVector` is expected and have the program know how to convert those representations into a `BitVec-tor`.

In one direction, we provide one or more conversion algorithms to change an object of the class type into a different type. Typically, these operators are specified as `implicit` because they should always succeed. This means that they are carried out automatically by the compiler, and therefore that they participate in overloaded-function resolution.

For example, the conversion of our `BitVector` into a `string` or `ulong` is well behaved. Here is how we might use it:

```
// our overloaded methods
public static void display( string s ){ ... }
public static void display( HashTable ht ){ ... }
```

```
public static void Main()
{
        BitVector bv = new BitVector( 32 );

        // implicitly convert bv into a string
        display( bv );

        // implicitly convert bv into a ulong
        ulong ul = bv;
}
```

Here is how we might declare the conversion operators to support these two implicit BitVector conversions:

```
public class BitVector
{
        static public implicit
                operator string( BitVector bv ){ ... }

        static public implicit
                operator ulong( BitVector bv ){ ... }

        // ... rest of BitVector class definition
}
```

Like an overloaded operator, a conversion operator must be both static and public. In addition, it must specify either implicit or explicit as a keyword. The type following the operator keyword is the return type of the conversion. The single parameter represents the source type to which the conversion should be applied. It cannot be either a ref or an out parameter. Either the return type or the parameter must be the type of the class to which the conversion operator belongs. In our example, both operators convert a BitVector object. In the first instance the operator turns the BitVector into a string type; in the second, into a ulong type.

In the other direction we provide one or more conversion algorithms to change an object of some other type into an object of the class type. We typically specify such conversions as explicit, meaning that to be carried out, the conversion requires an explicit cast by the user. There are two reasons for *not* making both conversion directions implicit.

The first reason is that if we specify both conversion directions as implicit, the compiler is likely to flag certain program situations as ambiguous. For example, imagine that we write the following:

```
classType + built-in-type;
```

The only two addition operators available are the addition operator taking two `classType` operands and the predefined addition operator taking two `built-in-type` operands. That is, for the addition shown here to be carried out, one or the other operand must be converted to the other. But which one?

If `classType` has defined two implicit conversion operators—one to convert the `classType` into the `built-in-type` and a second to convert the `built-in-type` into the `classType`—then the compiler is left with no clear choice, other than to flag the expression as ambiguous. By making one direction explicit, we make the ambiguity go away.

But how do we choose which conversion direction to make explicit? Experience has shown that the conversion of an object of some other type into an object of the class type is more likely to fail. For example, what should the conversion operator do if the `string` to be converted is `null`? The chance of the conversion failing is the second reason for choosing not to make a conversion implicit.

Here is how we might define our explicit pair of conversion operators:

```
static public explicit
    operator BitVec( string s )
{ ... }

static public explicit
    operator BitVec( ulong ul )

{ ... }
```

Here is how we might use them:

```
public static void display( BitVec bitvec ){ ... }
public static void display( HashTable ht ) { ... }

public static void Main()
{
    // both operators invoke display( BitVec );

    display( (BitVec) "0111001011010110" );
    display( (BitVec)43690 );
}
```

2.18   The Class Destructor

C# supports a nondeterministic destructor method, but its use is discouraged. It is nondeterministic in two respects. The first is that we are unable to predict when the destructor is called, or even if it is called. Second, we are unable to predict the order of destructor invocations. From a performance standpoint, classes with destructors have significantly greater overhead in their interaction with the garbage collector.

A destructor—or some sort of finalization routine—is necessary when a class object acquires unmanaged resources during its lifetime and we wish those resources to be released following a last use of that object. Resources might include window or file handles, or database connections. By convention, resource deallocation is factored into a method named `Dispose()`, which must be manually invoked by the user.

We return to this issue in Section 4.8 in a discussion of the `IDisposable` interface and a special `using` statement syntax for the automatic invocation of `Dispose()`.

2.19   The `struct` Value Type

The `struct` mechanism allows us to introduce new value types into our application. The declaration looks exactly the same as for a class, except that we use the `struct` keyword—for example,

```
public struct matrix
{
    private double[,] m_mat;
    private int       m_row;
    private int       m_col;

    // ...
}
```

A value type stores its data directly within the object. A `matrix` object, for example, directly holds the `m_row` and `m_col` integer values, as well as the handle to the two-dimensional reference type array, `m_mat`.

When we initialize or assign one `struct` object with another, a deep copy is carried out; the two objects hold the same values but remain independent, unlike the shallow-copy semantics of a reference type. This both simplifies and speeds up our addition operation—for example, since we just *bitblast* the one `matrix` object into a second:

```
public static matrix operator+( matrix m1, matrix m2 )
{
    check_both_rows_cols( m1, m2 );
    matrix mat = m1;

    for ( int ix = 0 ; ix < m1.rows; ix++ )
        for ( int ij = 0; ij < m1.cols; ij++ )
            mat[ ix, ij ] += m2[ ix, ij ];

    return mat;
}
```

A `struct` object is not allocated on the managed heap and is therefore not subject to garbage collection. When we create a new `struct` object, such as

```
public void func()
{
    matrix mat = new matrix();
    // ...
}
```

the `new` operator is not actually invoked. The `matrix` object is allocated directly within the function. It comes into existence when the function begins execution and ceases to exist when the function terminates.

Every value type is automatically provided with a default constructor—that is, a constructor that takes no arguments. The default constructor zeros out the data members stored within the object of the value type. It is an error to provide an explicit default constructor within a `struct` definition.

Invoking the `new` operator on a value type simply results in the execution of an associated constructor. If no arguments are passed to the invocation, the default constructor is invoked. If we provide arguments, the compiler searches for a constructor matching those arguments. For example, the statement

```
matrix mat = new mat( 4, 4 );
```

requires that we provide a `matrix` constructor that takes two arguments:

```
public struct matrix
{
    public matrix( int row, int col )
    {
        m_row = ( row <= 0 ) ? 1 : row;
        m_col = ( col <= 0 ) ? 1 : col;

        m_mat = new double[ m_row. m_col ];
    }
}
```

In addition to the restriction preventing a `struct` from introducing a default constructor, there are two other constraints: (1) The declaration of data members cannot include an initializer, and (2) a `struct` cannot provide a destructor.

This turns out to be problematic under some circumstances. For example, in computer graphics we generally define a specialized 4x4 matrix to perform geometric transformations such as rotation and scaling. Because we cannot define either a default constructor or an explicit member initializer, there is no straightforward way to define a 4x4 matrix as a `struct`—for example,

```
public struct Matrix44
{
    private double[,] mat; // the problem ...
```

The problem is that the array representing the matrix is a reference type. Its declaration does not represent the size of its two dimensions. Within a class definition, we would add the dimension, as in the following example:

```
public class Matrix44
{
    private double[,] mat = new double[ 4, 4 ];
```

but we can't do that inside a `struct`. Similarly, in the class definition we could have initialized `mat` within the default constructor. But we can't provide a default constructor within a `struct`.

There are tricks around these constraints, but having to resort to tricks is somewhat disappointing. In the sample programs for the book, I've provided a simple example of how one might program around these constraints. It is called `structFixMatrix`.

Why would we define a `struct` rather than a class? For improved runtime performance, primarily. For example, if `SmallInt` is a `struct`, the declaration

```
SmallInt [] vertices = new SmallInt[ 1000 ];
```

creates an array of a thousand `SmallInt` objects. If `SmallInt` is a class, the declaration results in an array of a thousand `null` handles. Each of the thousand objects still needs to be allocated on the managed heap through an additional thousand calls to operator `new`.

Remember that reference types declared as `struct` members still result in a shallow copy. That is, if our `Matrix44 struct` contains an array reference type member, copying one `Matrix44` to another by default results in both array members referring to the same heap array object.

When do we choose to make an abstraction a `struct`? The abstraction should be small; otherwise the deep-copy semantics can boomerang, particularly when we pass objects into functions by value. In addition, the abstraction should be heavily used; otherwise the performance benefit will probably be negligible. The predefined arithmetic types—`int`, `double`, and so on—are defined as value types under the .NET framework.

Chapter 3

Object-Oriented Programming

The primary use of a class is to introduce a new type that more directly represents an entity in our application. In a library checkout application, for example, it is generally easier to program the classes Book, Borrower, and DueDate directly than to translate the program logic to the underlying character, arithmetic, and Boolean data types.

A programming model based on unrelated classes proves cumbersome when an application begins to be filled with class types that represent *is-a-kind-of* instances of another class type. For example, imagine that over time our library checkout application must add support for a RentalBook class, an Audio-Book class, and an InteractiveBook class in addition to the original Book class. Each class is likely to share data members and the member functions to manage the data. Each class also will require additional unique data members to represent its state. Each class may (or may not) have a separate checkout and overdue fine algorithm, although each class will share the same interface.

The class mechanisms of the previous chapter cannot easily model both the commonality and the differences of these four *are-a-kind-of* Book classes. Why? The reason is that these mechanisms do not provide support for specifying relationships among classes. For this kind of support, we need the *object-oriented programming* model.

3.1 Object-Oriented Programming Concepts

The two primary characteristics of object-oriented programming are inheritance and polymorphism:

1. *Inheritance* allows us to group classes into families of related types, allowing for the sharing of common operations and data. For example, think of the family of exception classes that we looked at in Section 1.17.

2. *Polymorphism* allows us to program these families as a unit rather than as individual classes, giving us greater flexibility in adding or removing any particular class.

Inheritance defines a parent/child relationship. The *parent* defines the public interface and private implementation that are common to all its children. Each *child* adds to or overrides what it inherits to implement its own unique behavior.

An `AudioBook` child class, for example, in addition to the title and author it inherits from its parent `Book` class, introduces support for a speaker and a count of the number of cassettes or CDs it represents. In addition, it overrides the inherited `check_out()` member function of its parent.

In C#, the parent is called the *base class* and the child is called the *derived class.* The relationship between the parent or base class and its children is called an *inheritance hierarchy.* At a design review meeting, for example, we might say, "We intend to implement an `AudioBook` derived class. It will override the `check_out()` method of its `Book` base class. However, it will reuse the inherited `Book` class data members, properties, and member functions to manage its shelf location, author's name, and title."

Figure 3.1 pictures a portion of a possible library lending-material class hierarchy. The root of the class hierarchy is an abstract base class, `LibMat`. `LibMat` defines all the operations that are common to all the different types of library lending materials: `check_in()`, `check_out()`, `shelf_location()`, `fine()`, `due_date()`, and so on. `LibMat` does not represent an actual lending-material object; rather, it is an artifact of our design. In fact, it is the *key* artifact. We call it an *abstract base class.*

In an object-oriented program we indirectly manipulate the class objects of our application through an abstract base class rather than directly manipulating the derived-class objects of our application. Indirect manipulation allows us to add or remove a derived class without having to modify the existing program. For example, here is a possible implementation of a `loan_check_in()` member function of our `Library` class:

```
class Library
{
    public void loan_check_in( LibMat mat )
    {
            // mat refers to a derived-class object,
            // such as Book, RentalBook, Magazines, etc. ...
            mat.check_in();

            if ( mat.is_late() )
                    mat.assess_fine();

            if ( mat.waiting_list() )
                    mat.notify_available();
    }

    // ... rest of the Library class definition
}
```

There are no concrete `LibMat` objects in our application—only `Book`, `RentalBook`, and `AudioCD` objects, as well as actual library materials that users borrow. How does this function work? What happens, for example, when the `check_in()` operation is invoked through `mat`? For this function to make sense, `mat` must somehow refer to one of the actual class objects of our application each time `loan_check_in()` is executed. In addition, the `check_in()` member function that is invoked must somehow resolve to the `check_in()` instance of the actual class object to which `mat` refers. And this *is* what happens. The question is, How does it work?

The second unique aspect of object-oriented programming that we identified earlier in this section is polymorphism, the ability of a base-class object to refer transparently to any of its derived-class objects. In our `loan_check_in()` function, for example, `mat` always addresses an object of one of the classes derived from `LibMat`. Which one? That cannot be determined until execution of the program, and it is likely to vary with each invocation of `loan_check_in()`.

```
    mat.check_in();
```

the instance of `check-in()` to be executed is determined at compile time according to `mat`'s class type. Because the function to invoke is resolved before the program begins running, this is called *static binding*.

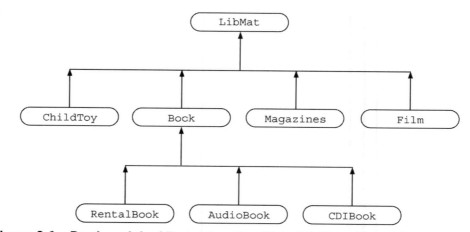

Figure 3.1   Portion of the Library Lending-Material Class Hierarchy

In object-oriented programming the compiler cannot know which instance of `check_in()` to invoke, and so the resolution is delayed until runtime. It is based on the actual derived-class object to which `mat` refers to with each invocation of `loan_check_in()`. This is what we mean by dynamic binding. It is a fundamental aspect of object-oriented programming.

Inheritance allows us to define families of classes that share a common interface, such as our library lending materials. Polymorphism allows us to manipulate objects of these classes in a type-independent manner. We program the common interface through an instance of an abstract base class. The operation is not determined until runtime, according to the type of the object addressed.

If the library decides no longer to lend interactive books, we simply remove the `InteractiveBook` class from the inheritance hierarchy. The implementation of `loan_check_in()` does not require any changes. Similarly, if the library decides to charge a rental fee for certain audio books, we simply implement a derived `AudioRentalBook` class. `loan_check_in()` still does not require changes. If the library decides to lend laptop computers or video game equipment and cartridges, our inheritance hierarchy can accommodate each of those options as well.[1]

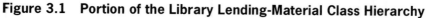

1. Note that `struct` declarations are not part of object-oriented programming. It cannot be the object of inheritance, nor can it participate in dynamic binding.

3.2 Supporting a Polymorphic Query Language

In the remainder of this chapter we implement a query language class hierarchy to introduce the C# language constructs and programming idioms that support object-oriented programming. What is a *query language?* It is part of a general text query application that allows users to search a text file for the occurrence of one or more words. For example, here is the text file against which our queries are directed:

> Alice Emma has long flowing red hair. Her Daddy says
>
> when the wind blows through her hair, t looks almost alive,
>
> like a fiery bird in flight. A beautiful fiery bird, he tells her,
>
> magical but untamed. "Daddy, shush, there is no such creature,"
>
> she tells him, at the same time wanting him to tell her more.
>
> Shyly, she asks, "I mean, Daddy, is there?"

Here is a sample execution of the text query system:

```
TextQuery: begin()

Reading c:\QueryManager\alice_emma.txt -- please wait!
Reading c:\QueryManager\alice_emma.txt -- OK, done!

The text file alice_emma.txt
        contains 6 lines in 357 bytes.

entering text into dictionary -- please wait!
entering text into dictionary -- OK, done!

        Time to read text file: 0.004 seconds
        Time to enter text into dictionary: 0.009 seconds

Please enter a query or 'q' to Quit: alice

alice

        1 line(s) match: [ 1 ]

[1]: Alice Emma has long flowing red hair. Her Daddy says
```

```
Please enter a query or 'q' to Quit: alice || daddy

alice
        1 line(s) match: [ 1 ]

daddy
        3 line(s) match: [ 1 4 6 ]

alice  || daddy
        3 line(s) match: [ 1 4 6 ]

[1]: Alice Emma has long flowing red hair. Her Daddy says
[4]: magical but untamed. "Daddy, shush, there is no such
creature,"
[6]: Shyly, she asks, "I mean, Daddy, is there?"

Please enter a query or 'q' to Quit: q

OK, bye!
TextQuery: end()
```

The query facility we have chosen to support consists of the following elements:

- A *name query*, represented as a single word, such as *Alice* or *untamed*. All lines in which the word appears are displayed with the line number in square brackets. (The lines are displayed in ascending order.)

- A *NOT query*, represented as the ! operator. For example, in the query !daddy, all the lines in which the word *daddy* does not appear are displayed:

```
Please enter a query or 'q' to Quit: ! daddy

daddy
    3 line(s) match: [ 1 4 6 ]

! daddy
    3 line(s) match: [ 2 3 5 ]

[2]: when the wind blows through her hair, it looks almost alive,
[3]: like a fiery bird in flight. A beautiful fiery bird, he tells
her,
[5]: she tells him, at the same time wanting him to tell her more.
```

- An *OR query*, represented as the `||` operator. For example, in the query `alice||daddy`, all the lines in which either of the two names appear are displayed.

- An *AND query*, represented as the `&&` operator. For example, in the query `alice&&daddy`, all the lines in which both words are present are displayed.

```
Please enter a query or 'q' to Quit: alice && daddy
alice
     1 line(s) match: [ 1 ]

daddy
     3 line(s) match: [ 1 4 6 ]

alice  && daddy
     1 line(s) match: [ 1 ]

[1]: Alice Emma has long flowing red hair. Her Daddy says
```

These elements can be combined, as in

```
fiery && bird || shyly
```

However, the order of evaluation is from left to right, with each element maintaining the same precedence level. The evaluation of the query here finds all lines in which the words *fiery* and *bird* appear on the same line, or a line in which *shyly* appears:

```
Please enter a query or 'q' to Quit: fiery && bird || shyly
fiery
     1 line(s) match: [ 3 ]
bird
     1 line(s) match: [ 3 ]
fiery  && bird
     1 line(s) match: [ 3 ]
shyly
     1 line(s) match: [ 6 ]
fiery  && bird  || shyly
     2 line(s) match: [ 3 6 ]

[3]: like a fiery bird in flight. A beautiful fiery bird, he tells
her,
[6]: Shyly, she asks, "I mean, Daddy, is there?"
```

To allow subgrouping of a query, our query facility must also support parentheses. For example, the query

```
fiery && ( bird || shyly )
```

finds all references in which either *fiery* and *bird,* or *fiery* and *shyly,* appear on the same line—for example,

```
Please enter a query or 'q' to Quit: fiery && ( bird || shyly )
fiery
        1 line(s) match: [ 3 ]
( bird
        1 line(s) match: [ 3 ]
shyly
        1 line(s) match: [ 6 ]
( bird  || shyly
        2 line(s) match: [ 3 6 ]

fiery  && ( bird  || shyly  )
        1 line(s) match: [ 3 ]
```

```
[3]: like a fiery bird in flight. A beautiful fiery bird, he tells
her,
```

So this is what we need to represent in our class hierarchy. How do we do that?

3.3 Designing a Class Hierarchy

Our first thought in terms of a class design is to represent each query operation as an individual class:

```
NameQuery       // Alice
NotQuery        // ! Alice
OrQuery         // Alice || fiery
AndQuery        // Alice && Daddy
```

At first blush, this design appears adequate. For example, each class provides an `eval()` method that solves the query for the operation it represents, and a `display_solution()` method to display its solution. A solution is represented as a unique collection of line numbers in ascending order.

The `eval()` method for `NameQuery` simply returns the numbers of the lines in which the name occurs. The `eval()` method for `OrQuery`, on the other hand, must build up a union of the line occurrences of its two operands. The `AndQuery` and `NotQuery` classes each must provide a unique implementation of `eval()` as well.

If the user enters the following query:

```
untamed || fiery
```

we create two `NameQuery` class objects to represent the strings *untamed* and *fiery*. We then create an `OrQuery` class object, passing in these two `NameQuery` objects as its operands. Next we invoke `OrQuery`'s `eval()` method to generate a solution. Finally, we call `print()` to display the solution. In fact, there seems to be no need to introduce object-oriented programming!

This design of four independent classes breaks down when we are handling compound queries such as the following:

```
Alice || Emma && Weeks
```

This query consists of two subqueries: an `OrQuery` object containing two `NameQuery` operands associated with the strings *Alice* and *Emma,* and an `AndQuery` object. The right-hand operand of the `AndQuery` object is the `NameQuery` object associated with the string *Weeks*. So far, so good: Every operand has been a `NameQuery` object, and that's easy enough to represent.

The left-hand operand, however, invalidates our simple design:

```
AndQuery
    // here is the problem!
    OrQuery
       NameQuery ("Alice")
       NameQuery ("Emma")
    NameQuery ("Weeks")
```

`AndQuery`'s left operand is the `OrQuery` object. More generally, we realize, the operand of a query object other than `NameQuery` can be any other query type. How can we internally represent an operand when we don't know what type it needs to be? Or rather, when we know it can be one of several different types? The problem is twofold:

1. We need to be able to declare the type of the operand within the `OrQuery`, `AndQuery`, and `NotQuery` classes such that each can hold each of the four different query class types.

2. We need to be able to invoke the class-specific instance of the `eval()` member function at runtime for each operand through whatever solution we come up with in item 1.

This is where the need for object-oriented programming comes in. Recasting our classes into a query inheritance hierarchy solves both problems.

Through inheritance we define a relationship among the four previously independent query class types. We do this by introducing an abstract `Query` base class from which the other classes can be derived. Inheritance provides an immediate solution to our first problem: A base-class object can transparently address objects of any of its derived-class types.

Inheritance confers a special type/subtype relationship between a base class and its derived classes. When a base-class object is initialized or assigned with a class derived from it, an implicit conversion is automatically carried out. In our `Query` class hierarchy, an object of type `Query` can transparently refer to an `OrQuery`, `AndQuery`, `NotQuery`, or `NameQuery` object.

To indicate that one class is inheriting from another, we write the following:

```
class NotQuery : Query
```

The colon following the `NotQuery` class name indicates that it is inheriting from the `Query` class name that follows. `NotQuery` is the derived class; `Query` is its immediate base class. The two primary constraints on a base class are

1. That it must already be defined, and

2. That it must be at least as accessible as the derived class.

Before we created our `Query` class hierarchy, the only way to define a function that could accept each of the query class types was to explicitly overload the function to accept each instance:

```
class testQuery
{
    public static void eval_print( OrQuery q )
      { q.eval(); q.print_solution(); }
```

```
    public static void eval_print( AndQuery q )
      { q.eval(); q.print_solution(); }

    public static void eval_print( NotQuery q )
      { q.eval(); q.print_solution(); }

    public static void eval_print( NameQuery q )
      { q.eval(); q.print_solution(); }

    // ...
}
```

Once we introduce our abstract `Query` base class and derive each of the query types from it, creating an inheritance hierarchy, we can reduce our four functions to a single instance:

```
class testQuery
{
    public static void eval_print( Query q )
      { q.eval(); q.print_solution(); }

    public static void Main()
    {
      NameQuery nq1 = new NameQuery( "Mason" );
      NameQuery nq2 = new NameQuery( "Dixon" );
      AndQuery  aq  = new AndQuery( nq1, nq2 );
      OrQuery   oq  = new OrQuery( nq1, nq2 );
      NotQuery  nq  = new NotQuery( nq1, nq2 );

      // OK: automatic conversion from a
      //     derived class to its base class

      eval_print( nq1 );   eval_print( aq );
      eval_print( nq );    eval_print( oq );

      // error: string is not derived from Query;
      //        no conversion
      eval_print( "MasonDixon" );
    }
}
```

A derived class is implicitly converted into an object of its base class when necessary, such as when we invoke `eval_print()`. However, when we attempt to assign a `string` object to the `Query` base-class object, the assignment fails. There is no relationship between the `Query` and `string` types.

What would you expect to happen if we assign two derived-class instances of a common base class to one another—for example, an `OrQuery` object to an object of type `AndQuery`? Once again, the assignment fails; no special relationship is defined between the derived classes of a common subtype.

Inheritance solves the problem of transparently *referring to* a family of types. However, it does not solve the problem of transparently *programming* these types; for this we need dynamic binding. Through dynamic binding, the invocation of `eval()` through the `Query` object, `q.eval()`, invokes the `eval()` function associated with the actual derived-class object to which `q` refers rather than the instance associated with the `Query` class.

By default, a member function is resolved through static binding—that is, at compile time based on the type of object through which the method is invoked. In other words, by default, `q.eval()` invokes the `eval()` method of `q`'s class type, which is `Query`.

To have a member function resolved through dynamic binding—that is, during runtime on the basis of the type of the object referred to—we must explicitly label the member function as `virtual`. Otherwise it is treated as nonvirtual. One part of object-oriented design under C# is deciding whether a base-class member function should be identified as `virtual`. (Note that static member functions do not support dynamic binding. The reason is that a static member function is not invoked through a class object.)

The design of an inheritance hierarchy, such as our `Query` class hierarchy, requires two primary design steps: (1) factoring a set of shared operations into an abstract base-class interface, and (2) deciding which of those methods (perhaps all) require dynamic binding. Before we turn to the design and implementation of that hierarchy, we need to step back a moment and reexamine the C# unified type system.

3.4 Object Lessons

In the preceding section we solved a perplexing storage and transmittal problem by introducing the abstract `Query` base class, from which the other query types inherit. For example, when declared as a `Query` object, the `NotQuery` operand is able to address all the derived query types—not only those we know about, but also any that are introduced in the future. This solves our transmittal problem as well. Each function parameter, if declared a `Query` type, can now correctly pass an object of any derived query type.

In this section we look at a similar problem—except that this one relates not to independent classes, but to independent class hierarchies. So far in this chapter we have defined two class hierarchies: the `LibMat` and the `Query` inheritance hierarchies. In Chapter 1 we saw portions of the `Exception` class hierarchy provided within the `System` namespace. Each class hierarchy represents an independent family of types.

Let's imagine that we need to write a function that can accept as a parameter any type defined within one of those three independent class hierarchies. One solution, of course, is to define a set of three overloaded functions:

```
class TheClassOfAllTypes
{
        public string ToString( LibMat m ){...}
        public string ToString( Query q ) {...}
        public string ToString( Exception e ){...}

        // ...
}
```

This set of three overloaded methods can accept every current and future class defined within the `LibMat`, `Query`, and `Exception` class hierarchies. The problem arises when a new class hierarchy or independent class is introduced that also wishes to invoke our `ToString()` method. Oops. Every time we have a new class or class hierarchy to support, we must go back to add a new function to our class. There has to be a better solution.

This is also a transport and storage problem, but one that cuts across independent type hierarchies such as `Query`. The various `Query` subtypes all represent a kind of specialized query. The shared commonality is the general set of operations of a query object.

There is no shared set of behaviorial operations upon which to define a relationship between the `LibMat` and `Query` class hierarchies, except that they both represent class types within the program's type system. The shared commonality is the general set of operations that we as programmers apply to the types in a runtime system.

The solution to this transport and storage problem is the same as our earlier solution: We introduce an abstract base class from which all the types within our program are derived. What should we call this base class, and what public operations, if any, should it provide?

I called it TheClassOfAllTypes because it represents what is common among all program types. Under .NET, it is called Object. Object is a class defined within the System namespace. It serves as the root of the type hierarchy under which all other types, such as Exception, string, int, LibMat, Query, and so on, are derived. The predefined object type in C# is an alias for this class.

Because all types are either directly or indirectly derived from object, an entity of type object can be initialized or assigned to an object of any other type—even literal values such as integer constants and strings. This solves our ToString() design dilemma: How can we define one function that can accept objects of all current and future types? By declaring it to take an object parameter:

```
class TheClassOfAllTypes
{
        static public string ToString( object o ){...}
        // ... what else?
}
```

An interesting question is, What member functions should the base class of all other classes provide? As you might guess, one operation the Object class provides is ToString(). A second public member function is Equals(). A third is GetType(). Each of these operations is inherited by every type in the system. We can invoke ToString(), Equals(), or GetType() on any object or literal value. An interesting question, of course, is what do these functions actually do?

One of the hard things about writing a function for all types is that it ends up doing very little of specific use to any particular type. This is especially true of both the ToString() and Equals() member functions. For example, how can we arbitrarily implement an equals operation that is meaningful for every possible type? The equality of two integers, for example, requires a different algorithm from that required by the equality of two `JulianCalendar` objects.

The solution is twofold. First, the default implementations within the `Object` class provide a least-common-denominator solution. For `Equals()`, the default implementation, called *reference equality*, returns `true` only if the two objects being compared are the *same* object. For `ToString()`, the default implementation prints out the type's fully qualified name. This is the functionality that each new class we define inherits.

The second aspect of the solution is to declare these two member functions as `virtual` functions. Doing so allows each derived class to optionally override the default implementation with an instance that provides more meaningful information about the data associated with the class object. For example, the arithmetic classes override `ToString()` to print out the value held by the object, and `Equals()` to implement *value equality*. As its name implies, value equality returns `true` if the two objects hold the same value.

A third function provided by the `Object` class is the nonvirtual `GetType()`. This function returns a `Type` object that encapsulates all the information about the actual type to which the object refers, such as a description of each of its properties, methods, constructors, and so on. It also contains a set of predicate properties—`IsClass`, `IsArray`, `IsPublic`, and so on—that answer questions about the type. It is nonvirtual because it provides a non-type-dependent operation that the derived class is not intended to override. The `Type` class serves as the gateway to runtime type reflection, the topic of Section 8.2.

Whenever we define a class without an explicit base class, that class implicitly inherits from the `Object` class. For example, let's look again at our `Query` class hierarchy. Here is how we might declare it:

```
class Query { ... }
class NameQuery : Query { ... }
class NotQuery  : Query { ... }
class OrQuery   : Query { ... }
class AndQuery  : Query { ... }
```

From this declaration it appears that `Query` is an independent class. Internally, however, its declaration is augmented to include `Object` as its base class:

```
// internally augmented to derive from System.Object
class Query : System.Object { ... }
```

`Query` serves as the immediate base class of each of the four derived query types. `Object` serves as an indirect base class of each of the derived query types as well. All five classes inherit the public methods defined within `Object`.

3.5 Designing an Abstract Base Class

In its design, an independent class such as `Matrix` or `Image` has generally one provider and many users. The provider designs and usually implements the class. The users exercise the public interface made available by the provider. This separation of activity is reflected in the division of the class into a `private` implementation and a set of `public` methods and properties.

Under inheritance, there are multiple class providers: one providing the base-class implementation (and possibly some derived classes), and one or more providing derived classes throughout the lifetime of the inheritance hierarchy. This activity is also an implementation activity. The provider of the subtype often (but not always) needs access to portions of the base-class implementation. To allow such access, while still preventing general access to the implementation, we provide an additional access level, `protected`. The data members and member functions of a `protected` section of a class, although still unavailable to the general program, are available to the derived class.

The criteria for designating a member `public` to a class does not change between the design of a class that is intended to serve as a base class and one that is not. What does change is whether to declare a nonpublic member as `protected` or `private`. Any member specified as `private` within the base class is *inaccessible* to the derived classes.

A member is made `protected` if we believe it provides an operation or represents data necessary for the effective implementation of the derived class, but that we do not wish to make available to the general user of the class hierarchy. For example, the `display_partial_solution()` member of our `Query` base class provides a common service for each derived class, but it is not intended to be invoked directly by users of the `Query` class hierarchy. If we declare this method `public`, we cannot prevent its general use. While declaring it `private` prevents its general use, it also prevents a derived class from accessing it. The `protected` acess level provides us with the right level of access to accommodate both users of the class and implementers wishing to extend the class through inheritance.[2]

What are the design considerations of a class that is intended to serve as a base class? We must identify the operations and properties that represent the public interface of the entire class hierarchy. We must then identify which of those operations are type dependent. These represent the virtual functions of our class hierarchy.

There is no magic formula for answering these questions or, once they have been answered, for guaranteeing either their correctness or their completeness. The process of object-oriented design is iterative and requires both additions to and modifications of our evolving class hierarchy. In the remainder of this chapter we walk through an iterative evolution of the `Query` class hierarchy.

3.6   Declaring an Abstract Base Class

`Query` represents the base class abstraction from which all the actual query types manipulated within our application are inherited. The user should never create an actual instance of a `Query` object. Rather, a `Query` object in our program always addresses one of the inherited query types. To enforce this usage model, we modify the `Query` class definition with the `abstract` keyword:

```
abstract public class Query { ... }
```

The `abstract` keyword tells both the compiler and readers of our program that it is illegal to create an actual `Query` class instance. For example, the following attempt to create a `Query` object triggers a compile-time error:

```
// error: Query is abstract
Query q = new Query();
```

---

2. There is some debate as to whether a derived class should directly access its base-class members or should access them through a base-class property. On the one hand, direct access results in a tight coupling between the base- and derived-class implementations—potentially inhibiting the evolution of the base class, or at least making that evolution more difficult. On the other hand, implementers of the derived class argue that direct member access is necessary to achieve acceptable performance.

Rather, a `Query` object can be used only to address one of the derived-class query types:

```
// OK: Query addresses a derived-class object
Query q = new AndQuery();
```

The two primary operations of the `Query` class hierarchy are to evaluate the query and to display the matching lines, if any. We'll name these methods `eval()` and `display_solution()`.

The implementation of `eval()` is specific to each derived-class query type. It therefore needs to be declared as a virtual function. How do we do that within a base class? We have two choices: We provide either a default implementation or simply an abstract placeholder.

If there is a meaningful default implementation of the method, we provide that definition and specify the function using the `virtual` keyword:

```
abstract public class Query
{
    virtual public void eval()
            { /* default implementation */ }
}
```

The `virtual` keyword identifies the method as type dependent. It also indicates that a definition of the method is associated with the function and serves as the default implementation for a subsequently derived class that does not provide its own instance.

The derived class may override the inherited base-class instance with its own implementation. A derived class, however, is *not required to override* the virtual function. The implementation of the base-class method may also be appropriate for a derived-class instance. In that case the derived class does not provide its own instance, but reuses (*inherits*) that of the base class. For example, whenever we define a class, we have the option of either overriding the virtual `ToString()` method of the `Object` base class or reusing its default implementation.

If, however, there is no meaningful default base-class implementation of the method, the method is declared with the `abstract` keyword and no function body is provided:

```
abstract public class Query
{
    // no function body is provided ...
    abstract public void eval();
}
```

An abstract function is also treated as a virtual function. Its declaration simply indicates that no meaningful implementation exists. An abstract method serves as a placeholder. It introduces the interface—that is, the method's name, access level, signature, and return type. The implementation is provided by each of the derived-class instances.

In the case of an abstract function, there is no default implementation for a derived-class instance to inherit. If the derived class does not provide a definition of the method, the derived class is also an abstract class, and no instance of that class can be directly created.

Why would we ever want to introduce an abstract derived class? An abstract derived class provides a way of subpartitioning a class hierarchy. For example, let's modify our class hierarchy so that the AndQuery and OrQuery classes are derived from an abstract BinaryQuery class. This change allows us to factor data members or methods common only to binary queries into a single, shared class:

```
abstract public class BinaryQuery : Query
{
    // inherits the abstract eval() method
}

public class AndQuery : BinaryQuery
{
    // OK: an implementation of eval() here
}
```

We say that both the Query and the BinaryQuery classes serve as abstract classes of the hierarchy, while AndQuery (and OrQuery) serves as a concrete class of the application domain.

The abstract keyword is required in the declaration of any class that either introduces or inherits an abstract method (or property or indexer). If we forget to specify the abstract keyword, its absence triggers a compile-time error.

Is the introduction of an abstract `BinaryQuery` class a better design? We can't really say until we understand how we use the `AndQuery` and `OrQuery` classes. If there are circumstances in which we manipulate the two queries collectively as binary queries, or if a shared set of operations is unique to binary queries but is not applicable to the other query types, this design makes sense. This sort of *refactoring* of a class hierarchy is common throughout the lifetime of the class hierarchy.

Properties and indexers can also be declared as either abstract or virtual. Let's look at an example of each.

One property associated with a `Query` object is the solution set—that is, the lines within the text that match the user query—which is represented by an array of integers. The solution-set array may or may not be present, depending on whether the query object has invoked `eval()`. If it is not set, the property must return `null`; otherwise it returns a handle to the array. We want to allow users to read the solution set, but we don't want users to modify it. Therefore, we specify only the `get` accessor:

```
abstract public class Query
{
    virtual public int [] Solution
    {
        get
        {
            return null;
        }
    }
}
```

The rule is that the `virtual` or `abstract` keyword is applied to the property (or indexer) as a whole rather than to the individual accessors. If the property is declared `abstract`, the accessor is not provided with a code block:

```
abstract public class Query
{
    abstract public int [] Solution
    {
        get;
    }
}
```

An indexer looks pretty much the same—for example,

```
abstract public class NumericSequence
{
    abstract public int this[ int index ]
    {
       get;
       set;
    }
}
```

3.7   Static Members of an Abstract Base Class

What about the text file against which the user queries are made? There is only one instance of the text file (or if we support multiple text files, one instance of each of the several text files). The text file, then, is represented as a static member, together with several supporting static methods and an indexer:

```
abstract public class Query
{
    static private [] string ms_textfiles;
    const  private    int    ms_maxFiles = 24;

    static protected void check_index( int ix )   {...}
    static public    void add_file( string name ) {...}

    static public int MaxFiles {
          get{ return ms_MaxFiles; }
    }

    static public string this[ index ix ]
    {
       get{ check_index( ix ); return ms_textfiles[ix]; }
       set{ check_index( ix ); ms_textfiles[ix] = value;}
    }
}
```

A static method, static indexer, or static property *cannot* be declared as either virtual or abstract. The class constructors and destructor cannot be declared as virtual.

How many instances of the static `ms_textfiles` or `ms_MaxFiles` actually exist? Only one, regardless of how many classes we derive from the base class. Even after we provide the four derived-class instances of `Query`, there exists only one instance of each `static` or `const` data member of the base class.

We have declared the two static members as `private`. A private member of the base class cannot be directly accessed within the derived class. This means that each derived-class instance must go through the associated public static property or static index in order to read (or write) the member.

The benefit of a `private` base-class member is a loose coupling between the base class and subsequent derived classes. If we allow the derived classes direct access to a base-class member, any change in the implementation of that member is likely to break the implementation of those derived classes as well.

The potential drawback is unacceptable overhead in the performance of the derived classes because of the inability to directly access a critical base-class member. The solution in this case is to declare the member as `protected`, thereby allowing the derived class direct access to the member but still preventing the general user from having access.

3.8   A Hybrid Abstract Base Class

The solution-set data member is the same for each derived-class query type: an array of integers indicating the matching lines of text. In our initial design, our `Query` class defines an abstract property encapsulating the solution set:

```
abstract public class Query
{
    abstract public int [] Solution { get; }
    // ...
}
```

Each derived class, in turn, defines the actual solution-set instance data member and provides the actual implementation of `get` for the `Solution` property—for example,

```
public class NotQuery : Query
{
    private int [] solution_set;
    virtual public int [] Solution
    {
            get{ return solution_set; }
    }
    // ...
}
```

Consider the following code fragment, in which `parseQuery()` represents a utility that transforms a string representation of the user's query into a corresponding class representation. It returns an abstract `Query` node that addresses the actual derived-class query type:

```
Query theQuery = parseQuery( userQueryString );
theQuery.eval();
int [] solution = theQuery.Solution;
```

In this sequence, both `eval()` and `Solution` are invoked at runtime through the virtual function mechanism. `eval()` is clearly dependent on the actual query type; the virtual mechanism is the only viable solution. Is the declaration of `Solution` as `abstract` equally as necessary?

The implementation of `Solution` is the same for each of the derived query types. The type of the instance member for `solution_set` is also the same. An alternative class design, in this case, is to refactor the definitions of the shared instance member and property into the abstract `Query` base class:

```
abstract public class Query
{
    abstract public void eval();

    protected int [] solution_set;
    public     int [] Solution
               { get{ return solution_set; }}
    // ...
}
```

This refactoring does not break source compatibility. The invocation

```
int [] solution = theQuery.Solution;
```

correctly returns the `solution_set` associated with the derived query object returned from `parseQuery()`. The difference is that it is now resolved statically at compile time.

There are various design implications when we introduce an instance member into the base class. For example, we now need a constructor for the `Query` class, which is odd if you think about it: The class is still an abstract base class, and independent instances of the class cannot be created. We look at these issues and others in the following subsections.

3.8.1 The Single-Inheritance Object Model

A derived class inherits *all* the members of its base class. (And all the members of the base class of its base class, and so on. Remember that all classes implicitly derive from `Object`.) Physically, each derived-class object contains a base-class *subobject* that consists of all the instance members of the base class. For example, a `NotQuery` object contains a `Query` subobject, and a `Query` subobject contains an `Object` subobject. You can think of the different subobjects as Lego blocks stacked atop one another. At the base of each is the `Object` subobject.

Although it may seem confusing to think of each base class as a separate subobject within the derived-class object, doing so provides for an efficient model of single inheritance:

- In terms of initialization, an associated base-class constructor is automatically applied to its subobject before the derived-class constructor is executed. When we create a `NotQuery` object, for example, first an associated `Object` constructor is invoked, then an associated `Query` constructor, and then the body of the `NotQuery` constructor. (In Section 3.9 we look at how to pass arguments to the immediate base-class constructor.)

- In terms of conversion, because a derived-class object contains a full subobject instance of its base class, no runtime work is required to accomplish the conversion. What is lost in the conversion is knowledge of the nonvirtual derived-class interface—for example,

```
NotQuery nq = new NotQuery( ... );
Query oper = nq.Operand; // OK

// still a NotQuery object,
// but now only the Query interface can be invoked
Query q = nq;

// OK: eval() is part of the Query interface,
//     and it is virtual: it invokes NotQuery.eval()
q.eval();

// OK: Solution is part of the Query interface,
//     but it is nonvirtual: it invokes Query.Solution
int [] solution = q.Solution;
```

```
// error: Operand is part of the NotQuery interface;
//         it cannot be invoked through Query
Query op = q.Operand;

// still a NotQuery object,
// but now only the Object interface can be invoked
Object o = q;

// error: eval() is part of the Query interface;
//         it cannot be invoked through Object
o.eval();
```

Now I'm going to contradict myself—but with an explanation. I've claimed that a derived class can directly access the inherited members of its base class. That's only partially true: Whereas the derived class inherits *all* the members of its base class, the derived class cannot access the inherited *private* members of its base class. (In fact, C# does not allow a function to be declared both `virtual` and `private`.)

If a private base-class member cannot be accessed by the derived class, why does the language bother to have it be inherited, especially given that this inheritance takes up space in each derived-class object? The reason is to maintain the integrity of the base-class subobject. The problem is that although we cannot directly access a private member, we often indirectly access it through a base-class property, indexer, constructor, or method. It has to be there.

3.8.2   How Is a Hybrid Abstract Class Different?

Once we introduce one or more instance members into an abstract base class, we must also introduce support for user-directed initialization of those members. This means introducing one or more constructors—for example,

```
abstract public class Query
{
    protected Query( int [] aSolution ){ ...}

    protected int [] solution_set;
    public    int [] Solution
             { get{ return solution_set; }}
    // ...
}
```

Notice that the constructor is `protected,` not `public`. A `Query` object is intended only to serve as a subobject of one of the derived query types. If the constructor is declared `protected`, only the derived query types can create an instance of `Query`.

By refactoring the shared instance data within the base class, we eliminate the abstract nature of the supporting property. There are two primary benefits:

1. *The `Solution` property executes significantly faster.* Rather than delaying until runtime the resolution of which `Solution` instance to invoke, the instance is resolved during compilation. A simple `get` accessor is almost certain to be expanded inline at each call point, eliminating the overhead of a function call altogether.

2. *The implementation of the derived-class instances is simplified.* In the pure abstract design, each derived class must provide not only the unique algorithms of the type, but the shared infrastructure for storing and returning the type. In the hybrid design, the designer of the derived class inherits the infrastructure support. The design of each derived type has therefore been simplified.

Is the performance improvement significant? That depends on how often the method or property is invoked. Were `Solution` heavily invoked in a critical portion of the application, the design change would be significant. Otherwise it would not.

Similarly, the simplification of the derived-class implementation may or may not prove significant. If the designer of the abstract base class is also providing the derived-class query types, and if the set of derived classes is not expected to grow very often, this hybrid design change is not likely to be significant. If, however, a primary activity of the hierarchy is the delivery of new query class types, and if that activity has been delegated to individuals more comfortable with library science than with programming, the refactoring makes for a better design.

So what's the rule? There is no rule—just a design choice to be aware of. An abstract base class can legitimately define both instance data members and nonvirtual methods. This is referred to as *implementation inheritance*. For example, if you come from the Component Object Model (COM) programming model, this sort of implementation refactoring is not an option. Under C# and .NET, however, it is. Even `Object` provides a nonvirtual `GetType()` method.

3.9 Defining a Derived Class

In general, a derived class needs to program only those aspects of its behavior that differ from or extend the behavior of its base class. `NotQuery`, for example, must provide an `eval()` definition that implements the *not* semantics. It must also introduce an instance member to store the query operand it is negating, and a property to allow get and set access to the operand, if appropriate. Both the `AndQuery` and `OrQuery` classes must support left and right operands. The `NameQuery` member must support a `string` member. All must provide definition of the abstract `eval()` virtual method.

The derived class is considered abstract if either it introduces an abstract member or it does not provide an implementation for an inherited abstract member. In either case it must explicitly be declared as an `abstract` class. The following example shows a `BinaryQuery` derived class. It is abstract because it does not provide an implementation of the abstract `eval()` method:

```
abstract public class BinaryQuery : Query
{
    protected BinaryQuery( Query leftOp, Query rightOp,
                           int [] solution )
        : base( solution )
        { m_lop = leftOp; m_rop = rightOp; }
    protected Query m_lop, m_rop;
    public Query LeftOp
        { get{ return m_lop; } set{ m_lop = value; }}
    public Query RightOp
        { get{ return m_rop; } set{ m_rop = value; }}
}
```

The use of the `base` keyword in the `BinaryQuery` constructor following the colon represents the invocation of the `Query` base-class constructor with `solution` as its argument. The base-class constructor is invoked before the body of the derived-class constructor is evaluated. This order of invocation guarantees that the inherited base-class members are initialized before execution of the body of the derived-class constructor within which they may be referenced.

C# does not permit the *invocation list* of the constructor to contain both a `base` and a `this` construct. If we need both, we must factor them into distinct constructor groups, such as in the following `3DPoint` class:

```
public class 3DPoint :  2DPoint
{
    // cannot have base() and this() in one constructor
    public point3D( float x, float y, float z )
            : base( x, y ){ m_z = z; }

    public 3DPoint() : this( 0.0F, 0.0F, 0.0F ){}

    public 3DPoint( float x ) : this( x, 0.0F, 0.0F ){}
    public 3DPoint( float x, float y )
                    : this( x, y, 0.0F ){}

    // ...
}
```

What about the `AndQuery` derived class? It inherits support for its two operands from its immediate abstract `BinaryQuery` class. It inherits support for the solution set from the `Query` base class from which `BinaryQuery` is derived. It seems that all it has to do is implement the inherited abstract `eval()` method. Well, almost.

There are two additional considerations. The first is the proverbial exception to the *we-inherit-everything-from-the-base-class* rule. Actually, a derived class does not inherit the constructor(s) of its base class. Even if all the derived-class constructor has to do is accept a set of parameters and pass them to its base-class constructor, it still has to be explicitly defined to do it. There is simply no inheritance of the base-class constructor(s).

The second consideration is that the derived class needs to define a constructor for each form of initialization it wishes to permit. For example, the `AndQuery` class allows an instance to be created only if it is passed either two operands of type `Query`, or two operands and an integer array:

```
public class AndQuery : BinaryQuery
{
    public AndQuery( Query leftOp, Query rightOp,
                    int [] solution )
        : base( leftOp, rightOp, solution ){}
```

```
        public AndQuery( Query leftOp, Query rightOp )
            : this( leftOp, rightOp, null ){}

        public virtual eval() { ... }
        // ... anything more ???
}
```

An attempt to create an `AndQuery` object with any other combination of arguments results in a compile-time error. This is true even for an attempt to create an `AndQuery` object with no arguments:

```
// OK: invokes the associated constructor
Query q1 = new AndQuery ( new NameQuery( "Cival" ),
                          new NameQuery( "War" ) );

Query q2 = new AndQuery ( q1, q1, q1.Solution );

// error: no constructor provided to support this
Query q3 = new AndQuery();
```

The no-argument constructor receives special treatment. If we provide no constructors for a class, the no-argument constructor is automatically supplied. Once we have defined one or more constructors, however, the no-argument constructor is no longer supplied automatically.

3.10   Overriding the Inherited Virtual Interface

A derived class can either inherit or override the virtual interface of its base class. To inherit a member, the class need do nothing. Inheritance is the default behavior. *To override an inherited abstract or virtual member, however, we must label the definition with the* `override` *keyword*. Otherwise the compiler treats the instance as an independent definition reusing the name of the inherited member. If you do this—accidentally or not—you'll receive a warning from the compiler. If the warning is spurious, you can turn it off by specifying the `new` keyword; we see how to do this in Section 3.12.

Both the base-class and derived-class instances of the virtual function must have the *same* access level, as well as the same signature and return type.[3] For

---

3. C# does not support *covariance of the return type*. That is, if a base-class virtual function returns an object of the base class, the derived-class instance must do so as well. The derived-class instance may not declare itself to return a derived-class object.

example, the following does not represent a legal override because the derived-class instance has a `ref string` parameter, which requires a different calling syntax:

```
public class Base
{
    public virtual void display( string msg ) { ... }
}

public class Derived : Base
{
    // error: signatures differ by ref keyword
    public override void display( ref string msg ){ ... }
}
```

The `Derived` class instance of `display()` results in a compile-time error because the `override` keyword instructs the compiler to look for the matching inherited instance, and it cannot find one.

When we override a property, we must specify the same property type and provide one or both of the accessors specified by the inherited property. The same holds true of an indexer, with the added requirement that the type and number of indices match as well.

3.11   Overriding the Virtual Object Methods

The second issue in the design of a derived class revolves around the three `virtual` methods that every class implicitly inherits from `Object`. Recall that by default, `ToString()` prints out the name of the class. It is generally more useful for a class to display a representation of its internal state. For example, here is the `ToString()` implementation of our `OrQuery` class (the `lparen` and `rparen` members keep track of any parentheses associated with the query):

```
override public string ToString()
{
    StringBuilder sb = new StringBuilder( 8 );

    if ( m_lparen != 0 )
        gen_lparen( ref sb, m_lparen );
```

```
    sb.Append( m_lop.ToString() );
    sb.Append( " || " );
    sb.Append( m_rop.ToString() );

    if ( m_rparen != 0 )
        gen_rparen( ref sb, m_rparen );

    return sb.ToString();
}
```

`ToString()` is intended primarily as a debugging aid, although no constraint is imposed on how we might choose to use it. However, many users may be reluctant to invoke `ToString()` for display purposes other than debugging. For that reason you may consider providing a `Display()` or `Print()` function as well.

Why do I use the `StringBuilder` class object rather than directly building up a `string`? Purely for efficiency. A `string` object is immutable. Each `string` modification results in the generation of a new `string` object. For example, to build up the following `OrQuery` representation directly in a `string` object:

```
(( alice && emma ) || weeks )
```

results in the generation of nine temporary `string` objects—one with the insertion of each new element. `StringBuilder` is mutable. It allows us to build up a string representation without generating multiple instances. After we have completed modifying our string, we extract it from the `StringBuilder` object using its `ToString()` member function.

By default, `Equals()` implements reference equality; that is, it returns `true` only if the two objects being compared are actually the same object. In general, when we implement a class, we'll want to override `Equals()` so that it represents value equality—that is, so that it returns `true` when two independent class objects contain the same values.

3.12 Member Access: The `new` and `base` Modifiers

The inherited members of the base class appear as if they are members of the derived class. This is why we are able to directly refer to them without qualification. However, they are not members of the derived class. Rather they maintain their membership within the declaration space of their base class.

The derived-class declaration space is searched first for an occurrence of a name within the derived class. If the name is not found there, the declaration space of the base class is searched. This is why a derived class can reuse the name of a base-class member without penalty. The derived instance is entered into the derived-class declaration space. All unqualified uses of the name within the derived class resolve to the derived-class instance. The derived-class instance is said to *hide* the inherited base-class instance—for example,

```
abstract public class Query
{
    public void func1( int i ) { ... }
    public virtual void func2( int ival )
            { func1( ival ); }

    // ...
}

public class OrQuery : Query
{
    // necessary because this definition
    // hides the inherited base-class member
    new public void func1( int i ) { ... }

    public override void func2( int ival )
    {
        // OK: we want the hidden base-class member
        //     invoked here
        base.func1( ival );

        // unqualified reference invokes the
        // OrQuery instance ...
        func1( ival );
    }

    // ...
}
```

Hopefully what is going on here is clear. The two `func1()` instances defined in both the base and the derived classes are nonvirtual. They have the same signature, so the derived-class instance hides that of the base class. To indicate to both the compiler and the readers of our program that the renaming is intentional, we modify the derived-class instance with the `new` keyword. In this context, the `new` keyword identifies the member definition as hiding the unqualified access of an inherited member with the same name. If we don't specify `new`, we get a warning because the compiler is not sure we are aware of the hidden base-class member.

To access the base-class member within the derived class, we must qualify its name with the `base` keyword:

```
base.func1( ival );
```

This statement invokes the `func1()` method defined as a member of the base class. In this case it invokes the `func1()` class member defined within `Query`. If `Query` has not defined a `func1()` member, the statement is flagged as an error.

Outside the derived class, the `base` keyword cannot be used. There is no syntax to support accessing a hidden base-class member through a derived-class object. If absolutely necessary, we can resort to an explicit cast:

```
static public void Main()
{
    OrQuery or = new OrQuery();

    or.func1( 1024 );           // OrQuery.func1( int )
    ((Query)or).func1(1024);    // Query.func1( int )

    // ...
}
```

Because `func1()` is not a virtual function, an invocation of `func1()` through a `Query` object always resolves to the member defined within `Query`, even if the `Query` object actually addresses an object of type `OrQuery`, as in the following example:

```
Query q = new OrQuery();
q.func1( 1024 ); // nonvirtual: Query.func1()
q.func2( 1024 ); // virtual: OrQuery.func2();
```

In general, you should be suspicious of a class hierarchy design in which nonvirtual methods reuse the same name. The potential for users to become confused as to which instance is being invoked is quite real.

A `virtual` function that provides a definition of an `abstract` method and the derived-class `override` method does not need to specify the `new` keyword because there is no hiding in such instances. The virtual mechanism invokes the appropriate method transparently according to the type of the runtime object through which the function is invoked.

3.12.1 Accessibility versus Visibility

Consider the following class hierarchy, with a member `s` defined in both the base and derived classes:

```
class aBase { public string s; }
class aDerived : aBase { new private string s; }
```

Within the base class, all references to `s` refer to its `public string` member. Similarly, within the derived class all unqualified references to `s` refer to its `private string` member. Within the derived class, the base-class member can be referenced through the `base` keyword:

```
base.s; // refers to aBase.s
```

The `new` keyword alerts the compiler (and readers of the program) that the designer of the derived class intended to hide the base-class member `s` within the declaration space of the derived class.

Now let's introduce another level of derivation:

```
class aMostDerived : aDerived
{
    // OK: which member 's' is assigned?
    public void foo( string str ) { s = str; }
}
```

Our new class inherits both member instances of `s`. Which of the two instances does an unqualified use of `s` within the `aMostDerived` class resolve to—that of `aBase` or of `aDerived`?

In C++ the member being referred to is resolved before its accessibility is considered. First the immediate scope of the method is examined, then the enclosing scope of the method's class, then the enclosing base-class scope. In C++ the `aDerived` class instance of `s` is selected. An error is subsequently generated because s is a private inherited member and is therefore not accessible. The intention is not to change the meaning of a program when the access level of a member is changed.

In C#, the member being referred to is resolved only after the accessible candidates are considered. That is, although the aDerived instance of s is the immediate derived-class instance, because it is private and therefore inaccessible, it is not considered an accessible candidate for resolving the reference. Rather the aBase instance is selected. If the class designer were later to redeclare the aDerived instance as protected, it would be selected instead.

3.12.2 Encapsulating Base-Class Access

Consider the following simplified Point/Point3D class hierarchy. The coordinate members span the base and derived classes:

```
class Point
{
    protected float x_, y_;
    public Point( float x, float y ){ x_ = x; y_ = y; }

    public virtual void display()
        { Console.Write( "{0}, {1}", x_, y_ ); }

    // ...
}

class Point3D : Point
{
    protected float z_;
    public Point3D( float x, float y, float z )...
    public override void display(){ ... }
}
```

First, how should we implement the Point3D constructor? Basically, we have two choices:

1. Pass the x and y coordinates to the Point constructor using the base keyword:

    ```
    public Point3D( float x, float y, float z )
            : base( x, y ) { z_ = z; }
    ```

2. Directly initialize the three members within the derived-class constructor:

```
public Point3D( float x, float y, float z )
   { x_ = x; y_ = y; z_ = z; }
```

The members are correctly initialized under both implementations. However, we should always prefer the first solution, in which the base-class constructor is given the responsibility of initializing the members of its class.

The primary reason is to maintain a loose coupling between the base class and the classes that inherit from it. This way, if the implementation of the base class were to change, the derived classes would not mysteriously then fail to compile. For example, point of contention among graphics programmers is whether to store coordinate members individually or as an array. I've actually seen implementations flip-flop between the two approaches as different programmers assumed responsibility to maintain the classes.

How, then, should we implement the Point3D instance of display()? The choices are pretty much the same: (1) directly print out all three members, or (2) invoke the base-class display() function to handle the base-class members and print out only the z coordinate member in the derived-class instance.

The preferred solution is to localize the responsibility to the class whose members are being displayed. Our derived instance should be concerned with only the display of its member(s):

```
class Point3D : Point
{
   public override void display()
   {
        base.display();
        Console.Write( ", {0}", z_ );
   }
   // ...
}
```

The use of the base keyword is necessary to invoke the Point instance of display(). An unqualified invocation of display() resolves to the Point3D instance, which results in an infinite recursion. Because the base keyword specifies which instance of display() to invoke, the invocation is performed at compile time rather than through the virtual mechanism.

3.13 Sealing a Class

To explicitly prevent derivation from a class, we specify the `sealed` keyword:

```
sealed public class BinaryTree { .. }
```

An attempt to inherit from a `sealed` class triggers a compile-time error:

```
// error: BinaryTree is a sealed class
public class RedBlackTree : BinaryTree { ... }
```

The `sealed` keyword cannot be applied to either a `struct`, which is already implicitly sealed, or class declared as `abstract`, which requires the inherited classes to provide a concrete implementation.

Why do we seal a class?

There is the philosophical aspect, of course. We're making a statement as to our perceived use of the class.

Unfortunately, our perception may be of limited perspicacity. For example, in the next chapter we will need to extend the `BitArray` collection class. However, the implementers have declared it as `sealed`, preventing inheritance. That's a real problem. Philosophy by itself is a poor design strategist!

There has to be a better reason for sealing a class. And there is: It can improve the performance of our classes.

Ordinarily the invocation of a virtual function or virtual accessor is unable to be resolved until runtime because the object through which we invoke the virtual member may refer not to an object of its class, but to an object of an unknown class derived from it. When we seal a class, we eliminate the unknown aspect of the invocation.

The invocation of a virtual member through an object of a sealed class can be resolved statically at compile time. Not only is the virtual mechanism unnecessary, but the opportunity for inline expansion, which is a compile-time optimization, becomes possible as well. This can significantly improve the performance of heavily used classes, such as that of the `string` and collection classes.

When an abstraction requires optimal performance but is not appropriate as a value type, a `sealed` class is a potential alternative design. A `sealed` class is still created on the managed heap, but its virtual interface is eliminated.

3.14 The `Exception` Class Hierarchy

An exception must represent either an `Exception` class object or an object of a class derived from `Exception`. The class framework provides many predefined exception classes. Alternatively, we can derive our own exception classes.

Consider the member function `find()`. It takes two parameters: a `string` array and a `string` item. If either or both arguments are `null`, `find()` throws the predefined `ArgumentNullException`:

```
public static bool find( string [] table, string item )
{
    if ( table == null || item == null )
    {
        Exception e = new ArgumentNullException();
        if ( table == null )
        {
            e.Source = "Argument One";
            if ( item == null )
                e.Source += " and Argument Two";
        }
        else e.Source = "Argument Two";
        throw e;
    }

    // ...
    return false;
}
```

The `Exception` class supports a pocketful of useful properties, including the following:

- `TargetSite`, which holds the name of the member function from which this exception is thrown. This is a read-only property. In our example, it is set to `Boolean find(System.String[], System.String)`.

- `Source`, which by default holds the name of the assembly from which this exception is thrown. We can explicitly assign it a value, however. In our example it is set to *Argument One, Argument Two,* or both.

- `Message`, which is set to a default message by each exception class. In our example the `ArgumentNullException` class sets it to *Value cannot be null.* We can override the default message string in the constructor only; the property is read-only.

- `StackTrace`, which is a trace of the call stack leading to the throw. The property is read-only. It includes path, file, and line information—for example,

```
at EntryPoint.find(String[] table, String item)
in c:\c#programs\exceptions\class1.cs:line 17

at EntryPoint.Main()
in c:\c#programs\exceptions\class1.cs:line 29
```

- `InnerException`, which holds a reference to the inner exception, if any. The property is read-only.

The concept of an *inner exception* may be unfamiliar. Let's imagine that `find()` is invoked in a member function named `queryText()`, as follows:

```
public static void queryText()
{
    try
    {
        if ( find( get_text_array(), get_item() ))
            // ...
    }
    catch( ArgumentNullException ane )
    {  /* what should we do here? */ }
}
```

Within `queryText()`, `ArgumentNullException` indicates that either one or both of the retrieval routines failed. (We can determine that by examining the `Source` property of the caught exception.)

To the caller of `queryText()`, however, the `null` argument problem is of less concern than the failure of the retrieval routines. What we'd like to do within `queryText()` is throw back a more explicit exception object, but also return the original exception. We do this through the inner exception.

In other words, an inner exception is an exception that has been only partially handled within a `catch` clause. Rather than rethrowing the same exception, the developer chooses to create a new and usually more informative exception object. The original exception is passed to the `InnerException` property in the constructor of the exception, allowing the next exception handler access to both—for example,

```
catch( ArgumentNullException ane )
{
    string msg;

    switch ( ane.Source )
    {
        case "Argument One":
            msg = "get_text_array() failed";
        break;

        case "Argument Two":
            msg = "get_item() failed";
        break;

        default:
            msg = "both get_text_array() " +
                    "and get_item() failed";
        break;
    }

    throw new InvalidProgramException( msg, ane );
}
```

The `Exception` class hierarchy is broken down into two primary subtrees. All the exception classes thrown by the runtime environment are derived from `SystemException`, which in turn is derived from the `Exception` class. `ArgumentException`, `ArithmeticException`, `FormatException`, and so on, are all derived from `SystemException`. These classes are then further derived into the more specialized `ArgumentNullException` or `DivideByZeroException` classes.

If we wish to introduce exception classes of our own, the recommendation is to derive them from `ApplicationException`. This class is directly derived from `Exception`. It is also recommended that our exception classes provide a default constructor that initializes the class object with default properties—for example,

```
class TextQueryException : ApplicationException
{
    public TextQueryException()
            : this( "A TextQueryException has been thrown", null )
    {}
```

```
public TextQueryException( string message )
    : this( message, null ){}

public TextQueryException( string msg, Exception innerE )
    : base( msg, innerE ){}

// application-specific members go here ...
}
```

We may wish subsequently to provide more specific subclass exceptions, such as the following:

```
class ProhibitedQueryException : TextQueryException
{ ... }
```

When we set up a series of `catch` clauses, we should always order them such that the more derived class occurs before that of its base. For example, we should always try to catch a `TextQueryException` object before we try to catch either its immediate base class (`ApplicationException`) or the base of the base class, and so on.

The reason is that the resolution of an exception is based on a *first* match rather than on a *best* match. If a base-class `catch` clause occurs before that of a derived class, the match is made on the base-class instance and the remaining clauses are not considered. The following ordering of `catch` clauses handles the most-derived class instances first:

```
try {
    // ...
}
catch( ProhibitedQueryException pqe )
{ ... }

catch( TextQueryException tqe )
{ ... }

catch( ApplicationException ae )
{ ... }

catch( SystemException se )
{ ... }

catch( Exception e )
{ ... }
```

Function matching employs a best-match rather than a first-match resolution algorithm. This is why function matching is independent of declaration order. The matching of exception objects is not. Under function matching, the matching of two derived-class objects takes precedence over the matching of a derived-class object with an object of its base class. Under exception matching, the two are treated in effect as equal. This is why we must place the base class exception object after that of its derived instances.

Chapter 4

Interface Inheritance

An interface specifies a set of abstract methods and properties. Like an abstract base class, an interface is made concrete by each of its derived classes. Unlike an abstract base class, an interface cannot provide a default implementation or define state, such as an instance data member or constant.

An abstract base class provides a common interface for a family of related types. In computer graphics, for example, `Light` may serve as an abstract base class for a family of lights. Users are likely to manipulate the lights in a scene independently of the actual type—turning them on or off, repositioning them, changing their color and intensity, and so on. The delivery of a `Light` hierarchy includes the abstract base class and several common derived instances, such as classes representing a spotlight, a directional light, and a point light (think of the sun). We can either make use of these prebuilt instances or derive a new instance(s). For example, in the Disney film *Dinosaur* we introduced a class to represent a barn-door light.

An interface, on the other hand, provides a common service or characteristic for otherwise unrelated types. For example, any type wishing to be the target of the `foreach` statement must implement the `IEnumerable` interface.[1] For example, the `ArrayList`, `BindingManager`, `DataView`, and `BitArray` classes are all derived from the `IEnumerable` interface, but otherwise they have little in common.

---

1. By convention, interfaces under .NET begin with a capital *I* followed by a mnemonic identifier with a capitalized first letter. This is a carryover from COM-based programming, which has interfaces such as `IUnknown` or `IDirectDraw`.

Unlike classes, which support single inheritance only, interfaces support multiple inheritance. The `System.String` class, for example, is derived from four interfaces provided within the `System` namespace:

```
public sealed class String:
    IComparable, ICloneable, IConvertible, IEnumerable { ... }
```

As C# programmers, we have three different experiences of interfaces: (1) as users of concrete instances of either the `System` or user-introduced interfaces, (2) as providers of a new class implementation of either the `System` or user-introduced interfaces, (3) as providers of a new interface class. We look at each of these three aspects in this chapter.

4.1   Implementing a System Interface: `IComparable`

Let's start by implementing our own class instance of a predefined interface within the `System` namespace. The motivational context is the following: We need to sort an `ArrayList` of strings in ascending order by the length of the string. OK. That sounds simple enough. So how are we going to do that? If we look at the public methods of `ArrayList`, we see that it provides an overloaded pair of `Sort()` member functions:

```
System.Collections.ArrayList

Sort: Overloaded.
Sorts the elements in the ArrayList, or a portion of it.
```

Let's look at the documentation for the two different methods and see which one, if either, fits the bill. Here's the one with an empty parameter list:

```
public virtual void Sort()

Sorts the elements in the entire ArrayList using
the IComparable implementation of each element.
```

Just by its name we know that `IComparable` is an interface. The element held by our `ArrayList` is a string. The `String` class implements the `IComparable` interface. The no-parameter `Sort()` method of the `ArrayList` uses the `IComparable` implementation of the `String` class to determine the ordering of two string objects. This imposes a dictionary order on the words—not an ordering by length. This instance, then, is not of use to us.

Okay. Maybe the next overloaded instance is useful:

```
public virtual void Sort( IComparer ic )

Sorts the elements in the entire ArrayList using the
special comparer ic.
```

This instance provides us with a way to override the default ordering algorithm associated with the String class. We'll create a special implementation of the IComparer interface that sorts the strings by length. (If we were defining a class, we would include an implementation of the IComparable interface if we wanted to support sorting within the ArrayList container.)

How do we do that? What are the IComparer methods, and what do they do? Not only do we have to provide a definition of every interface member, but we must implement the documented behavior of each member if we want our implementation to transparently meld with the other implementations of that interface.

In addition, we need to throw the same exceptions under the same abnormal conditions. The compiler cannot enforce this. Recognizing and throwing the exceptions are responsibilities of the interface implementation.

It turns out there is only one method to implement. Phew! Not only that, but the implementation seems doable:

```
int Compare( object x, object y )

Compares two objects and returns a value indicating whether
one is less than (negative number), equal to (zero), or greater
than (positive number) the other.
```

What about any exceptions the method can throw? Again we have to look at the documentation. As it turns out, there is just one, and it also seems doable:

```
ArgumentException

Neither x nor y implements the IComparable interface.
-or- x and y are of different types and neither one
can handle comparisons with the other.
```

This means that our implementation of the `IComparer` interface requires only one method: `Compare()`. It should throw an `ArgumentException` if one or both of the two arguments are invalid; in our case, that simply means that the two arguments are not both strings. Let's call the class `StringLengthComparer`:

```
public sealed class StringLengthComparer : IComparer
{
    // first obligation: the Compare() method
    public int Compare( object x, object y ){…}
}
```

Our `Compare()` instance must define two parameters of type `object`, even though our implementation is interested in only two parameters of the `string` type. This is necessary because `Compare()` is implicitly a virtual function (as are all interface member functions), and therefore the signature of the overriding instance must exactly match the signature of the inherited method.

This is something of an inconvenience. It means we have to check within `Compare()` that the arguments are both of type `string`. If we were able to explicitly declare them as type `string`, the compiler would enforce that type requirement automatically. We'll see how to get around that—at least partially—in Section 4.4.

The only thing left now is the implementation of `Compare()`. We can break that down into two primary steps. First we must confirm the validity of the two arguments. That done, we must compare the lengths.

We have two parameters of type `object`, and we must confirm that they are really instances of type `string`. One strategy is to use the `is` operator:

```
if (( ! ( x is string )) || ( ! ( y is string )))
    throw new ArgumentException( "some dire message" );

// OK: arguments are valid;
//      let's cast them to string objects

string xs = (string) x; string ys = (string) y;
```

Alternatively, we can allow the `as` operator to do the downcasting. We throw an exception if either `xs` or `ys` is set to `null`:

C# PRIMER

```
string xs = x as string;
string ys = y as string;

if ( xs == null || ys == null )
  throw new ArgumentException( "some dire message" );
```

That's really the only tricky part. Here is the length comparison:

```
int ret_val = 1;

if ( xs.Length < ys.Length )
    ret_val = -1;
else
if ( xs.Length == ys.Length )
    ret_val = 0;

return ret_val;
```

So we've implemented our first concrete instance of an interface class. Here is how we might invoke Sort():

```
ArrayList stringList = new ArrayList();
// fill it up
stringList.Sort( new StringLengthComparer() );
```

4.2   Accessing an Existing Interface

In this section we implement a generic binary tree that holds node values of any type. As you know by now, the way we do that in C# is to declare the node to be of type object. As an additional wrinkle, a node value is inserted only once within a tree. If it occurs another time, we increment an occurrence count. This gives us the chance to look at the IComparable interface. The node class is called TreeNode:

```
public sealed class TreeNode
{
    private int       m_occurs;
    private object    m_nval;
    private TreeNode  m_lchild, m_rchild;

    // ...
}
```

For our tree we'll implement several policies that provide opportunities for exercising some of the interfaces defined within the .NET framework. For example, we want to fix the type of the tree after inserting the first element. The tree class is called `BinaryTree`:

```
public class BinaryTree
{
    public delegate void Action( ref TreeNode node);
    private Type        m_elemType;
    private TreeNode    m_root;
    private Action      m_nodeAction;
    // ...
}
```

When the user creates a `BinaryTree` object, we want it to be able to hold a value of any type. We support that capability by using the type `object`. Once the user inserts a value, however, we want all the remaining values inserted in that tree to be of the same type. The insertion of a first value locks the type of that tree.

For example, here is how our tree must behave. When we create a new tree, it can hold objects of any type. Once we have inserted an element, however, the tree can store only other elements of that type. For example, when we write

```
BinaryTree bt = new BinaryTree();
```

`bt` can potentially store elements of any type. However, once we write

```
bt.insert( "Piglet" );
```

`bt` becomes a binary tree that holds elements of type `string`. Subsequent insertions of `string` elements, such as

```
bt.insert( "Eeyore" );
bt.insert( "Roo" );
```

are fine. Each element is inserted within the tree according to the ordering supported by the `IComparable` interface.

What we want to prevent is a subsequent attempt by the user, after having inserted an object of one type, to insert an object of a different type. For example, if the user writes

```
bt.insert( 1024);
```

we want to recognize and flag that the type being inserted is different from the type to which we've previously bound our tree. To do this, we'll throw an exception.

We'll make no further constraints on objects in order for them to be accepted as tree node values. Only types that implement the `IComparable` interface are accepted. Why? Because each element is passed to us through the `object` parameter, so we have lost all compile-time type information. The interface provides an ordering service that is type independent—for example,

```
private IComparable confirm_comparable( object elem )
{
    IComparable ic = elem as IComparable;
    if ( ic == null ){
        string msg = "Element type must support IComparable -- "
                + elem.GetType().Name
                + " does not currently do so!";
        throw new ArgumentException( msg );
    }
    return ic;
}
```

Here is how we might invoke `confirm_comparable()`:

```
public void insert( object elem )
{
    // if this is the first element
    if ( m_root == null ){
        confirm_comparable( elem );
        m_elemType = elem.GetType();
        m_root = new TreeNode( elem );
    }
    else
    {
        confirm_type( elem );
        m_root.insert_value( elem );
    }
}
```

`insert()` checks the element's suitability only with the first insertion of an object of that type. Subsequently, it simply confirms that the new object is of the same type as the initial object. If it is, we insert the element within the tree, as shown here:

```
public void insert_value( object val )
{
    // assumption is that BinaryTree has confirmed this ...
    IComparable ic = val as IComparable;

    // OK: zero means the two objects are equal
    if ( ic.CompareTo( m_nval ) == 0 ){
        m_occurs++;
        return;
    }

    // OK: less than; insert within left subtree
    if ( ic.CompareTo( m_nval ) < 0 ){
        if ( m_lchild == null )
            m_lchild = new TreeNode( val );
        else m_lchild.insert_value( val );
    }
    else { // insert within right subtree
        if ( m_rchild == null )
            m_rchild = new BTreeNode( val );
        else m_rchild.insert_value( val );
    }
}
```

When we manipulate an object's actual type, we can pretty much ignore whatever interfaces that type implements. When we manipulate an entity of type `object`, however, the discovery and use of an interface becomes critical because all compile-time type information is lost. (Alternatively, we can query the object at runtime as to its actual type. We look at *type reflection* in Section 8.2.)

4.3   Defining an Interface

In Section 4.1 we implemented a new instance of an existing interface. In Section 4.2 we simply discovered and used the interface associated with a given type. In this section we introduce an interface definition. This interface supports the generation and display of sequences of numbers based on a unique algorithm. Here is the general set of operations we wish to support (two methods, a property, and an indexer):

- `GenerateSequence()`, which generates the unique sequence of elements
- `Display()`, which outputs the elements
- `Length`, which returns a count of the number of elements
- `Indexer`, which allows the user to access a specific element

An interface definition begins with the keyword `interface` followed by a name. Recall that in .NET, interfaces by convention begin with a capital *I*. The name follows, beginning with a capital letter, although this convention is not enforced by the compiler. We'll call our interface `INumericSequence`:

```
public interface INumericSequence{}
```

Yes, it is legal to define an empty interface, so this represents a complete interface definition.

The members that an interface is permitted to define are a subset of those permitted for a class. An interface can declare only methods, properties, indexers, and events as members—for example,

```
public interface INumericSequence
{
     // a method
     bool generate_sequence( int position );

     // a set of overloaded methods
     void display();
     void display( int first );
     void display( int first, int last );

     // a property
     int Length { get; }

     // a one-dimensional indexer
     int this[ int position ]{ get; }
}
```

All members of an interface are implicitly abstract. We cannot provide a default implementation, however trivial. In addition, the members of the interface are implicitly public. We cannot modify a member with either the `abstract` or the `public` keyword.

An interface cannot define instance data members. Nor can it define either a constructor or a destructor. (Without state members, neither is required.) In addition, an interface cannot declare `static` members. Because a `const` member is implicitly static, `const` members are not allowed, and neither are operators nor, not surprisingly, a static constructor.

An interface can inherit from another interface:

```
public interface INumericSequence : ICollection { ... }
```

or from multiple interfaces:

```
public interface INumericSequence
                : ICollection, ICloneable { ... }
```

but an interface cannot explicitly inherit from a class or `struct`. All interfaces, however, implicitly inherit from the root `Object` class.

4.3.1 Implementing Our Interface: Proof of Concept

Once we have defined our interface, how can we tell if it is any good? Typically, in addition to defining the interface, we deliver at least one implementation—as a kind of proof of concept or sanity check to confirm the viability of the interface. Let's provide a `Fibonacci` implementation to test our interface.

The first two elements of the *Fibonacci sequence* are both 1. Adding the two previous elements generates each subsequent element. For example, the first eight Fibonacci elements are 1, 1, 2, 3, 5, 8, 13, 21.

So what do we do first?

An interface is implemented by either class or `struct` inheritance. A `struct` isn't appropriate in this case: We don't expect to be creating and manipulating lots of Fibonacci objects in time-critical portions of the application. We'll declare `Fibonacci` as a class then. Because we do not expect it to be subsequently derived from, we'll declare it to be `sealed` as well:

```
public sealed class Fibonacci : INumericSequence {}
```

This empty definition, however, is illegal. A class inheriting from an interface must provide an implementation of every interface member. Leaving out even one member results in a compile-time error. (The exception is any case in which the class implementing the interface is abstract. It can then declare one or more of the interface member functions abstract. This is illustrated in Section 4.5.)

Before we can implement the interface members, we must determine the state information necessary to support the sequence abstraction. In this case we'll need an array to hold the sequence elements, and two additional members to hold the size and capacity of the array. Because the elements of the sequence are invariant, we need only a single array. We'll declare the array and its two supporting members as `static`.

The implementation of an interface has two main elements: (1) providing the underlying infrastructure, if any, to support the abstraction, and (2) providing a definition for each member of the interface, including the members of all inherited base interfaces. Here is the skeleton of a `Fibonacci` class design:

```
public sealed class Fibonacci : INumericSequence
{
    // infrastructure to support sequence abstraction
    private static int   [] m_elements;
    private static short    m_count;
    private static short    m_capacity = 128;

    // Fibonacci-specific methods:
    //    all for infrastructure supports
    static Fibonacci(){ … }
    private void check_pos( int pos ) {…}
    private void grow_capacity() { … }

    // INumericSequence inherited members
    public bool generate_sequence( int pos ) { … }

    public void  display(){ … }
    public void  display( int first ) { … }
    public void  display( int first, int last ) { … }

    public int Length { get{ return m_count; }}
    public int this[ int position ] { … }
}
```

The indexer has to verify the validity of the position, of course. I've factored that verification into a private member function, `check_pos()`. If the position is invalid, an exception is thrown. Otherwise the indexer returns the element, decrementing the position by one:

```
public int this[ int position ]
{
    get
    {
            check_pos( position );
            return m_elements[ position-1 ];
    }
}
```

Because array indexing in C# is zero based—that is, the first element is retrieved with an index of 0—we must adjust the position specified by the user. Why not require the user to make that adjustment explicitly? Whether that's a good decision or not depends on the perceived sophistication of our users. If they are other software developers, requiring the index to be zero based might well make sense. Nonprogrammers, however, often find the notion of a first element being at position zero very unnatural. By encapsulating the adjustment within the class, we shoulder the burden and make using our code safer and more pleasant for our users.

Here is how we might exercise our implementation. First we program an instance directly as a Fibonacci class object. Next we program it indirectly as a generic INumericSequence object:

```
public static void Main()
{
    // just some magic numbers - used as positions
    const int pos1 = 8, pos2 = 47;

    // let's directly use interface through class object
    Fibonacci fib = new Fibonacci();

    // invokes indexer;
    // indexer invokes generate_sequence( pos1 );
    int elem   = fib[ pos1 ];
    int length = fib.Length;

    string msg = "The length of the INumericSequence is ";
    Console.WriteLine( msg + length.ToString() );
    Console.WriteLine(
            "Element {0} of the Fibonacci Sequence is {1}",
                        pos1, elem );
```

```
    fib.display();

    // OK: let's now use interface generically
    INumericSequence ins = fib;

    elem = ins[ pos2 ];
    length = ins.Length;

    Console.WriteLine( msg + length.ToString() );
    Console.WriteLine(
        "Element {1} of the Fibonacci Sequence is {0}",
                    elem, pos2 );

    ins.display( 44, 47 );
}
```

As it turns out, our implementation is somewhat flawed. (That's the point of testing it.) The problem is self-evident in the program's output:

```
The length of the INumericSequence is 8
Element 8 of the Fibonacci Sequence is 21
Elements 1 to 8 of the Fibonacci Sequence:
        1 1 2 3 5 8 13 21

The length of the INumericSequence is 47
Element 47 of the Fibonacci Sequence is -1323752223
Elements 44 to 47 of the Fibonacci Sequence:
        701408733 1134903170 1836311903 -1323752223
```

What's going on here? The program claims that the forty-seventh element of the Fibonacci sequence is -1323752223. That's *really* not right. If we look at the display of elements 44 through 47, what has happened is pretty clear:

```
Elements 44 to 47 of the Fibonacci Sequence:
        701408733 1134903170 1836311903 -1323752223
```

We have declared m_elements to hold elements of type int. Unfortunately the forty-seventh Fibonacci element is too large to be contained within an int. The value overflowed into the sign bit, so the value is incorrectly displayed as negative. To better handle large Fibonacci values, we need to redefine m_elements as a type able to hold larger values.

What type is the most appropriate? In addition to the integral types, there are two floating-point types (the single-precision `float` and the double-precision `double`) and the 28-digits-of-precision `decimal` type. Let's redeclare m_elements to be, in turn, a `uint`, a `ulong`, a `decimal`, and a `double`. At position 50, only the `ulong`, `decimal`, and `double` are left standing:

```
Fibonacci Element #50 : (int)     :   -298632863
Fibonacci Element #50 : (uint)    :   3996334433
Fibonacci Element #50 : (ulong)   : 12586269025
Fibonacci Element #50 : (decimal) : 12586269025
Fibonacci Element #50 : (double)  : 12586269025
```

At position 100, only the `decimal` and `double` are capable of representing the value. However, the `double` begins to lose precision by rounding, which is unacceptable. Only the `decimal` values do not round off. Our best choice for representing the elements of the Fibonacci sequence is thus the `decimal` type:

```
Fibonacci Element #100 : (ulong)   :    3736710778780434371
Fibonacci Element #100 : (decimal) : 354224848179261915075
Fibonacci Element #100 : (double)  :    3.54224848179262E20
```

Still, however, this is not a complete solution. The `decimal` type reaches its 28-digit limit at position 139:

```
Fibonacci Element #139 :(decimal): 50095301248058391139327916261
Fibonacci Element #139 :(double) :       5.0095301248058406E28
```

When we attempt to calculate position 140, the `decimal` object overflows and the following exception occurs:

System.OverflowException:

Value is either too large or too small for a Decimal.
    at System.Decimal.Add(System.Decimal, System.Decimal)
    at System.Decimal.op_Addition(System.Decimal, System.Decimal)
    at Project1.Fibonacci.version_decimal(Int32)
    at Project1.MainObj.Main()

We can store and display only the first 139 Fibonacci elements using the pre-defined C# arithmetic types. Unless we plan to implement our own numeric class supporting very large integral values, we'll need to define a limit to the element position a user can request. Because this holds true for any numeric sequence, we should add that limit definition to the INumericSequence interface, as follows:

```
public interface INumericSequence
{
    // the two new properties
    int Length      { get; }
    int MaxPosition { get; }

    // ... rest the same ...
}

public sealed class Fibonacci : INumericSequence
{
    // infrastructure to support sequence abstraction
    private static int  [] m_elements = new int[ m_maxpos ];
    private static short   m_count·
    private const  short   m_maxpos = 128;

    public int MaxPosition { get{ return m_maxpos; }}

    // ... rest the same, except no longer need to grow array
}
```

This means that there is an infinite set of Fibonacci element positions that are legitimate but that we can't easily support and, in fact, have chosen not to support. In addition, the user might specify an invalid position—any value less than or equal to zero. How should we handle these two invalid conditions? The convention in both C# and .NET programming is to report all program anomalies through the raising of an exception.

But which exception should it throw? Should it throw separate exceptions for an invalid position and an unsupported position? There is no single right answer. Who should decide? If each interface implementation is allowed to decide whether and what exceptions to throw, if any, it becomes nearly impossible to safely program the interface generically. For example, to write the following code sequence:

```
INumericSequence ins = o as INumericSequence;
if ( ins != null )
    elem = ins[ pos2 ];
```

we must know that every implementation of the indexer reports an invalid position in exactly the same way.

This means that the interface definition must decide under what conditions an exception must be thrown and what the exception should be. Unfortunately, we can do that only through documentation. There is no way within C# to directly associate a member with one or a set of exceptions it may throw.

4.3.2 Integrating Our Interface within the System Framework

Is INumericSequence a good interface? In isolation, it seems to do the job. In the context of .NET, the interface probably will be a disappointment. Users will want to enumerate over the elements, for example, both explicitly and using the foreach loop. How do we support that functionality?

We need to have each INumericSequence implementation also provide an implementation of the IEnumerable interface. By having our interface inherit from IEnumerable, we ensure that each implementation of our interface also implements the IEnumerable interface:

```
public interface INumericSequence : IEnumerable
{ ... }
```

We do not list any of the IEnumerable base-interface members within our INumericSequence definition. However, when a user attempts to implement INumericSequence, he or she must provide a definition of not only all the INumericSequence members, but all the members of IEnumerable as well. Otherwise the compilation fails with a list of the missing interface members.

What are those members, and what do we need to do to implement them? Again, we have to turn to the documentation, where we discover that IEnumerable has only one member:

```
IEnumerator GetEnumerator();
```

GetEnumerator() returns an IEnumerator object. IEnumerator is yet another interface. It is defined in the System.Collections namespace. It encapsulates the knowledge of how to iterate through its associated collection.

Generally, when we implement the IEnumerable interface, we must also implement an associated instance of the IEnumerator interface. However, the instance of `IEnumerator` that supports terating over a numeric sequence is implemented as an independent class:

```
class NSEnumerator : IEnumerator { ... }
```

rather than as a base interface of `INumericSequence`. This way, the enumerator need be implemented only once. Multiple implementations of the interface can reuse it. Here is our implementation of `GetEnumerator()`:

```
public sealed class Fibonacci : INumericSequence
{
    private static int [] m_elements = new int[ m_maxpos ];
    private static short m_count;

    public IEnumerator GetEnumerator()
        { return new NSEnumerator( m_elements, m_count ); }

    // ...
}
```

How do we implement the `NSEnumerator` constructor? Again, we need to look the `IEnumerator` documentation. Here is what it says:

> `IEnumerator` is the base interface for all enumerator types. When an enumerator is instantiated, it takes a snapshot of the current state of the collection.

This is why we pass the array and a count of its size to `NSEnumerator`. This represents our snapshot.

The `IEnumerator` interface has three members: a property, `Current`, that returns the current element in the iteraticn; and two methods—`MoveNext()`, which advances `Current` to the next element of the collection, and `Reset()`, which sets `Current` to its initial position. As it happens, special semantics are associated with the initial position of an `IEnumerator` instance:

> The enumerator is initially positioned before the first element in the collection, and it must be advanced before it is used.

This behavior is slightly nonintuitive, and it is easy for beginners to get this wrong. Users learn soon enough, however. Accessing `Current` before an invocation of `MoveNext()` results in a runtime exception:

```
public void iterate( ArrayList al )
{
    IEnumerator it = al.GetEnumerator();

    // oops: this access of Current before MoveNext()
    // generates an exception
    while( it.Current != null )
    {
        Console.WriteLine( it.Current.ToString() );
        it.MoveNext();
    }
}
```

The correct use of `IEnumerator` invokes `MoveNext()` before accessing `Current` for the first time. If `MoveNext()` has a next element to access, it returns `true`. Here is the corrected implementation:

```
public void iterate( ArrayList al )
{
    IEnumerator it = al.GetEnumerator();

    while( it.MoveNext())
            Console.WriteLine( it.Current.ToString() );
}
```

The essential point is that whenever we implement an interface that someone else has defined, we must be sure to understand and provide the *exact* semantics as described for its members. Otherwise, when our implementation is used through an interface object, it will behave unexpectedly. The compiler cannot enforce this level of conformance.

The next example shows a partial implementation of `NSEnumerator` without providing an implementation of the three interface members yet. This represents just the interface necessary to support iteration across the collection of elements:

```
class NSEnumerator : IEnumerator
{
    decimal [] m_elems;

    int        m_count;
    int        m_curr;
```

```
public NSEnumerator( decimal [] array, int count )
{
    // these are exceptions defined within System
    if ( array == null )
        throw new ArgumentNullException( "null array" );

    if ( count <= 0 )
        throw new ArgumentOutOfRangeException(
                                    count.ToString() );

    m_elems = array;
    m_count = count;
    m_curr  = -1; // required semantics!
}

// ...
}
```

`Current` is a property. It returns an object addressing the current element in the collection. If `Current` is positioned either before or after the last element of the collection, it must throw the `InvalidOperationException` :

```
public object Current
{
    get{
        if ( m_curr == -1 || m_curr >= m_count )
            throw new
                InvalidOperationException( ToString() );

        return m_elems[ m_curr-1 ];
    }
}
```

Notice that `Current` does not advance `m_curr` to address the next element. Why didn't we do that? Because the documentation told us we can't.

> `Current` does not move the position of the enumerator. Consecutive calls to `Current` will return the same object until either `MoveNext()` or `Reset()` is called.

If we had either initialized `m_curr` to the first sequence element or incremented it within `Current`, our users would have silently dropped elements as they iterated across our sequences.

To allow `Current` to represent elements of any program type, the `IEnumerable` definition defines the type of the element to be `object`. This is somewhat disappointing. Within `NSEnumerator`, for example, we know that the element type is `decimal`. Returning it as an `object` means that it is implicitly boxed within `Current` and the user must unbox it with an explicit cast. We'll see how to design around this problem in the next section.

`MoveNext()` returns `true` if the enumerator advances to a next element. If the enumerator advances past the last valid element, it returns `false`:

```
public bool MoveNext()
      { return m_count < ++m_curr;}
```

`Reset()` sets the enumerator to its initial position. Remember that the documentation states that the value of this position must be set as one less than the first element in the collection:

```
public void Reset(){ m_curr = -1; }
```

The code to implement the interface is quite straightforward. The challenge of the implementation is in providing interface semantics consistent with its documentation.

4.4 Explicit Interface Member Implementations

Given an entity of type `object`, how can we discover if it supports a particular interface? One way is simply to ask, using the `is` operator:

```
public static void iterate( object o )
{
      // true if o implements IEnumerable
      if ( o is IEnumerable )
      {
            IEnumerable ie = (IEnumerable) o;
            IEnumerator iter = ie.GetEnumerator();

            while ( iter.MoveNext() )
                  Console.WriteLine( "{0} ",
                              iter.Current.ToString() );
      }
}
```

`iterate()` is an example of a *generic function* in C#. We have no idea as to the actual type that o refers to. We ask if it supports the `IEnumerable` interface. If it does not, that's an end to it. If it does, we access it through an abstract `IEnumerator` object, moving through the elements in turn. We have no idea of either the enumerator type or the type of collection element. This function can be invoked with any program type as its argument.

Generic programming provides an almost magically flexible implementation. We can invoke `iterate()` with an object of our `Fibonacci` class:

```
Fibonacci fib  = new Fibonacci();
// ...
iterate( fib );
```

or with an instance of an `ArrayList`, or a built-in array, and so on. In each case, everything works fine.

However, if we wish to iterate across our `Fibonacci` class object directly using an `NSEnumerator` object, the generic support begins to trip us up. We have to treat the return values generically, even though we know the actual type being returned—for example:

```
NSEnumerator nse = (NSEnumerator) fib.GetEnumerator();
while ( nse.MoveNext() )
{
    decimal el = (decimal) nse.Current; // downcast
    // ...
}
```

There are two ways to provide multiple instances of an interface member—one to be used when we are programming generically through the interface, and one to be used when we are programming an explicit instance of the interface, such as `NSEnumerator`. We do this through explicit interface member implementations—for example:

```
class NSEnumerator : IEnumerator
{
    private void checkIntegrity(){
        if ( m_curr == -1 || m_curr >= m_count )
            throw new InvalidOperationException( ToString() );
    }
```

```
        // invoked through an NSEnumerator object
        public decimal Current
            { get{ checkIntegrity(); return m_elems[ m_curr-1 ]; }}

        // the explicit interface member,
        // invoked only through a generic IEnumerator object
        object IEnumerator.Current
            { get{ checkIntegrity(); return m_elems[ m_curr-1 ]; }}

        // ...
    }
```

We identify an explicit interface member implementation by prefixing the member name with the name of the interface in which the member is declared, followed by the scope operator (.):

```
object IEnumerator.Current { ... } // explicit member
public decimal Current      { ... }
```

The access level of an explicit member is implicitly public. An explicit access level, even that of `public`, is not allowed. If the interface that is used to identify an explicit member does not contain the member, an error results.

The explicit interface instance is invoked whenever `Current` is accessed through an `IEnumerator` object, such as in `iterate()`:

```
NSEnumerator nse = (NSEnumerator) fib.GetEnumerator();

// downcast from object is no longer necessary
decimal el = nse.Current;
```

I(If we wish to eliminate the downcast of `GetEnumerator()`, we provide an explicit instance returning an `IEnumerator` and a nonexplicit instance returning an `NSEnumerator`.)

4.5   Inherited Interface Members

Here is a puzzle for you. Given the following three-level hierarchy:

```
interface IControl
{
    void Paint();
}
```

```
class Control: IControl
{
    public void Paint() { ... }
}

class TextBox: Control
{
    new public void Paint() { ... }
}
```

which instance of `Paint()` is invoked in the following code sequence?

```
IControl it  = new TextBox();

// which instance of Paint() is invoked?
it.Paint(); // which instance of Paint() is invoked?
```

Most people's first response is `TextBox.Paint()`. After all, it addresses a `TextBox` object. The `IControl` interface instance of `Paint()` is treated as an abstract method. Therefore, the actual method to invoke must be resolved at runtime according to the type of the actual object addressed by `it`. In this case that object is `TextBox`, so the method must be `TextBox.Paint()`.

Of course, this whole discussion is justified only if that answer is wrong. In fact, the `Paint()` method invoked is resolved statically. It is the `Control`, not `TextBox`, instance of `Paint()` that is invoked. The giveaway clue is the use of the `new` keyword in the definition of `TextBox.Paint()`.

Recall from Chapter 3 that the `new` keyword is used to identify a derived member that hides the name of an inherited base-class member. Our confusion derives from our assumption that the `Paint()` instance provided by `Control` is automatically treated as virtual.

If the implementation of an interface wants its implementation of a member to be treated as virtual, it must explicitly label it using the `virtual` keyword, just as we do for a derived class of an abstract base class—for example:

```
class Control: IControl
{
    virtual public void Paint() { ... }
}
```

In order for the derived `TextBox` class instance of `Paint()` to override the inherited `Control.Paint()` instance, it must specify the `override` keyword:

```
class TextBox : Control {
    override public void Paint() { ... }
}
```

Now when we invoke the original code sequence:

```
IControl it  = new TextBox();
it.Paint();
```

the `TextBox` instance of `Paint()` really is invoked!

What if the implementers of both the `Control` and `TextBox` classes insist that the performance of the associated `Paint()` instances is too critical to have it be virtual? Okay. We can support that eventuality as well:

```
class Control: IControl
{
    public void Paint() { ... } // nonvirtual
}

class TextBox: Control, IControl
{
    public new void Paint() { ... } // nonvirtual as well!
}
```

By explicitly adding `IControl` to its list of base interfaces, `TextBox` in a sense leapfrogs the implementation provided by `Control`. Now if we invoke the original code sequence:

```
IControl it  = new TextBox();
it.Paint();
```

the `TextBox` instance of `Paint()` is again invoked, but this time statically, rather than through the runtime virtual mechanism.

It is also possible for a class to defer the implementation of one or more interface members by explicitly labeling the member with the `abstract` keyword. For example, an abstract `NumericSequence` class defers the type-dependent implementation of the sequence generation, but it provides shared infrastructure. For example:

```
public abstract class NumericSequence : INumericSequence
{
    // type-dependent method remains abstract
    public abstract bool generate_sequence( int pos );

    // concrete infrastructure of shared state
    private const int m_maxpos = 128;
    public int MaxPosition { get{ return m_maxpos; }}

    // ...
}
```

The concrete sequence abstractions are then derived from the abstract base class rather than from the interface:

```
public class Fibonacci :  NumericSequence
{
    virtual public bool generate_sequence( int pos ){ ... }
    // ...
}

public class Pell :  NumericSequence
{
    virtual public bool generate_sequence( int pos ){ ... }
    // ...
}
```

4.6 Overloaded, Hidden, or Ambiguous?

Consider the following class hierarchy:

```
class Base
{
   public void f( int ival ){ ... }
}

class Derived : Base
{
    public void f( ref int ix ){ ... }
}
```

Does the definition of `f()` within the `Derived` class require a `new` specifier? Or, to put it in program terms, which of the following invocations, if any, result in a compile-time error?

```
public static void main()
{
    Derived d = new Derived;
    int ival = 1024;

    d.f( ref ival ); // OK?
    d.f( ival );     // OK?
}
```

The answers are (1) no, the new specifier is *not* required, and (2) *none* of the invocations result in a compile-time error. That is, the definition of f() within the Derived class does not hide the base-class instance. Within the Derived class, both instances are visible and thus able to be invoked.

Why? Recall that functions that share the same name are treated as over-loaded, provided that the signatures are unique. When two members of a class or interface hierarchy share the same name and are methods, the derived instance is treated as hiding the base-class instance only if the two signatures are the same.

In our example, the two signatures are not equivalent. Two methods can be overloaded on the basis of the presence or absence of the ref parameter. In fact, we can introduce an overloaded third instance distinguished only by an out parameter.

Multiple interface inheritance leaves open the possibility of inheriting the same member name from two or more interfaces, resulting in a name ambiguity. For example, consider the following inheritance hierarchy, in which two instances of doSomething() are visible within aMed:

```
interface a {
    void doSomething(object o);
}

interface b {
    void doSomething(object o);
}

class aMed : a, b {
    // oops! which doSomething?
    public void doit(){ doSomething(); }
}
```

We can fully resolve the potential name ambiguity within the aMed class by providing explicit declarations for both inherited interface instances. In addition, we provide a synthesized instance to be used when an aMed class object is being manipulated directly—for example:

```
class aMed : a,b
{
    public void doSomething( string s ){ ... }


    public void a.doSomething( object o ) { ... }
    public void b.doSomething( object o ) { ... }


    // ...
}

class EntryPoint
{
    public static void Main()
    {
        aMed am = new aMed();
        am.doSomething( "OK" ); // aMed.doSomething


        a aaa = am as a;
        aaa.doSomething( am );   // aMed.a.doSomething


        b bbb = am as b;
        bbb.doSomething( am );   // aMed.b.doSomething
    }
}
```

4.7 Mastering Copy Semantics: `ICloneable`

When we copy one reference type with another, as in the following example:

```
Matrix mat = new Matrix( 4, 4 );
// ...
Matrix mat2 = mat;
```

the result is a shallow copy; that is, both mat and mat2 now refer to the same Matrix object on the managed heap. A problem occurs when the object is modified through one handle, as in this example:

```
// changes are seen through mat2 as well
mat[0,0]=mat[1,1]=mat[2,2]=mat[3,3]=1;
```

while the second handle still requires the object to be in its original state.

If we are users, we cannot modify the class implementation to provide deep-copy semantics. Rather we'll need to explicitly implement a deep copy. First we allocate a new instance of the reference types. Next we copy each value in turn:

```
public class DeepCopy
{
    public static Matrix copyMatrix( Matrix m )
    {
        Matrix mat = new Matrix( m.Rows, m.Cols );

        for ( int ix = 0; ix < m.Rows; ++ix )
            for ( int iy = 0; iy < m.Cols; ++iy )
                mat[ix,iy] = m[ix,iy];

        return mat;
    }
}

Matrix mat = new Matrix( 4, 4 );
Matrix mat2 = DeepCopy.copyMatrix( mat );
```

The result is a second, independent copy of the object. We have cloned it.

By default, the copy of a reference type results in a shallow copy. If we are designers of a class, we need to think about whether we wish to also provide deep-copy semantics. We do that by implementing the ICloneable interface. ICloneable specifies a single function, Clone(). Clone() returns a deep copy as an instance of type object—for example:

```
class matrix : ICloneable
{
    public matrix( int row, int col )
    {
        m_row = ( row <= 0 ) ? 1 : row;
        m_col = ( col <= 0 ) ? 1 : col;

        m_mat = new double[ m_row, m_col ];
    }
```

```
        public object Clone()
        {
                matrix mat = new matrix(m_row,m_col);
                for ( int ix = 0; ix < m_row; ++ix )
                        for ( int iy = 0; iy < m_col; ++iy )
                                mat.m_mat[ ix, iy ] = m_mat[ ix, iy ];
                return mat;

        }

}
```

The user now has a choice of using a shallow or a deep copy. Knowing when to choose which one is really what's important here. Consider the following overloaded addition operator:

```
public static matrix operator+( matrix m1, matrix m2 )
{
    check_both_rows_cols( m1, m2 );

    // not: matrix mat = m1;
    matrix mat = (matrix) m1.Clone();

    for ( int ix = 0 ; ix < m1.rows; ix++ )
       for ( int ij = 0; ij < m1.cols; ij++ )
            mat[ ix, ij ] += m2[ ix, ij ];

    return mat;
}
```

There are four copies of a `matrix`. Of those four, only one needs a deep copy.

The default shallow copy is the right mechanism for passing the two `matrix` objects into the function and returning the resulting `matrix` object. A deep copy in this case would be unnecessary and inefficient.

On the other hand, a shallow copy inside the addition operator is a serious mistake. Initializing `m1` to the local matrix through a shallow copy means that each assignment to `mat` modifies `m1` as well. This is where a deep copy is necessary to keep the two objects independent.

4.8 Mastering Finalize Semantics: `IDisposable`

Garbage collection solves an important problem: that of automatically managing the allocation and freeing up objects on the heap. But that solution introduces the smaller problem of *deterministic finalization*. What this means in a very broad sense is that we cannot predict when (or if) an object is finalized by the garbage collector.

One case in which the time of finalization matters occurs when a class object acquires *unmanaged resources,* such as a window or file handle or a database connection—resources that we don't want tied up too long, or at least no longer than necessary. What we would like, ideally, is to have such a resource freed automatically after a last use of the object holding it. Unfortunately, we cannot automate that—at least in a timely manner. The reason is that there is no deterministic finalization under .NET.

The garbage collector has knowledge of the memory available in the managed heap. When it determines that the available memory is below a particular threshold, it performs a collection. Until then, an unreferenced object continues to exist in memory.

The garbage collector has no knowledge of external resources such as database connections. If the availability of database connections is low, there is no equivalent mechanism to automatically perform a collection.

An unreferenced object maintaining a database connection, for example, continues to hold onto that connection until either the garbage collector finalizes the object or the user explicitly frees the resource. This is the problem that the `IDisposable` interface is intended to manage.

A class that is expected to acquire unmanaged resources should implement `IDisposable`. `IDisposable` declares a single member: `Dispose()`. All resources held both by the object and by any object contained within this object should be freed up within this implementation of `Dispose()`.

How is `Dispose()` invoked? In most cases, the user must manually invoke it after a last use of the object. In case the user forgets, we also provide a destructor within which `Dispose()` is called. If the user manually invokes `Dispose()`, we disable the destructor instance through a call of the `SuppressFinalize()` member function of the `GC` garbage collection class. For example, :

```
class ResourceWrapper : IDisposable
{
    // ...
```

C# PRIMER

```
    public void Dispose()
    {
        Dispose( true );

        // take us off of the finalization queue
        GC.SuppressFinalize( this );
    }

    protected virtual void Dispose( bool disposing )
    {
        if ( disposing ) {
            // dispose of managed resources ...
        }

        // dispose of unmanaged resources ...
    }

    // just in case Dispose() is not explicitly invoked
    ~ResourceWrapper() { Dispose(false); }
}
```

Optionally we may wish to maintain an `IsDisposed` class member that indicates whether `Dispose()` has yet been invoked on the object. This allows us to avoid attempting to free the same resources multiple times. It also allows us to trap an attempt to use an object on which `Dispose()` has been invoked. In the latter case we are advised to throw an `ObjectDisposedException` object.

When we program under .NET, it is important that we always be aware of the possibility of an exception being thrown. For example, the following code is not exception safe:

```
foo()
{
        FileStream fin = new
                FileStream(@"c:\fictions\alice.txt", FileMode.Open);
        StreamReader ifile = new StreamReader( fin );

        while (( str = ifile.ReadLine()) != null )
        {
                // ...
        }

        ifile.Close();
}
```

If `ReadLine()` throws an exception, the `Close()` method is never invoked; the file handle remains open until `ifile` is collected. In this case `Close()` wraps the invocation of `Dispose()`.

A safer but more complex implementation introduces a `finally` clause to guarantee the invocation of either `Close()` or `Dispose()` whether or not an exception occurs:

```
foo()
{
        FileStream fin = new
                FileStream(@"c:\fictions\alice.txt", FileMode.Open);
        StreamReader ifile = new StreamReader( fin );

        try
        {
            while (( str = ifile.ReadLine()) != null )
                        // ...
        }
        finally
          { ifile.Close(); }

}
```

A special instance of the `using` statement provides a shorthand notation for the invocation of an object's `Dispose()` method—for example:

```
foo()
{
    // equivalent to the earlier try/finally block
    using ( File f = new File( "c:\tmp" ))
            { byte[] b = f.Read(); }
}
```

This `using` statement expands internally into the `try/finally` block of code explicitly programmed in the previous example.

4.9 `BitVector`: Extension through Composition

The `BitArray` class is provided within the `System.Collections` namespace. It manages an array of Boolean objects as if it were a *bit vector*. A `true` value indicates that the bit is turned on; `false`, that it is off. `Count` returns the number of elements in the array. It is a property of the `ICollection` interface, from which `BitArray` is derived.

We can turn a bit on or off either by subscripting into the array:

```
bat1[ 2 ] = bat2[ 4 ] = true;
```

or by explicitly setting the element:

```
1bat.Set(ix, bat[ ix ] );
```

A function called `SetAll()` sets all the bits in the array to either `true` or `false`. The value of an element can be read either through subscripting or by the `Get()` method:

```
// both return the value of the first element
bool b1 = bat1[ 0 ];
bool b2 = bat1.Get( 0 );
```

To reverse the values of the `BitArray` object, we use the `Not()` method:

```
bat1.Not(); // bits are now reversed
```

Six constructors support the creation of a `BitArray` object. The following code segment illustrates their use.

```
const int  elemSize  = 6;
const bool elemValue = true;

// create a BitArray of size elemSize;
// each element is initialized to false
BitArray bits0 = new BitArray( elemSize );

// create a BitArray of size elemSize;
// each element is initialized to elemValue
BitArray bits1 = new BitArray( elemSize, elemValue );

// create a BitArray copied from another BitArray
BitArray bits2 = new BitArray( bits1 );

// create a BitArray with the number and value
// of elements from a bool array
bool [] bvals  = { false, true, false, true, false, true };
BitArray bits3 = new BitArray( bvals );
```

```
// create a BitArray initialized to an array of bytes
// in which each byte represents 8 consecutive bits
byte [] byteValues = { 255, 0 };

// evaluates to 1111111100000000
BitArray bits5 = new BitArray( byteValues );

// create a BitArray initialized to an array of ints
// in which each int represents 32 consecutive bits
int [] intValues = { -7 };

// evaluates to 10011111111111111111111111111111
BitArray bits6 = new BitArray( intValues );
```

In addition, we can perform a bitwise AND operation between two BitArray objects using the And() method:

```
BitArray andResult = bat1.And( bat2 );
```

andResult holds true for each element that is set for both bat1 and bat2; each other element is set to false.

There is also support for bitwise OR using the Or() method (an element is evaluated as true if it is set in either bat1 or bat2), and for bitwise XOR using the Xor() method. (The bitwise exclusive OR operation returns true if exactly one operand is set, and returns false if both operands have the same Boolean value.)

One small disappointment in the BitArray class is the absence of a provision for displaying the collection of bits. The inherited ToString() method prints out only the class type:

```
System.Collections.BitArray
```

rather than displaying the elements as a string, such as

```
00000101
```

In the documentation, an example of displaying a BitArray object has the user iterating across the elements, printing out the literal true or false values:

```
False False False False False True False True
```

This approach really doesn't scale to BitArray objects with many elements.

Another minor complaint is that there is no support for converting the container of bits into a numeric value. For example, given a `BitArray` object with an eight-element configuration of `00000101`, it would be useful to retrieve an unsigned numeric representation—in this case, a return value of `5`.

While at DreamWorks Animation, I was technical lead on a pencil test animation system released to the studio as ToonShooter. Animators use the system to transfer their drawings to the computer through a GUI-driven digital video camera. The sequences of drawings animating a scene are entered as *levels*. Each level represents an element in the scene. Each character, for example, is drawn as a separate level. There may be a background level, and levels for foreground images, shadows, vehicles, cute animals, and so on.

One use of the tool is to allow the animator to check the smoothness of the animation. A second use is to check the correctness of the lip movements of the characters with the soundtrack. A third use is to play back scenes with or without audio for director approval. The user can turn levels on or off prior to and during playback.

Playback has to occur at a minimum of `24` frames per second if the animation is to appear smooth. Before an image is displayed, it may require *compositing*. That is, if more than one level is active, the active levels, each of which represents an image, must be combined to form one composite image. Levels are combined pixel by pixel across the set of active levels. Compositing is done on the fly as it delivers frames to the playback engine. If compositing takes too long to deliver a frame, the tool can no longer play at speed without either dropping frames or breaking up the audio. Needless to say, both conditions are extremely annoying to the user.

One way to speed up compositing is to cache the composited images. Before we invoke the compositor, we check that the resulting image is not already available in the cache. Failing an exact match, we look for a best match—perhaps two, three, or four required levels have already been composited, so we composite only the missing level(s). To look up and retrieve images quickly, we need to be able to uniquely tag the different composited images efficiently. A unique signature for each image consists of its frame number and the set of its active levels.

An array of `BitArray` objects captures this information perfectly. Each element of the array represents the frame. The `BitArray` object represents the levels turned on for that frame. So for a six-level scene with a bit configuration of 00000101, levels 6 and 8 are turned on, and the unique tag retrieval code is 5.

Let's implement a `BitVector` class that provides the additional functionality absent from `BitArray`. My first idea is to derive the `BitVector` class from `BitArray`. In this way `BitVector` inherits all of the `BitArray` infrastructure, and we simply need to program what is different. Unfortunately, the `BitArray` class is sealed, so we cannot inherit:

```
public sealed class BitArray :
        ICollection, IEnumerable, ICloneable
```

An alternative design choice to inheritance is *composition*, in which we wrap our `BitVector` class around an internal `BitArray` member:

```
public sealed class BitVector :
        ICollection, IEnumerable, ICloneable
{
    private BitArray m_array;
    // ...
}
```

Although we do not inherit the `BitArray` members, we duplicate their functionality through small dispatch methods. For example,

```
// ICollection
public int Count { get { return m_array.Count; }}
public bool IsReadOnly { get { return m_array.IsReadOnly; }}
public object SyncRoot { get { return m_array.SyncRoot;    }}
public bool IsSynchronized
        { get{ return m_array.IsSynchronized; }}

public void CopyTo( Array array, int index )
        { m_array.CopyTo( array, index ); }

// IEnumerable
public IEnumerator GetEnumerator()
{
    return m_array.GetEnumerator();
}
```

```
// ICloneable
public object Clone()
{
        BitVector bv = new BitVector( m_array.Count );
        bv.m_array = (BitArray)m_array.Clone();
        return bv;
}
```

The next example shows the `ToString()` implementation. It iterates over the `BitArray` member, building up the string representation by appending either `'1'` or `'0'`, depending on whether the bit is turned on. Because this algorithm modifies the `string` representation with each element, building up the representation by using a `string` object is not efficient.

The string class is immutable. If we append a character to a `string` object after examining a `BitArray` of 132 elements, we will have created 133 different `string` objects. One `string` object is actually sufficient. This is why we use a `StringBuilder` object instead.

The `ToString()` method is identified with the `override` keyword because it replaces the inherited virtual method defined within the `object` class:

```
override public string ToString()
{
    StringBuilder sb = new StringBuilder( m_array.Count );
    for ( int ix = m_array.Count-1; ix >= 0; --ix )
        sb.Append( m_array[ ix ] ? '1' : '0' );

    return sb.ToString();
}
```

The `StringBuilder` class is within the `System.Text` namespace. Its only purpose is to allow string modifications, such as removing, replacing, or inserting a character, without creating a new string with each modification. For example, to replace an *ies* ending of a word with *y*, using one of the overloaded `StringBuilder Replace()` methods, we write

```
if ( word.EndsWith( "ies" ))
    theWord.Replace( "ies", "y", theWord.Length-3, 3 );
```

We retrieve the `string` representation within the `StringBuilder` object through its `ToString()` method once our modifications are complete.

Here is an implementation of `ToUlong()` that turns our underlying bit vector into an unsigned `long` numeric value:

```
public ulong ToUlong()
{
        ulong bv = 0ul;
        for ( int ix = 0; ix < m_array.Count; ++ix )
        {
                if ( m_array[ix] )
                {
                        ulong bv2 = 1;
                        bv2 <<= ix;
                        bv += bv2;
                }

                Console.WriteLine( "{0} :: {1}", ix, bv );
        }

        return bv;
}
```

`<<=` is the bitwise compound left-shift assignment operator. When we assign `bv2` a value of `1`, internally this value is represented as the first bit in the underlying representation being turned on. A left shift moves the bits `ix` positions. For example, when `ix` is set to `1`, each bit is shifted by one position. Shifting the 1-bit to the second position equals the value `2`, shifting the 1-bit to the third position equals `4`, and so on.

For example, the following is the `ToString()` and `ToUlong()` output of a small sequence of `BitArray` 24-element configurations:

```
000000000000000000000010 :: 2
000000000000000000001010 :: 10
000000000000000000101010 :: 42
000000000000000010101010 :: 170
000000000000001010101010 :: 682
```

To allow a `BitVector` to be used in any situation in which a `BitArray` can be used, we provide an implicit conversion from `BitVector` to `BitArray`:

```
public static implicit operator BitArray( BitVector bv )
        { return bv.m_array; }
```

By returning the private array member by reference, we are allowing multiple handles to this internal object. This means that it can be changed from outside the class. An alternative implementation returns a copy of the member by invoking the associated `Clone()` function:

```
return (BitArray)m_array.Clone();
```

Chapter 5

Exploring the System Namespace

The `System` namespace provides at least three distinct levels of support for the C#/.NET programmer.

1. At the most basic level it provides the underlying implementation of all the fundamental types, including the numeric types, `string`, `enum`, `delegate`, and `array`.

2. At a second level it serves as a system class library, providing support for input/output, collection classes, exceptions, regular expressions, sockets, threads, Web requests, and so on.

3. At a third level it provides a framework for complex application domains, such as Windows Forms (Chapter 6), Web Forms (Chapter 7), eXtensible Markup Language (XML), and the tabular display of data, often retrieved from a database.

This chapter provides a tour of many of the classes and class hierarchies. Unfortunately, space does not allow a full treatment of any single topic.

5.1 Supporting the Fundamental Types

On its simplest level, the `System` namespace provides support for the fundamental data types of the language. In C#, all the primitive types, such as `int`, `double`, `bool`, and `string`, are aliases for types provided within the `System` namespace. These aliases are listed in Table 1.3 in Section 1.18.2.

The methods associated with these types can be invoked through objects of the aliased C# types. For example, to discover the range of values supported by one of the numeric types, we can access the `MaxValue` and `MinValue` properties:

```
int imaxval = int.MaxValue;
int iminval = int.MinValue;
```

One useful member function of each numeric type is `Parse()`. For example, given the `string` object

```
string bonus = "$  12,000.79";
```

the following invocation of `Parse()` initializes `myBonus` with the value `12000.79`:

```
double myBonus = double.Parse( bonus, ns );
```

where `ns` represents a bitwise OR operation of `NumberStyles` enumerations to direct the handling of leading white space, the currency symbol, a decimal point or comma, and so on. We set that up as follows:

```
NumberStyles ns = NumberStyles.AllowLeadingWhite;
             ns |= NumberStyles.AllowCurrencySymbol;
             ns |= NumberStyles.AllowThousands;
             ns |= NumberStyles.AllowDecimalPoint;
```

We can explicitly convert between types either using the C# cast notation:

```
int ival = (int) myBonus;
```

or using one of the conversion methods of the `System.Convert` class, such as `ToDouble()`, `ToInt32()`, `ToDateTime()`, and so on—for example,

```
int ival2 = Convert.ToInt32( myBonus );
```

The difference between these two approaches is that the explicit cast results in truncation, so `ival` is assigned `12000`. The `Convert` members perform rounding, so `ival2` is assigned `12001`.

5.2   The Array Is a `System.Array`

All C# array types have access to the `System.Array` class public methods and properties. For example, the `Length` property returns the number of elements in an array:

```
for ( int ix = 0; ix < fib.Length; ++ix )
```

If the array is multidimensional, `Length` is a less useful property. For example, for the following array declaration:

```
static float [,] mat = new float[4,5]
{
        { 1f, 0f, 0f, 0f, 0f },
        { 0f, 1f, 0f, 0f, 0f },
        { 0f, 0f, 1f, 0f, 0f },
        { 0f, 0f, 0f, 1f, 0f }
};
```

the result of `Length` is `20`. To retrieve the length of the individual dimensions of a multidimensional array, we use `GetLength(int dim)`, where `dim` represents the number of the dimension: `0`, `1`, `2`, and so on. To discover the number of dimensions associated with an array, we query its `Rank` property:

```
int rank = mat.Rank;
Console.WriteLine( "Array of {0} dimensions", rank );

for ( int dim = 1, ix = 0; ix < rank; ++ix )
{
    dim = mat.GetLength( ix );
    Console.WriteLine( "size of dimension {0} is {1} elements",
                       ix, dim )
}
```

When compiled and executed, this code generates the following output:

```
Array of 2 dimensions
      size of dimension 0 is 4 elements
      size of dimension 1 is 5 elements
```

The `CopyTo()` member function copies the elements of a one-dimensional array into a second array passed in as the first argument. Copying begins in the target array at the index specified as the second argument. If the index is invalid or the target array is too small, an exception is thrown—for example,

```
int [] fib;

// assign fib to an array ...
int [] notfib = new int[ fib.Length ];
fib.CopyTo( notfib, 0 );
```

To copy a range of elements from one one-dimensional array to another, we must use the static `Copy()` method. We pass in the source array, target array, and number of elements to copy. Copying begins at the first elements of both arrays—for example,

```
Array.Copy( fib, notfib, fib.Length );
```

If we wish to start copying somewhere other than at the first element of either of the two arrays, we must invoke the five-parameter instance of `Copy()`. For example, the following invocation copies `Length-1` elements of `fib` beginning at index `1` into `notfib` beginning at its first element:

```
Array.Copy( fib, 1, notfib, 0, fib.Length-1 );
```

If the two arrays hold elements of different types and an implicit conversion exists between those types, the conversion is carried out as part of `Copy()`.

To reset all or a portion of an array to `0` (for the numeric types), `false` (for the `bool` type), or `null` (for a reference type), we invoke the static `Clear()`. For example, the following invocation zeros out our `fib` array starting at index `0` for the length of the array:

```
Array.Clear( fib, 0, fib.Length );
```

We can sort, reverse, and search one-dimensional arrays as well. For example, consider the following integer array:

```
int [] ivalues = new int[]{ 14, 8, 2, 16, 8, 7, 14, 0 };
```

To search for the first occurrence of `8`, we use the static `IndexOf()` method:

```
int index = Array.IndexOf( ivalues, 8 );
if ( index != -1 ) /* found! */ ;
```

If the value is found, `IndexOf()` returns the index of its first occurrence; otherwise it returns `-1`. `LastIndexOf()` searches for the last occurrence of the search value, returning either the index or `-1`.

The following code sequence finds all occurrences of a value. The trick is to invoke `IndexOf()` repeatedly until it returns `-1`. To do that, we pass in, as a third parameter, the index at which to begin its search. We begin at `0`, of course, and then increment one beyond each matching index:

```
int index = -1;
ArrayList found = new ArrayList();

while( true )
{
    index = Array.IndexOf( ivalues, search_value, index+1 );

    if ( index == -1 )
        break;

    found.Add( index );
}

Console.Write( "{0} occurrences of {1} found at ",
               found.Count, search_value );

foreach ( int ix in found )
        Console.Write( "{0} ", ix );
```

When `search_value` is `8`, this code results in the following output:

```
2 occurrences of 8 found at 1 4
```

The `IndexOf()` search algorithm is linear; that is, it looks at each element of the array in turn until either a match is achieved or all the elements have been examined. For large arrays, a binary search is more efficient, but it requires our array to be sorted:

```
Array.Sort( ivalues );
index = Array.BinarySearch( ivalues, search_value );
if ( index >= 0 ) /* found! */
```

`BinarySearch()` returns the value's index, if present; otherwise, it returns a negative value rather than always returning `-1`. There is also a `Reverse()` static method. It reverses the order of the elements in the array.

5.3 Querying the Environment

Let's implement a small program to query the local machine environment about the user, processes running on the machine, and the logical drives associated with the machine. Our output looks like this:

```
Hello, stanley lippman!
Your machine PROUST is running Microsoft Windows NT 5.0.0.2195
Service Pack 1

The current process running is 'HelloEnvironment'
Startup Path is C:\C#Programs\HelloEnvironment\bin\Debug
There are 46 other processes running on PROUST

Process Name: Idle
        has been running for 3 days
        total: 3.22:59:33.0130432

Machine PROUST Process Statistics
        Longer than a day:     1
        Longer than an hour:   0
        Longer than a minute: 12
        Less than a minute:    34

The logical drive subdirectory structure:
        A:\ :: 2 subdirectories.
            The subdirectories: ParamPassing Visibility
        C:\ :: 50 subdirectories.
        D:\ :: 4 subdirectories.
            The subdirectories: interfaces xml efficiency munich
        E:\ :: 1 subdirectories.
            The subdirectories: Art
        F:\ :: is currently unavailable.
```

5.3.1 The Environment Class

By using the System.Environment class, we can retrieve the name of the user, the name of the machine, and the name and version of the operating system. GetEnvironmentVariable() is a static method of the Environment class. We pass it the name of the environment variable that interests us. It returns the string value of the variable if it is defined; otherwise it returns null. The two environment variables of interest to us are USERNAME and COMPUTER-NAME:

```
string user_name =
      Environment.GetEnvironmentVariable( "USERNAME" );

string mach_name =
      Environment.GetEnvironmentVariable( "COMPUTERNAME" );
```

```
OperatingSystem os_ver = Environment.OSVersion;

Console.WriteLine( "Hello, {0}!", user_name );
Console.WriteLine( "Your machine {0} is running {1}\n",
        mach_name, os_ver.ToString() );
```

OSVersion returns an OperatingSystem object that stores properties about the current operating system. This code generates our first lines of greeting:

```
Hello, stanley lippman!
Your machine PROUST is running Microsoft Windows NT 5.0.0.2195
Service Pack 1
```

As it turns out, USERNAME is defined under the Windows NT, Windows 2000, and Windows XP environments but not under Windows 95, Windows 98, or Windows ME. Under these latter operating system versions, user_name is initialized to null. We could test user_name to see if it is null, of course. Instead, let's conditionally execute alternative greetings depending on the operating system. Here's how we do that:

```
if ( os_ver.Platform == PlatformID.Win32NT )
    Console.WriteLine( "Hello, {0}!", user_name );
else Console.WriteLine( "Hello!");
```

PlatformID is an enum type. Platform is a static property of the OperatingSystem class that holds a PlatformID value. PlatformID currently defines three values: (1) Win32NT, which represents those versions based on the NT code base; (2) Win32S, which represents a version of the operating system prior to Windows 95; and (3) Win32Windows, which represents everything else.

5.3.2 Accessing All the Environment Variables

To access all the environment variables as a collection of key/value pairs, we use GetEnvironmentVariables(). It returns an instance of the IDictionary interface. The following function collects, sorts, and prints each environment variable, asking if the user would like to see its associated value as well:

```
public static void displayEnvironment()
{
    IDictionary dict =
        Environment.GetEnvironmentVariables();

    Console.WriteLine( "There are {0} environment variables",
                        dict.Count );

    string [] keys   = new string[ dict.Count ];
    string [] values = new string[ dict.Count ];

    int ix = 0;
    foreach ( DictionaryEntry de in dict )
    {
        keys[ ix ]   = (string) de.Key;
        values[ ix ] = (string) de.Value;
        ++ix;
    }

    Array.Sort( keys, values );

    for ( ix = 0; ix < keys.Length; ++ix )
    {
        Console.Write( "Variable is {0} -- value? (y/n)",
                        keys[ix]);
        string rsp = Console.ReadLine();
        if ( rsp == "y" || rsp == "Y" )
            Console.WriteLine( "\t==> {0} ", values[ix] );
        else Console.WriteLine();
    }
}
```

You might wonder why I store the keys and values in separate string arrays. The order of the entries returned from GetEnvironmentVariables() is not alphabetical. I want to sort the environment variables alphabetically but also want to retain their associated values in the corresponding index. Happily, this is exactly the semantics provided with the following invocation of Sort():

```
// sorts the keys array --

// that is, maintains the values array
// in the order of the associated keys element
Array.Sort( keys, values );
```

The environment variables stored within `keys` are sorted alphabetically. The associated elements stored in `values` are moved to corresponding indices as `keys` is sorted. The one-to-one mapping between the two arrays is maintained.

5.3.3 The `Process` Class

The `Process` class, defined within the `System.Diagnostics` namespace, provides access to the executables running on a local or remote computer through two static retrieval methods:

1. `GetCurrentProcess()` returns a `Process` class object with information about our currently executing program:

   ```
   Process currProc = Process.GetCurrentProcess();
   Console.WriteLine( "The current process running is \'{0}\'",
                      currProc.ProcessName );
   ```

2. `GetProcesses()` returns an array of `Process` objects representing all the running processes on the local computer:

   ```
   Process [] procs = Process.GetProcesses();
   string msg="There are {0} other processes running on {1}\n";
   Console.WriteLine( msg, procs.Length-1, mach_name );
   ```

Through the `Process` class object we have access to a great many properties of a process, including `Id` (its unique identifier) and `ProcessName`. Execution time of the process is available as user time (`UserProcessorTime`); privileged (i.e., system) time (`PrivilegedProcessorTime`); or total time, which is the sum of user and privileged time (`TotalProcessorTime`). For example, the statistics generated by our program:

```
Process Name: Idle
        has been running for 3 days
        total: 3.22:59:33.0130432

Machine PROUST Process Statistics
        Longer than a day:     1
        Longer than an hour:   0
        Longer than a minute: 12
        Less than a minute:   34
```

are collected by the following code sequence:

```
foreach ( Process proc in procs )
{
    TimeSpan totalTime = proc.TotalProcessorTime;
    if ( totalTime.Days > 0 )
    {
        dayCnt++;
        Console.WriteLine( msg, proc.ProcessName,
                    totalTime.Days, totalTime.ToString() );
    }
    else
    if ( totalTime.Hours > 0 )
        hourCnt++;
    else
    if ( totalTime.Minutes > 0 )
        minCnt++;
    else lessMinCnt
}
```

TimeSpan is a struct within the System namespace for representing a period (or span) of time, such as the extent of time a process is active or the difference between two DateTime objects. Properties such as Days and Hours return the number of whole units (in this case days or hours) represented by the value. For example, if the TimeSpan object represented 25 hours and 20 minutes, the value of Days would be 1, the value of Hours would be 1, and the value of Minutes would be 20. For example, the following code subtracts one DateTime object from another:

```
DateTime theNow = DateTime.Now;
DateTime backThen = new DateTime( 1945, 11, 11, 11, 11, 0, 0 );

TimeSpan soFar = theNow - backThen;
Console.WriteLine( soFar.ToString() );

Console.WriteLine( "Days since: {0}", soFar.Days );
Console.WriteLine( "Years since: {0}", soFar.Days/356 );
```

5.3.4 Finding the Logical Drives

In the last portion of our program we list the computer's logical drives and print the top-level directories of each drive, provided that the number of directories is less than ten:

```
The logical drive subdirectory structure:
    A:\ :: 2 subdirectories.
            The subdirectories: ParamPassing Visibility

    C:\ :: 50 subdirectories.

    D:\ :: 4 subdirectories.
            The subdirectories: interfaces xml efficiency munich

    E:\ :: 1 subdirectories.
            The subdirectories: Art

    F:\ :: is currently unavailable.
```

GetLogicalDrives() is a public static method of both the `Directory` and the `Environment` classes. It returns an array of string elements representing the logical drives in the form *C:*, where *C* represents the drive letter:

```
string [] logical_drives = Directory.GetLogicalDrives();
```

The `Directory` class is defined within the `System.IO` namespace. Let's look at that next.

5.4 `System.IO`

The `System.IO` namespace provides support for input and output. Support for file and directory manipulation is factored across four classes. A `Directory` and `File` pair of classes provide support for static members only. We use these classes when we do not have an actual directory or file. To manipulate an actual file or directory object, we use the `DirectoryInfo` and `FileInfo` pair of classes. These provide instance member functions to operate on a particular directory or file object. In addition, a `Path` utility class provides file and directory path string support.

Read and write support is separated into three general categories: the byte-oriented `Stream` class hierarchy (1), and specialized classes for handling character (2) or binary (3) input/output. Rather than listing the various classes and itemizing each interface, let's walk through an implementation of the file read and write portions of the text query system introduced in Chapter 3. The two primary routines we'll need are the following:

1. `request_text_file()`, which requests the path of either a directory or a file. It checks that the file exists and has a file extension, such as *.txt*, that is supported by our application.

2. `handle_directory()`, which confirms that the directory exists. It collects all files with file extensions supported by our application, and it displays the list of files and associated characteristics (length, last opened, and so on).

A path name entered by the user, such as `C:\fictions\araby.txt` or `C:\fictions`, may represent a file, as in the first example, or a directory, as in the second, or it may be an invalid path name. How do we determine which of these is the case?

```
// text_file holds a string entered by the user
file_check = File.Exists( text_file );

if ( file_check == false )
{
    if ( Directory.Exists( text_file ))
        return handle_directory();

    Console.WriteLine( "Invalid file: {0}: ", text_file );
}
```

The `File` class provides static operations for querying, creating, copying, deleting, moving, and opening files. `Exists(string path)` returns `true` if the file represented by `path` exists, and `false` *if either the file does not exist or* `path` *specifies a directory.*

The `Directory` class provides analogous static operations for the support of directories. The `Directory` instance of `Exists(string path)` returns `true` if the directory given by `path` exists, and `false` otherwise.

5.4.1 Handling File Extensions: The `Path` Class

Once we have a valid file name, we still need to ensure that we support the file type. The type of a file, by convention, is indicated by the file extension. For example, a C# program text file is indicated by the *.cs* file extension, a C++ file by *.cpp,* an XML file by *.xml,* a simple text file by *.txt,* and so on.

The extension is identified by the embedded period within the file name. The file name is interpreted as the sequence of characters following the last directory or volume separator. For example, in the path

```
@"c:\fictions\current\word.txt"
```

the file name is `word.txt`, and the extension is `.txt`.

The `Path` utility class provides a set of static operations on a directory or file path string—picking them apart or combining them. (It does not require that the file or directory path actually exist.) We can use the following three static methods to query, retrieve, or change the extension of a file or directory:

1. `bool HasExtension(string path)`, which returns `true` if the file name contains an embedded period. Otherwise it returns `false`.

2. `string GetExtension(string path)`, which returns the file extension, such as `.txt`, including the period, or else returns `String.Empty`.

3. `string ChangeExtension(string path,string newExt)`, which strips off the extension associated with the file name if the second parameter is `null`. Otherwise the new extension replaces the old extension. If the file name lacks an extension, the new extension is added.

Here is a brief code sequence that illustrates these and other members of the `Path` class. The names of the members are reasonably self-describing:

```
string thePath = @"C:\fictions\Phoenix\alice.txt";

Console.WriteLine( "The file is named " +
    Path.GetFileNameWithoutExtension( thePath ));

if ( Path.HasExtension( thePath ))
    Console.WriteLine( "It has the extension: " +
                        Path.GetExtension( thePath ));

Console.WriteLine( "The full path is " +
                    Path.GetFullPath( thePath ));

if ( Path.IsPathRooted( thePath ))
    Console.WriteLine( "The path root is " +
                        Path.GetPathRoot( thePath ));

string tempDir = Path.GetTempPath();
```

```
Console.WriteLine( "The temporary directory is " + tempDir );

// combine two path strings ...
string tempCombine =
  Path.Combine( tempDir, Path.GetFileName( thePath ));

Console.WriteLine( "Path of file copy " + tempCombine );

// creates the path of a unique file name within the
// system's temporary directory ...

string tempFile = Path.GetTempFileName();
Console.WriteLine( "Temporary file is " + tempFile );
```

When this code sequence is packaged into a member function and executed, it generates the following output:

```
The file is named alice
It has the extension: .txt
The full path is C:\fictions\Phoenix\alice.txt
The path root is C:\
The temporary directory is C:\DOCUME~1\STANLE~1\LOCALS~1\Temp\
Path of file copy C:\DOCUME~1\STANLE~1\LOCALS~1\Temp\alice.txt
Temporary file is C:\DOCUME~1\STANLE~1\LOCALS~1\Temp\tmp337.tmp
```

5.4.2 Manipulating Directories

Given a string that represents a valid directory, we'd like to (1) find all the files in that directory with a file extension that we support, such as *.txt,* and (2) find all the subdirectories in that directory and examine each of them in turn. The following code fragment does that:

```
try
{
    // if unable to open for any reason, throws exception
    DirectoryInfo dir = new DirectoryInfo( text_file );

    // holds all supported file types

    ArrayList candidate_files = new ArrayList();

    // holds array of files returned from GetFiles()
    FileInfo [] curr_files;
```

```
    foreach ( string ext in m_supported_files )
    {
            // returns a file list from the current directory
            // that matches the given search criteria,
            // such as "*.txt"
        curr_files = dir.GetFiles( "*" + ext );
        candidate_files.AddRange( curr_files );
    }


    // get all subdirectories within our directory
    DirectoryInfo [] directories = dir.GetDirectories();

    // OK: let's do it again
    foreach ( DirectoryInfo d in directories )
        foreach ( string ext in m_supported_files )
        {
          curr_files = d.GetFiles( "*" + ext );
          candidate_files.AddRange( curr_files );
        }
```

The `DirectoryInfo` class member `GetFiles()` comes in two flavors. The empty-signature instance returns an array of `FileInfo` objects representing each of the files in a directory. A second instance takes a search criteria string and returns only the files that meet those criteria. In our case, we want all files ending with a particular file extension. For example, the following returns all files ending with the *.txt* file extension:

```
FileInfo [] curr_files = dir.GetFiles( "*.txt" );
```

The asterisk (*) serves as a *wild card* in the search process. Provided that the file name ends with *.txt,* all characters prior to that are accepted.

`GetDirectories()` comes in two flavors: the empty-signature instance that returns all directories, and the search criteria instance that returns only those directories that match.

The following member function creates a directory, creates a file and a subdirectory within it, and then deletes them all. Static methods such as `Exists()` are invoked through the `Directory` class; instance methods, such as `CreateFile()` and `CreateSubdirectory()`, are invoked through a `DirectoryInfo` class object:

```
public static void testDirCreateDelete( string workDir )
{
    DirectoryInfo wd;

    // create the directory if it does not exist
    if ( ! Directory.Exists( workDir ))
            wd = Directory.CreateDirectory( workDir );
    else    wd = new DirectoryInfo( workDir );

    // create a file and a subdirectory
    FileStream    f = wd.CreateFile( workDir + "test.txt" );
    Directoryinfo d = wd.CreateSubdirectory( "subdir" );

    // delete directory and its contents
    d.Delete();

    // delete directory and all subdirectories
    f.Close();
    wd.Delete( true );
}
```

This routine is invoked through the following call:

```
testDirCreateDelete( Path.GetTempPath() + "foobar" +
                     Path.DirectorySeparatorChar );
```

`DirectorySeparatorChar` is a read-only property of the `Path` class. It is set to the backslash (\) under Windows; under Unix, to the slash (/); and under the Macintosh operating system, to the colon (:) .

The `DirectoryInfo` class provides a collection of properties that encapsulate different directory characteristics, such as whether the directory exists (e.g., a disk or CD-ROM drive that is empty, when asked if it exists, returns `false`). The following code sequence exercises several `DirectoryInfo` class properties—their names are pretty much self-documenting:

```
public static void testDirProperties( string workDir )
{
    DirectoryInfo dir = new DirectoryInfo( workDir );
    if ( dir.Exists )
    {
        Console.WriteLine("Directory full name ", dir.FullName);
```

```
        // refreshes object --
        dir.Refresh();

        DateTime createTime = dir.CreationTime;
        DateTime lastAccess = dir.LastAccessTime;
        DateTime lastWrite  = dir.LastWriteTime;
        // ... display these ...

        DirectoryInfo parent = dir.Parent;
        DirectoryInfo root   = dir.Root;

        FileInfo []        has_files = dir.GetFiles();
        DirectoryInfo [] has_dirs  = dir.GetDirectories();
    }
}
```

5.4.3 Manipulating Files

As in the handling of directories, the operations for creating, copying, moving, deleting, querying, and modifying the characteristics of a file are separated into two classes. The `File` class provides a collection of static members that can be invoked without having an actual file object. The `FileInfo` class provides instance members to apply to a file object.

The `FileInfo` class provides a set of properties. These are similar to those of the `DirectoryInfo` class. For example, the output

```
Creation Time        : 11/29/2000 7:02 PM
Last Access Time     : 5/7/2001 12:00 AM
Last Write Time      : 3/13/2001 1:59 PM
File Size in Bytes   : 703
```

is generated from the following code sequence:

```
DateTime createTime = fd.CreationTime;
DateTime lastAccess = fd.LastAccessTime;
DateTime lastWrite  = fd.LastWriteTime;
long     fileLength = fd.Length;
```

where `fd` represents a `FileInfo` object.

We can query a `File` using the `Attributes` property to discover its file attributes, including `Archive`, `Compressed`, `Encrypted`, `Hidden`, `Normal`, and `ReadOnly,` among others. These are all `FileAttributes` enumerators. The object returned by the `Attributes` property can be thought of as a bit vector in which each attribute associated with the file is turned either on or off. For example, here is how we might query a `FileInfo object` as to its attributes:

```
public static void displayFileAttributes( FileInfo fd )
{
        // Attributes returns a FileAttributes object
        FileAttributes fs = fd.Attributes;

        // use bitwise operators to see if attribute is set
        if (( fs & FileAttributes.Archive ) != 0 )
            // OK: file is archived ...

        if (( fs & FileAttributes.ReadOnly ) != 0 )
            fd.Attributes -= FileAttributes.ReadOnly;

        // ... and so on ...
}
```

To modify a file attribute, we can either subtract or add the associated `enum` value, provided of course that we have the required permissions.

5.4.4   Reading and Writing Files

There are multiple ways of opening an existing text file for reading or writing. The actual reading and writing of a text file is done with the `StreamReader` and the `StreamWriter` classes, respectively—for example,

```
public static void StreamReaderWriter()
{
        StreamReader ifile =
            new StreamReader( @"c:\fictions\word.txt" );

        StreamWriter ofile =
            new StreamWriter( @"c:\fictions\word_out.txt" );

        string str;
        ArrayList textLines = new ArrayList();
```

```
while (( str = ifile.ReadLine()) != null )
{
        Console.WriteLine( str ); // echo to Console
        textLines.Add( str );     // add to back ...
}

textLines.Sort();

foreach ( string s in textLines )
        ofile.WriteLine( s );

ifile.Close();
ofile.Close();
}
```

If the file is unable to be opened, for whatever reason, an exception is thrown. In production code, then, we should check that we can open both files before attempting to bind them to a `StreamReader` and a `StreamWriter`. For example, here is an alternative implementation strategy using the `OpenText()` and `CreateText()` member functions of the `FileInfo` class:

```
public static void FileOpen( string inFile, string outFile )
{
    FileInfo ifd = new FileInfo( inFile );
    FileInfo ofd = new FileInfo( outFile );

    if ( ifd.Exists && ofd.Exists &&
       ((ofd.Attributes & FileAttributes.ReadOnly)==0))
    {
        StreamReader ifile = ifd.OpenText();
        StreamWriter ofile = ofd.CreateText();

        // rest is the same as above
    }
}
```

If we wish to append text to an existing output file rather than overwrite the existing text within the file, we invoke `FileInfo`'s `AppendText()` method rather than `CreateText()`:

```
StreamWriter ofile = ofd.AppendText();
```

We use the Stream class hierarchy to read a file as a sequence of bytes rather than as a text file—for example,

```
FileInfo ifd = new FileInfo( inFile  );
FileInfo ofd = new FileInfo( outFile );

Stream ifile = ifd.OpenRead();
Stream ofile = ofd.OpenWrite();
```

The File class methods OpenRead() and OpenWrite() return a derived-class instance of Stream. We pass into the Read() method of the Stream an array in which to deposit the bytes, an index indicating where to begin writing the bytes, and a count of the maximum number of bytes to read. Read() returns the number of actual bytes read. A value of 0 indicates the end of the file. Similarly, to write the Stream using the Write() function, we pass in an array holding the bytes, an index indicating where to begin extracting the bytes, and the number of bytes to write:

```
const int max_bytes = 124;
byte  []  buffer    = new byte[ max_bytes ];
int       bytesRead;

while (( bytesRead =
        ifile.Read( buffer, 0, max_bytes )) != 0 )
{
     Console.WriteLine( "Bytes read: {0}", bytesRead );
     ofile.Write( buffer, 0, bytesRead );
}
```

Several enum types defined within the System.IO namespace allow us to specify the read/write and sharing attributes of a file when we open it—for example,

```
Stream ifile = ifd.Open( FileMode.Open, FileAccess.Read,
                         FileShare.Read );


// default FileShare of None
Stream ofile = ofd.Open(FileMode.Truncate,FileAccess.ReadWrite);
```

There are six FileMode enumerators:

1. `Append`, which opens a file if it exists and searches to the end of it. Otherwise it creates a new file.

2. `Create`, which creates a new file. If the file exists, it is overwritten.

3. `CreateNew`, which creates a new file. If the file exists, an exception is thrown.

4. `Open`, which opens an existing file.

5. `OpenOrCreate`, which opens a file if it exists; otherwise it creates a new file.

6. `Truncate`, which opens an existing file and truncates it to 0 bytes.

The `FileAccess` enumeration defines three modes of accessing a file being opened (by default, a file is opened for both reading and writing):

1. `Read`, which specifies read access. Data can be read from the file, and the current position can be moved. This is the mode for `File.OpenRead()`.

2. `ReadWrite`, which specifies read and write access to the file. Data can be both written to and read from the file, and the current position can be moved.

3. `Write`, which specifies write access to the file. Data can be written to the file, and the current position can be moved. This is the mode for `File.OpenWrite()`.

The `FileShare` enumeration defines alternative values for controlling the kind of access that other `Stream` objects can have to the same file. For example, if a file is opened and `FileShare.Read` is specified, other users can open the file for reading but not for writing. Here are `FileShare`'s access modes:

- `None`, which indicates no sharing of the current file. Any request to open the file (by this process or another process) will fail until the file is closed.

- `Read`, which allows subsequent opening of the file for reading.

- `ReadWrite`, which allows subsequent opening of the file for reading or writing.

- `Write`, which allows subsequent opening of the file for writing.

The `Stream` class hierarchy allows us to adjust the current position within the stream using `Seek()`. We can then read and/or write either a byte or a chunk of bytes stored within an array. To discover if a `Stream` supports read, write, or seek permission, we access the following Boolean properties:

```
public void StreamSeek( Stream file, int offset )
{
    Console.WriteLine( "CanRead: {0}",  file.CanRead  );
    Console.WriteLine( "CanWrite: {0}", file.CanWrite );
    Console.WriteLine( "CanSeek: {0}",  file.CanSeek  );

    if ( ! file.CanWrite || ! file.CanSeek )
        return;

    // ...
}
```

For example, let's open our two streams using the `File` class `Open()` method with the mode, access, and share `enum` values we saw earlier:

```
public void BytesReadWrite( string inFile, string outFile )
{
    FileInfo ifd = new FileInfo( inFile );
    FileInfo ofd = new FileInfo( outFile );

    if ( ifd.Exists && ofd.Exists &&
        (( ofd.Attributes & FileAttributes.ReadOnly )==0))

    {
        Stream ifile = ifd.Open( FileMode.Open,
                                 FileAccess.Read,
                                 FileShare.Read );

        Stream ofile = ofd.Open( FileMode.Truncate,
                                 FileAccess.ReadWrite );

        // ... we read the same as before ...
    }
}
```

The following code sequence illustrates how we can reposition ourselves within a file for both read and write operations. Both `Length` and `Position` are `Stream` properties. `Length` holds the size in bytes of the file. `Position` maintains the current position within the stream:

```
// it's just been written to by ifile;
// let's flush it, just to be on the safe side
ofile.Flush();

long offset = ofile.Length/4 - 1,
     position = 0L;

for ( ; position < ofile.Length; position += offset )
{
    ofile.Seek( position, SeekOrigin.Begin );
    int theByte = ofile.ReadByte();
    ofile.WriteByte((byte)'X' );

    Console.WriteLine( "Position: {0} -- byte replaced: {1}",
                       ofile.Position, theByte.ToChar() );
}

ifile.Close(); ofile.Close();
```

Seek() takes two arguments. The first represents the byte offset relative to a reference point represented by the second. TSeekOrigin is an enum with three enumerators: (1) Begin, which sets the reference point to the beginning of the stream; (2) Current, which sets it to the current position; and (3) End, <which sets the reference point to the end of the stream.

5.5   A System Miscellany

In this section we review several useful classes that don't fit into any common category other than miscellaneous. The presentation represents more of a peek than a formal introduction. All of these classes reside directly in the System namespace unless otherwise noted.

5.5.1   The System.Collections.Stack Container

The System.Collections namespace contains a variety of container classes, such as ArrayList (discussed in Section 1.13), Hashtable (Section 1.16), and BitArray (Section 4.9). In general, the container classes store the elements as objects of type object. Value types are boxed and unboxed with each read and write operation. Let's briefly look at the Stack class of the Collections namespace.

The `stack` class interface is characterized as follows:

- `Clear()` removes all elements from the stack.
- `Contains(object)` searches for `object` in the stack.
- `Count` returns the number of elements in the stack.
- `Peek()` returns an object at the top without removing it.
- `Pop()` removes and returns an object at the top.
- `Push()` inserts an object at the top.
- `ToArray()` copies the stack elements to an array.

To illustrate how we might use `stack`, consider the following problem. When the TextQuery application needs to evaluate a compound query, such as

```
Alice && ( fiery || untamed )
```

it finds incomplete operators and independent operands that it needs to tuck away for subsequent retrieval. One way of doing this is to define two stacks—one to hold the current operator, such as `&&` or `||`, and one to hold unattached operands—for example,

```
public class QueryManager
{
    // query operand and operator stacks for
    // processing the user query

    private Stack m_query_stack;
    private Stack m_current_op;
}
```

When we see *Alice* in the preceding query, we process it as a `NameQuery`. There is no operator with which to associate it yet, so we push it onto `m_query_stack`. When we encounter an operator, such as `AndQuery`, we pop `m_query_stack` to retrieve the left `AndQuery` operand. The right `AndQuery` operand, however, is not yet available, so we push the `AndQuery` onto the `m_current_op` stack—for example,

```
case ')':
{
    // ...
```

```
if ( m_paren < m_current_op.Count )
{
        if ( m_query_stack.Count==0 ||
            m_current_op.Count==0 )
        {
                throw new Exception( "Internal Error: " +
                    "Empty query or operator stack " +
                    "for closing right paren!" );
        }

        Query operand = (Query) m_query_stack.Pop();
        Query op      = (Query) m_current_op.Pop();

        op.add_op( operand );
        m_query_stack.Push( op );
    }

    break;
}
```

There is also a `Queue` class. It is implemented as a *circular array;* that is, objects are inserted at one end and removed from the other. When the number of elements reaches its capacity, the capacity is automatically increased. The `Queue` class interface is characterized as follows:

- `Clear()` removes all elements from the queue.
- `Contains(object)` searches for `object` in the queue.
- `Count` returns the number of elements in the queue.
- `Peek()` returns an object at the front without removing it.
- `Dequeue()` removes and returns an object at the front.
- `Enqueue()` inserts an object at the back.
- `ToArray()` copies the queue elements to an array.

5.5.2 The `System.Diagnostics.TraceListener` Class

The `System.Diagnostics` namespace provides a `TraceListener` family of classes with which the user can turn on and direct diagnostic output. For example, in the `WordCount` program of Chapter 1, the user determines if and where tracing output should be generated:

```
    if ( m_trace != traceFlags.turnOff )
        switch ( m_trace )
        {
            case traceFlags.toConsole:
                 cout = new TextWriterTraceListener( Console.Out );
                Trace.Listeners.Add( cout );

            break;

            case traceFlags.toFile:
                m_tracer =
                        File.CreateText(startupPath + @"\trace.txt");
                cout = new TextWriterTraceListener( m_tracer );
                Trace.Listeners.Add( cout );

            break;
        }
```

The `TextWriterTraceListener` class is initialized either with a `Stream` or a `TextWriter` object. In our example we initialize it either to the console or to a file called `trace.txt`. We then add it to the `Listeners` collection monitoring the trace output. The trace output is what we implement—for example,

```
    private void writeWords()
    {
        Trace.WriteLine( "!!! WordCount.writeWords: " +
                            m_file_output );
        timer tt = null;

        if ( m_spy ){
                tt = new timer();
                tt.context = "Time to write file ";
                tt.start();
        }

        ArrayList aKeys = new ArrayList( m_words.Keys );
        aKeys.Sort();
        foreach ( string key in aKeys )
        {
                m_writer.WriteLine("{0} : {1}", key, m_words[ key ]);
                Trace.WriteLine( "!!! " + key + " : " +
                                    m_words[ key ].ToString() );
        }
```

```
    if ( m_spy )
    {
        tt.stop();
        m_times.Add( tt.ToString() );
    }
}
```

`Trace.WriteLine()` represents the output to which `Listeners` is attending. If our user has added something to the `Listeners` collection within `Trace`, the `WriteLine()` output is now directed at that target.

By default, tracing is turned on in Visual Studio for both *Debug* and *Release* builds. This means that the tracing code is always present. The benefit of this configuration is that anyone can tap into the code without having to recompile everything. The downside, of course, is that it is always there.

To eliminate the code in the *Release* build, we can use the `Debug` class rather than `Trace`. Debugging is turned off under *Release*, so no debugging code is generated for `Debug` methods.

5.5.3 `System.Math`

The `Math` class within the `System` namespace provides static methods for trigonometric (e.g., `Cos()`, `Sin()`, `Tan()`), logarithmic (`log()`, `log10()`), and other common mathematical functions (`Abs()`, `Ceiling()`, `Floor()`, `Exp()`, `Min()`, `Max()`, `Pow()`, `Round()`, and so on). It defines two fields: `E` and `PI`. Here is an example of a `Vector` class invoking the square root method, `Sqrt()`:

```
public class Vector
{
    public double length()
        { return Math.Sqrt( length_() ); }

    public double distance( vector v )
        { return Math.Sqrt( distance_( v )); }

    // ...
}
```

`Math` is an example of a class that serves primarily as a bucket in which to toss a somewhat random set of operations whose only commonality is that they represent one or another math routine. In a procedural language like C, these static members are presented as independent functions grouped in a library named `math`. The important thing for you to know about the `Math` class is just that it exists. Whenever you need a standard math routine, this is the first place to look.

5.5.4 The `DateTime` Class

The `DateTime` class represents a date and a time value. Two static properties of the `DateTime` class are `Ncw`, which represents the current date *and* time, and `Today`, which retrieves the current date (the time is set to midnight)—for example,

```
DateTime theDate = DateTime.Now;
```

To access the time and date as individual strings, we can invoke one of the following `DateTime` methods:

```
Console.WriteLine( "The current long date is {0}",
                   theDate.ToLongDateString() );

Console.WriteLine( "The current short date is {0}",
                   theDate.ToShortDateString() );

Console.WriteLine( "The current long time is {0}",
                   theDate.ToLongTimeString() );

Console.WriteLine( "The current short time is {0}",
                   theDate.ToShortTimeString() );
```

When executed, these statements generate output like the following:

```
The current long date is Tuesday, February 27, 2001
The current short date is 02/27/2001
The current long time is 14:31:30
The current short time is 14:31
```

There are also many format strings we can use. The set of `DateTime` formats is listed in Table 5.2. For example, my favorite is the *full* format, indicated in code by a capital `F`:

```
// generates this format: Tuesday, May 08, 2001 6:23:51 PM
Console.WriteLine( "{0:F}", theDate );
```

Table 5.1   The DateTime Format Strings

Format	Output	Description
"{0:d}"	5/8/2001	Short date
"{0:D}"	Tuesday, May 08, 2001	Long date
"{0:f}"	Tuesday, May 08, 2001 6:23 PM	Full (long date + short time)
"{0:F}"	Tuesday, May 08, 2001 6:23:51 PM	Full (long date + long time)
"{0:g}"	5/8/2001 6:23 PM	General (short date + short time)
"{0:G}"	5/8/2001 6:23:51 PM	General (short date + long time)
"{0:M}"	May 08	Month/day date
"{0:R}"	Wed, 09 May 2001 01:23:51 GMT	RFC standard
"{0:s}"	2001-05-08T18:23:51	Sortable without time zone
"{0:t}"	6:23 PM	Short time
"{0:T}"	6:23:51 PM	Long time
"{0:u}"	2001-05-09 01:23:51Z	Universal with sortable format
"{0:U}"	Wednesday, May 09, 2001 1:23:51 AM	Universal with full format
"{0:Y}"	May, 2001	Year/month date

The `DateTime` class supports many instance properties that return different portions of the current `DateTime` object: `Date`, `Day`, `Hour`, `DayOfWeek`, `DayOfYear`, `Millisecond`, `Minute`, `Month`, `Second`, `Ticks`, `TimeOfDay`, and `Year`.

The `DateTime` class offers a large number of methods: `AddMinutes()`, `AddMilliseconds()`, `Parse()` (to make a `DateTime` object from a string), `IsLeapYear()`, `AddDays()`, `AddHours()`, `DaysInMonth()`, and so on.

There are seven overloaded constructors, including the following four:

```
DateTime( long Ticks );

DateTime( int year, int month, int day );

DateTime( int year, int month, int day,
          int hour, int min, int sec );

DateTime( int year, int month, int day,
          int hour, int min, int sec,
            int millisecond );
```

5.6 Regular Expressions

The *Firebird* segment of *Fantasia 2000* has only three characters: a sprite, the firebird of the title, and a somewhat fastidious elk. Although the elk is the least remarked of the three, he is actually one of the more remarkable figures. His body and facial expressions are hand-drawn by traditional Disney animation techniques. His antlers, however, are a three-dimensional computer model. The challenge was to match the movement of the antlers with the hand-drawn two-dimensional animation. Solving this problem brought not only the elk to *Fantasia 2000;* it brought me along as well.

My computer-generated imagery (CGI) supervisor, Chyuan, came up with the splendid idea of capturing the stream of camera positions mapping the movements of the hand-drawn elk. These movements were then transformed into a set of curves and fed into the three-dimensional animation package. The antler was manually positioned at the start of the scene to sit atop the elk's head. The curves match the antlers' movement with that of the elk as the scene unfolds.

Chyuan patiently explained the math to me; I did the actual programming, first in C++, then in Perl, a scripting language. The Perl implementation was considerably smaller than the equivalent implementation in C++, largely because of the regular-expression support built into Perl. Regular-expression support under .NET is found in the `System.Text.RegularExpressions` namespace. This is the topic of this section.

What is a *regular expression?* It is a pattern of characters and symbols representing a character sequence of arbitrary length. For example, let's say we need to find all lines of text that begin with the number 5. The number can be any length, but it must be followed by a dash and then the letter *a, b,* or *c,* followed by one or more letters or characters. It must end with the sequence *2001.* To use a regular expression, we need symbols to do the following:

- Indicate that we wish to begin the search at the beginning of the line. We do this with the caret (^). So, for example, ^5 means we want the line to begin with a literal value of 5 .

- Indicate that we wish to match on a particular flavor of character. So, for example, \d means that we wish to match on a single digit between 0 and 9. \D means that we wish to match on a single character that is not a digit.

C# PRIMER

\s means that we wish to match on a single white-space character, and \S means that we wish to match on a single character that is not white space. \w matches on any alphanumeric character (*a* to *z*, *A* to *Z*, 0 to 9). \W matches any character that is not alphanumeric.

- Indicate that we wish to match on any character, regardless of its type. For example, the period matches any non-new-line character.

- Indicate that we wish to match on multiple (or no) instances of a character type. The plus operator (+) means that we wish to match on one or more characters of the same type. \d+, for example, matches on 2, 22, 1217, and so on. The asterisk (*) means that we wish to allow for no matches as well. For example, the regular expression

```
^5\d+\D+2001
```

matches on any line that begins with 5 followed by one or more additional digits, followed by one or more nondigit characters followed by the literal *2001*. The regular expression

```
^5\d*\D*2001
```

matches on every line that begins with 5 and ends with the literal *2001*. Between the 5 and *2001*, there may or may not be some digits followed by some nondigit characters.

- Indicate that we wish to match on a fixed number of characters. For example, the regular expression

```
\d{3}-\d{4}
```

requires three digits followed by a hyphen, followed by four digits, such as 375-4128.

- Indicate that we wish to match on one of a set of different characters. We do this by placing a set of alternative characters within parentheses, separated by the bool OR operator (|). For example, the expression a|e|i|o|u means that we wish to match on one of the five English vowels. Adding the addition operator—(a|e|i|o|u)+, that is—means that we wish to match on one or more consecutive occurrences of the five English vowels. Following the expression with an asterisk means that we wish to allow for no matches as well.

Regular expressions take some getting use to. In the beginning they seem quite complicated because they offer such compact notation. To facilitate your exploration of regular expressions, I've written a small regular-expression test program. You enter a string, a regular expression, or both, and the program identifies which matches, if any, occur—for example (note that my console input is highlighted in bold),

```
Would you like to enter a string to match against? (Y/N/?) y
Please enter a string, or 'quit' to exit.
    ==> 5abc2001

Would you like to change regular expressions? (Y/N/?) y
Please enter regular expression:
    **> ^5\d*(a|d|e)\w+2001

original string:  5abc2001
attempt to match: ^5\d*(a|d|e)\w+2001

The characters 5abc2001 match beginning at position 0

Would you like to enter a string to match against? (Y/N/?) y
Please enter a string, or 'quit' to exit.
    ==> 5abc2001

Would you like to change regular expressions? (Y/N/?) n

original string:  527ar2001
attempt to match: ^5\d*(a|d|e)\w+2001
The characters 527ar2001 match beginning at position 0
```

Of course, there can be multiple matches as well—for example,

```
original string:  r24d2
attempt to match: \d+
The characters 24 match beginning at position 1
The characters 2 match beginning at position 4
```

Let's try our hand at programming regular expressions under .NET. First let me show you the code that does the matching; then I'll explain what's going on:

```
public static void doMatch()
{
    Console.WriteLine( "original string:  {0}", inputString );
    Console.WriteLine( "attempt to match: {0}", filter );
```

```
Regex regex = new Regex( filter );
Match match = regex.Match( inputString );

if ( ! match.Success )
{
   Console.WriteLine( "Sorry, no match of {0} in {1}",
                       filter, inputString );
   return;
}

for ( ; match.Success; match = match.NextMatch() )
{
   Console.WriteLine(
     "The characters {0} match beginning at position {1}",
     match.ToString(), match.Index
   );
}
}
```

The `Regex` class represents our regular expression. We pass its constructor the string representation of the expression, which is compiled into an *immutable* internal representation. We cannot change the regular expression associated with a `Regex` object. A two-parameter constructor takes a second string argument containing option characters that modify the matching pattern.

`Match()` performs the matching algorithm of the regular expression against its `string` argument. It returns a `Match` class object that holds the results of the pattern matching. The `Match` object is also immutable.

To discover if the match succeeded, we query the `Success` property of the `Match` class. Each match is spoken of as a *capture*. The `Index` property returns the position in the original string where the first character of the captured substring was found. `Length` returns the length of the captured substring. The `ToString()` method returns the captured substring.

The `Match` object that `Match()` returns holds the results of the first capture. If the regular expression captures multiple substrings, we use `NextMatch()` to access the second and each subsequent capture. Before we manipulate the next object, we must test that it represents a success. A sentinel `Match` object for which `Success` evaluates to `false` marks the end of the captured substrings. A typical `for` loop might look like this:

```
for ( Match match = regex.Match( inputString );
        match.Success;
        match = match.NextMatch() )
{ ... }
```

Consider the following three lines:

```
5040        bez( 99,    -3.194, 43.8,   85     )
4930.7823 bez( 10.7, 19.59,  -20,   -20.48 )
-5123       bez( -3.5,  2.46,   89,     0.02 )
```

These are samples of lines that we need to match. First we have to come up with a regular expression that can match each of these lines.

We see that each line begins with a number. The number can be either positive or negative, and it can represent either a scalar or a floating-point value. The number is followed by a space, then the literal substring *bez*. Four comma-separated numbers follow that, enclosed within parentheses. The numbers can be negative or positive. They can be either integers or floating-point values. Before you look at my solution, try your hand at coming up with a regular expression that captures each of these lines in its entirety.

Once we have our regular expression, we're still not done. Our next problem is how to gain access to the individual parts of the line. That is, our regular expression captures the entire string; we now need to pick it apart to access the five numeric fields.

The regular-expression syntax supports a grouping mechanism in which we assign numbers to particular subfields of the match. We can subsequently use these numbers to access the subfields. For example, the following identifies a group associated with the index 1 using the special ?<1> syntax:

```
(?<1>(-*\d+\.\d+)|(-*\d+))
```

Can you read this? It represents an alternative pair of regular expressions. The first one,

```
-*\d+\.\d+
```

matches a floating-point number that may or may not be negative. The second,

```
-*\d+
```

matches an integer value that also may or may not be negative. The entire regular expression, with five identified groups, looks like the following. For clarity, I've broken it up and identified each subfield. For realism, I've listed it as a string literal with the necessary double backslash (\\) escape:

```
string filter = "
    // the digit before the bez literal
    (?<1>(-*\\d+\\.\\d+)|(-*\\d+))

    // arbitrary white space, bez literal, and open paren
    \\s*bez\\(

    // the four internal numeric values and literal comma
    (?<2>(-*\\d+\\.\\d+)|(-*\\d+)),
    (?<3>(-*\\d+\\.\\d+)|(-*\\d+)),
    (?<4>(-*\\d+\\.\\d+)|(-*\\d+)),
    (?<5>(-*\\d+\\.\\d+)|(-*\\d+))
";
```

Now we attempt the match on the line of text:

```
Regex regex = new Regex( filter );
Match match = regex.Match( line );
```

If the match is successful, we need to grab each of the five numeric subfields and translate them into values of type `float`:

```
float loc = Convert.ToSingle(match.Groups[1].ToString());
float m_xoffset1 = Convert.ToSingle( match.Groups[2].ToString());
float m_yoffset1 = Convert.ToSingle( match.Groups[3].ToString());
float m_xoffset2 = Convert.ToSingle(match.Groups[4].ToString());
float m_yoffset2 = Convert.ToSingle(match.Groups[5].ToString());
```

The `Group` class represents a capturing group within the returned `Match` class object. We access each `Group` object through its associated index. The `ToString()` method returns the captured substring. In this case we invoke the `Convert.ToSingle()` method on each string to convert the value into type `float`.

A useful `Regex` class method is `Split()`. This method is similar to the `String` class `Split()` method—both return a `string` array. Unlike the `String` class `Split()` method, however, the `Regex` class version separates the input string on the basis of a regular expression rather than a set of characters—for example,

```
string textLine =
    "Danny%Lippman%%Point Guard%Shooting Guard%%floater";

string splitMe = "%+";
Regex  regex = new Regex( splitMe );

foreach ( string capture in regex.Split( textLine ))
        Console.WriteLine( "capture: {0}",
                                        capture );
```

In this example we are splitting `textLine` at each point where one or more % characters appear. When executed, this code generates the following output:

```
capture: Danny
capture: Lippman
capture: Point Guard
capture: Shooting Guard
capture: floater
```

Another useful `Regex` class method is `Replace()`, which allows us to replace captured substrings with alternative text. Here is a simple example:

```
public static void testReplace()
{
    string re = "XP.\\d+";
    Regex regex = new Regex( re );

    string textLine =
        "XP.109 is currently in alpha. " +
        "XP.109 represents a staggering leap forward";

    string replaceWith = "ToonPal";

    Console.WriteLine ( "original text: {0}", textLine );
    Console.WriteLine ( "regular expresion : {0}", re );

    string replacedText = regex.Replace( textLine, replaceWith )
    Console.WriteLine ( "replacement text: {0}", replacedText );
}
```

When compiled and executed, this code generates the following output (reformatted slightly for better display):

C# PRIMER

```
original text: XP.109 is currently in alpha. XP.109 represents a
        staggering leap forward

regular expresion : XP.\d+

replacement text: ToonPal is currently in alpha. ToonPal
        represents a staggering leap forward
```

5.7 `System.Threading`

Multithreading allows a process to execute multiple tasks in parallel. Each task is given its own thread of control. For example, in our text query system, we might choose to have each independent subquery executed simultaneously by spawning a thread for the evaluation of each. We could then either pause our controlling program (or main thread) until all the evaluation threads are complete, or perform auxiliary tasks while the executing threads run to completion.

One benefit of multithreading is the potential increase in performance. In a single-threaded program, the time cost of the query evaluation is the sum of the evaluation of each subquery, each executed one after the other in turn. In a multithreaded program, the time cost is now reduced to the time cost of the subquery that takes the longest time to evaluate, since all the queries are run in parallel, plus the overhead incurred by the support for multithreading.

A second benefit of multithreading is the ability of the main thread to package and deploy subtasks into parallel threads of execution. This frees the main thread to maintain communications with and monitoring of its users.

The primary drawback of multithreaded programming is the need to maintain the integrity of shared data objects and resources, such as forms, files, or even the system console. As we'll see, monitors help keep the multiple threads synchronized in their access to critical sections of our programs.

Thread support is provided within the `System.Threading` namespace. It includes classes such as `Thread`, `Mutex`, `Monitor`, `Timer`, and `Thread-Pool`. First let's look at a simple program exercising the `Thread` interface. The program needs to create two threads—one responsible for writing the word *ping,* the other responsible for writing the word *PONG:*[1].

---

1. This program is a variation of an excellent threads example in *The Java™ Programming Language* by Ken Arnold and James Gosling, Addison-Wesley, 1996.

```csharp
using System.Threading;
public static void Main()
{
    PingPong p1 = new PingPong( "ping", 33 );
    Thread ping = new Thread( new ThreadStart( p1.play ))
    ping.Start();

    while ( ! ping.IsAlive )
            Console.Write( "." );

    // OK: now Main() and ping are executing in parallel

    PingPong p2 = new PingPong( "PONG", 100 );
    Thread PONG = new Thread( new ThreadStart( p2.play ));
    PONG.Start();

    // OK: now Main(), ping, and PONG are executing ...

    // OK: let's rest this puppy for 100 milliseconds;
    //      both ping and PONG continue to run in parallel
    Thread.Sleep( 100 );

    /*
     * OK: another way of resting this puppy
     *
     * this main thread waits until either
     *      ping completes or 100 milliseconds pass ...
     *
     * the PONG thread is unaffected;
     * both threads continue to run in parallel
     */
    ping.Join(100);


    // let's suspend PONG for a moment while we determine
    // if ping completed or Join() timed out ...
    PONG.Suspend();

    if ( p1.Count != PingPong.Max )
        // Join() timed out ...
        // ping must still be executing

    // OK: let's resume PONG
    PONG.Resume();
```

```
        // let's absolutely wait for PONG to complete
        PONG.Join();

        Console.WriteLine( "OK: ping count: {0}", p1.Count );
        Console.WriteLine( "OK: PONG count: {0}", p2.Count );
}
```

Each `PingPong` class object is initialized with its display string and a delay time, in milliseconds, between each display:

```
PingPong p1 = new PingPong( "ping", 33 );
PingPong p2 = new PingPong( "PONG", 100 );
```

`play()` is a `PingPong` class method that prints out the associated string. The only unfamiliar aspect of its implementation is its use of the static `Sleep()` method of the `Thread` class to accomplish the millisecond delay:

```
public void play()
{
    for ( ; ; )
    {
        Console.Write( theWord+ " " );

        Thread.Sleep( theDelay );
        if ( ++theCount == theMax )
            return;
    }
}
```

`theCount` keeps a running count of the displayed instances. `theMax` is a `const` member set to the maximum number of instances to display.

`Sleep()` suspends the *current thread* for a specified time, in milliseconds. The current thread is, broadly put, whatever is currently executing. When `play()` is invoked by the `ping` thread, `ping`, of course, is the current thread, `theDelay` is set to 33, and `ping` sleeps for the duration.

The current thread is not always a named thread object such as we're discussing here. For example, if we don't use threads at all in our program, we don't call it a *no-threaded* program. We call it a *single-threaded* program. The main thread of control begins with the invocation of `Main()`. In our program, when we invoke `Sleep()` within `Main()`, as shown here:

```
public static void Main()
{
    PingPong p1 = new PingPong( "ping", 33 );
    Thread ping = new Thread( new ThreadStart( p1.play ))
    ping.Start();

    Thread.Sleep( 100 );
}
```

it's the main thread, not `ping`, that goes to sleep for 100 milliseconds.

The `Thread` constructor takes a single argument—a delegate type named `ThreadStart`. When a thread begins, it invokes the method addressed by `ThreadStart`. Both our thread objects are initialized to invoke `play()`, through either the `p1` or the `p2` `PingPong` class object:

```
Thread ping = new Thread( new ThreadStart( p1.play ));
Thread PONG = new Thread( new ThreadStart( p2.play ));
```

A thread does not begin execution until we explicitly invoke `Start()`:

```
ping.Start();
```

When `ping` starts execution, it invokes `play()` through `p1`. When `play()` completes execution, `ping` ceases to exist. We describe it as *dead*.

What can we do with a thread once we start it? There are several options:

- We can ignore it completely—just let it run its course. We don't have to do anything with it once we have kicked it off by invoking `Start()`.

- We can stop it by invoking `Suspend()`. Suspended threads are collected somewhere where they won't bother us.

- If it has been suspended, we can start it back up by invoking `Resume()`. If it hasn't been suspended, invoking `Resume()` causes no harm. We can invoke `Suspend()` on a suspended thread without penalty. Similarly, we can invoke `Resume()` without penalty on a thread that is not suspended.

- If suspension is too severe, we can put the thread to sleep by invoking `Sleep()`, but only if it is the current thread. There is no instance `Sleep()` method that can be applied to a named thread.

- We can query a thread as to whether it is alive or not through its `IsAlive` property. `IsAlive` returns `true` only if the thread has been started and is not yet dead. A thread dies after it has completed executing its `Thread-Start` object. We can directly kill a thread by invoking `Abort()`.

Through the `Join()` method we can also have the current thread wait until a particular thread completes execution and terminates:

```
public static void Main()
{
        // OK: we resume PONG
        PONG.Resume();

        // OK: we sit here until PONG completes
        PONG.Join();
}
```

In this example, `Main()` is told absolutely to wait and not move until PONG has completed and presumably made available the results of its execution. Now if PONG were infinitely recurring, of course, `Main()` might never stop waiting. So sometimes we may want to add a condition to our imperative by providing `Join()` with an explicit time limit to wait:

```
// OK: let's rest this puppy for 100 milliseconds;
//      both ping and PONG continue to run in parallel
Thread.Sleep( 100 );

/*
 * OK: another way of resting this puppy
 *
 * this main thread waits until either
 *      ping completes or 100 milliseconds pass ...
 *
 * the PONG thread is unaffected;
 * both threads continue to run in parallel
 */

ping.Join(100);
```

The hard part of thread programming is maintaining the integrity of memory and other shared resources. For example, here is a portion of the program output. The nonbold text beginning with *OK* is generated from `Main()`. The text highlighted in bold is generated by the `ping` and PONG *asynchronous* threads:

```
OK: about to start ping thread
OK: ping thread is now alive!
OK: ping is now running in parallel
OK: 0 Within PingPong.play() for ping!!!
ping 1 2 3 4 5 6 7 8 9 10 11 12 13 14 15 16 17 18 19

OK: creating PONG object
OK: creating PONG thread object
OK: about to start PONG thread
OK: ping and PONG are now running in parallel
OK: 0 1 2 3 4 5 6 Within PingPong.play() for PONG!!!
PONG 7 8 9 10 11 12 13 14 15 16 17 18 19

OK: about to put main thread to sleep for 600 milliseconds
ping ping PONG ping ping ping PONG ping ping PONG
ping ping ping PONG ping ping PONG ping ping ping
PONG OK: here after sleep

OK: about to wait to Join(400) ping
ping ping PONG ping ping ping PONG ping ping PONG
ping ping ping OK: back now -- hi.
```

In this program, the interleaving of output among the three parallel threads is amusing—well, somewhat amusing, anyway. In real-world code, of course, we need to guarantee the integrity of resources from the competing demands of parallel independent threads. One way to do that is with monitors.

The `Monitor` class allows us to synchronize thread access to critical code blocks through an `Enter()` and `Exit()` lock and unlock pair of methods—for example,

```
Monitor.Enter( this );
try
{
    // critical text goes here ...
}
finally{
   Monitor.Exit( this );
}
```

When the static `Enter()` method is invoked, it asks for a lock to associate with the object passed to it. If the object is already associated with a lock, the thread is not permitted to continue execution. We say that it *blocks*.

If the object currently lacks a lock, however, the lock is acquired, and the code following `Enter()` is executed. Until the lock is no longer associated with the object, our thread has exclusive access to the code following `Enter()`.

The static `Exit()` method removes the lock on the object passed to it. If one or more threads are waiting for the lock to be removed, one of them is unblocked and allowed to proceed. If we fail to provide an `Enter()`/`Exit()` pair using the same object, the code segment could remain locked indefinitely.

`TryEnter()` does not block, or blocks only for a specified time in milliseconds, before giving up and returning `false`—for example,

```
if ( ! Monitor.TryEnter( fout, maxWait ))
    { logFailure( file_name ); return;  }
```

`Monitor` allows us to guarantee exclusive access to a critical block of code by associating a lock with an object. C# provides an alternative shorthand notation for the `Monitor.Enter()`/`Monitor.Exit()` pair of calls through a use of the `lock` keyword. For example, the following code segment:

```
// equivalent to the earlier
// Monitor.Enter()/Monitor.Exit() code block
lock( this );
{
     // critical text goes here ...
}
```

is equivalent to the earlier code block that begins with `Monitor.Enter()`.

Let me end with a brief mention of the `ThreadPool` class. It manages a pool of preallocated threads. `ThreadPool` allows us to associate a callback method with the wait state of an object. When the wait is open, one of the available pool threads invokes the associated callback method. Alternatively, we can simply queue a method to be added to the thread pool and invoked when a thread becomes available.

5.8   The Web Request/Response Model

In this section we'll walk through the steps necessary to access a page over the Internet. We use the `WebRequest`, `WebResponse,` and `Uri` classes. They are defined within the `System.Net` namespace. Let's create a class called

`PageReader`. First, we need a Uniform Resource Locator (URL) address. The user may optionally pass in a string representation to the `PageReader` constructor; otherwise, by default, we use the address of my company's home page:

```
public class PageReader
{
    private Uri uri;
    private bool validateUrl( string url ) { ... }

    public PageReader( string url )
    {
        if ( url != null && url != String.Empty &&
            validate_url( url ))
                uri = new Uri( url );
    }

    public PageReader()
            : this( "http://www.objectwrite.com" ) {}

    // ...
}
```

The `Uri` constructor parses the string, translating it into a lowercase canonical notation. (For example, C# is turned into *C%23*.) An invalid string results in an `UriFormatException` being thrown. The string must represent an absolute path. For example, passing it `www.amazon.com` is not acceptable. The prefix *http://* (or *file://)* *must* be present in the string.

The `Uri` class provides read-only access to various aspects of the resource, such as `Host`, `HostNameType`, `Port`, `Query`, and so on. For example, given the following `url` string with an embedded query:

```
string url = @"http://www.amazon.com//exec/obidos/search-handle-
form/002-9257402-0511232?index=book&field-keywords=C#";
```

we can query various properties of the resource within the `Uri` as follows:

```
Uri uri = new Uri( url );
Console.WriteLine( "Uri: "           + uri.AbsoluteUri );
Console.WriteLine( "Uri host: "      + uri.Host );
Console.WriteLine( "Uri host type: " + uri.HostNameType );
```

```
Console.WriteLine( "Uri port: "      + uri.Port );
Console.WriteLine( "Uri path: "      + uri.AbsolutePath );
Console.WriteLine( "Uri query: "     + uri.Query );
Console.WriteLine( "Uri toSting: "   + uri.ToString() );
```

When compiled and executed, this code generates the following output:

```
Uri path: http://www.amazon.com/exec/obidos/search-handle-form/
002-9257402-0511232?index=book&field-keywords=C%23
Uri host: www.amazon.com
Uri host type: Dns
Uri port: 80
Uri path: /exec/obidos/search-handle-form/002-9257402-0511232
Uri query: ?index=book&field-keywords=C%23
Uri toSting: http://www.amazon.com/exec/obidos/search-handle-
form/002-9257402-0511232?index=book&field-keywords=C#
```

The representation within the `Uri` object is immutable. If we wish to modify the properties, we should use the `UriBuilder` utility class. `Uri` and `Uri-Builder` are analogous to `String` and `StringBuilder` in terms of when we use each.

Once we have the `Uri` object, the next step is to create a `WebRequest` object. We do this through the static member function `Create()`, passing it the `Uri` object—for example,

```
WebRequest wreq = WebRequest.Create( uri );
```

The `WebRequest` object returned by `Create()` represents a derived class that supports a specific protocol, such as HTTP or FTP. The details of that protocol, however, are encapsulated within the class hierarchy that `WebRequest` represents.

We program a simpler and less error-prone protocol-neutral set of general operations that shield us from the low-level intricacies of making the Internet connection. The network expertise is encapsulated within the specialized derived classes that are by default shielded from us.

If the high-level interface is not flexible enough for our request requirements, we can explicitly downcast the `WebRequest` object to one of its derived classes. For example, the `HttpWebRequest` class manages the details of an HTTP Internet connection:

```
WebRequest wreq = WebRequest.Create( uri );

// the downcast to the specific derived instance
HttpWebRequest hwreq = ( HttpWebRequest )wreq;
```

GetResponse() sends the request from the client application to the server identified in the Uri object. It returns a WebResponse object that provides access to the data returned by the server—for example,

```
WebResponse wresp = wreq.GetResponse();
```

The data returned by the server is accessed through a System.IO.Stream class object that is returned from GetResponseStream(). At this point, we're back to our input-from-a-stream processing model. For example, in this fragment we tuck away each line within an ArrayList object:

```
Stream        wrespStream = wresp.GetResponseStream();
StreamReader wsrdr        = new StreamReader(wrespStream);
ArrayList     webData      = new ArrayList();
string        data         = null;

while (( data = wsrdr.ReadLine()) != null )
        webData.Add( data );
```

The following code segment examines each element of the array, looking for an explicit URL address beginning with *http://*:

```
Console.WriteLine( "read {0} lines of text from {1}",
                        webData.Count, uri.AbsoluteUri );

ArrayList webUrls = new ArrayList();
foreach ( string s in webData )
{
        int  pos, nextPos;
        int  spacePos, quotePos;
        char space = ' ', quote = '\"';

        if (( pos = s.IndexOf( "http://" )) != -1 )
        {
            spacePos = s.IndexOf( space, pos );
            quotePos = s.IndexOf( quote, pos );
            nextPos = spacePos < quotePos
                        ? spacePos : quotePos;
```

```
                if ( nextPos > pos )
                {
                        string surl = s.Substring( pos, nextPos - pos );
                        if ( ! webUrls.Contains( surl ))
                                webUrls.Add( surl );
                }
        }
    }

    Console.WriteLine("There are {0} url references",webUrls.Count);
    webUrls.Sort();

    foreach ( string s in webUrls )
            Console.WriteLine( "\t{0}", s );
```

When this code is executed against my home Web page, the following output is generated:

```
read 117 lines of text from http://www.objectwrite.com
There are 5 url references
http://cseng.awl.com/bookdetail.qry?ISBN=0-201-30993-9&ptype=0
http://www.amazon.com/exec/obidos/ASIN/0135705819/
qid%3D902875557/sr%3D1-6/002-5252584-4839230
http://www.awl.com/cseng/titles/0-201-82470-1/
http://www.awl.com/cseng/titles/0-201-83454-5/
http://www.objectwrite.com/
```

5.9 `System.Net.Sockets`

The `System.Net.Sockets` namespace provides a `Socket` class encapsulating Windows Sockets functionality. Transmission Control Protocol (TCP) support is provided by the `TcpListener` and `TcpClient` classes. To illustrate how we can use these classes, we'll create a client/server phone directory from the sample Northwind SQL database. On separate threads, the server retrieves the database information and sets up a `TcpListener` object to accept incoming requests. The client creates a `TcpClient` object, acquires a `NetworkStream` object, and then packages and sends a request over the network. A client session is pictured in Figure 5.1. The port number of the client request is displayed in square brackets. The server line with the phone number is data received across a `NetworkStream` from the `TcpListener`.

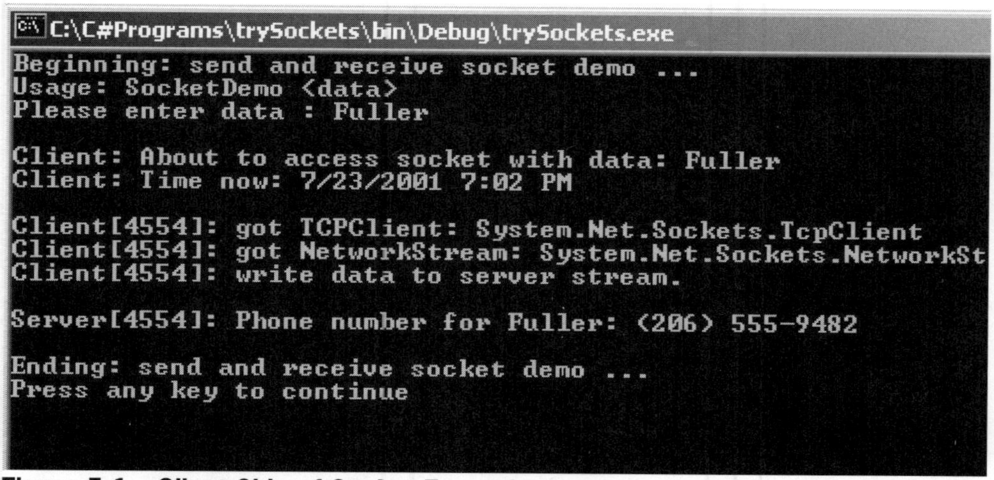

Figure 5.1   Client Side of Socket Example

A server session handling three incoming requests is pictured in Figure 5.2. The server start-up traces the various operations, including the starting of the `TcpListener` and retrieving the SQL database information. The port number of the server is displayed in square brackets. Let's solve the server-side implementation first.

5.9.1   The Server-Side `TcpListener`

`TcpListener` is a class object that listens for connections from TCP clients. The first step is to create an instance; in our case we pass the constructor a port number. This is the same port to which clients direct their requests. Once the object has been constructed, we invoke its `Start()` method to have it begin listening for incoming requests—for example,

```
public class SocketDemo_Server
{
    static private int port = 4554;
    private TcpListener        tcpl;

public SocketDemo_Server()
{
    // start listening on the assigned port
    tcpl = new TcpListener(port) ;
    tcpl.Start();
```

C# PRIMER

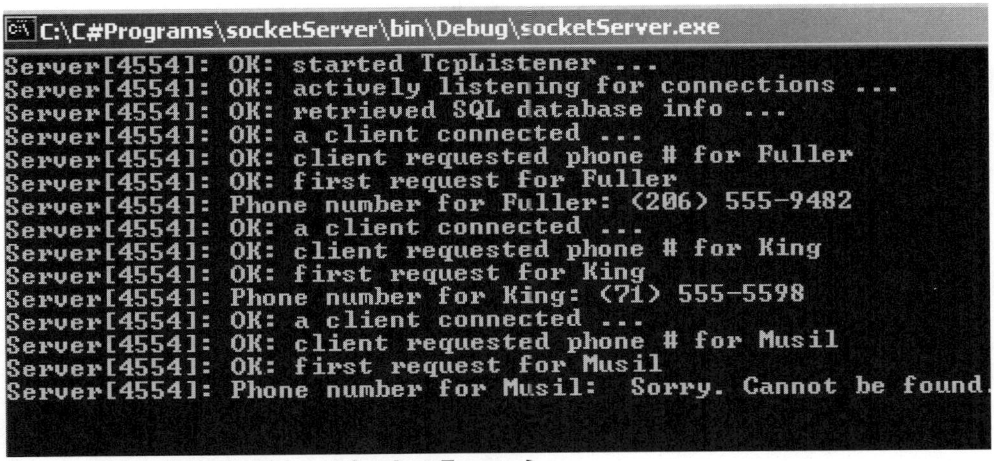

Figure 5.2   Server Side of Socket Example

The next step is to implement the connection logic to handle an incoming request. In this case we expect the input to represent an individual's last name. We'll grab the data, clean it up a bit, and attempt to retrieve a phone number associated with the name. We'll then package our response and send it back to the client. Let's see how we do that.

The client is ephemeral. It comes into existence to post its request, then to wait for and handle the response. Once that is done, the client is generally done and exits. The server, on the other hand, can run as long as the host machine is running. This means that it must continually poll to discover if a connection has docked in the port. The `AcceptSocket()` member function serves as a poll mechanism. It blocks on the call until a client connects; at that point it returns a `Socket` connection object. Here is that portion of the code:

```
public void handleConnection()
{
      while( true )
      {
            // blocks until a client connects
            Socket aSocket = tcpl.AcceptSocket();
            if( aSocket.Connected ) {
```

Next a byte array is created to receive the client's data. We pass it to the `Receive()` member function of the `Socket` class, together with the size of the array, and the index identifying where to begin placing the data. `Receive()` returns the number of bytes transferred. The `byte` array is converted into a string. We toss away any extraneous filler characters within it:

```
Byte [] packetBuffer = new Byte[ maxPacket ];
int byteCnt =
    aSocket.Receive( packetBuffer, packetBuffer.Length, 0 );

string clientPacket =
        Text.Encoding.ASCII.GetString( packetBuffer );

// get rid of unused buffer space ...
char [] unusedBytes = { (char)clientPacket[ byteCnt ] };
clientPacket = clientPacket.TrimEnd( unusedBytes );
```

Once the request has been processed, the next step is to package the result and return it to the client. The response is built up as a string then turned into a `byte` array and passed to the `Send()` member function of the `Socket` class:

```
Byte [] resultBuffer =
        Text.Encoding.ASCII.GetBytes( response.ToCharArray() );
aSocket.Send( resultBuffer, resultBuffer.Length, 0 );
```

The code sequence we've walked through here represents a complete handling of the client connection. The `while` loop reevaluates, and `TcpListener` again invokes `AcceptSocket()`, waiting for the next client connection.

5.9.2 The Client-Side `TcpClient`

`TcpClient` is a class object that provides network connection to a specified port on a specified host. In our example the `TcpClient` object is initialized with the host name and port. The connection is made implicitly within the constructor. Following that, we invoke `TcpClient`'s `GetStream()` method to retrieve a `NetworkStream` object. All data between the client and server goes through this `NetworkStream` object—for example,

```
public class SocketDemo_Client
{
        private TcpClient tcpc;
        private static int port = 4554;
        private static string host = "localhost";
```

```
public bool sendRequest( string data )
{
        tcpc = new TcpClient( host, port);
        NetworkStream netstream = tcpc.GetStream();
```

Next we have to prepare the data we wish to transmit. As we did with our server-side implementation, we create a `byte` array. We invoke `Write()`, passing in the array, a beginning index, and a count of bytes to be transmitted:

```
Byte[] outPacket =
        Text.Encoding.ASCII.GetBytes( data.ToCharArray() );


netstream.Write( outPacket, 0, outPacket.Length );
netstream.Flush();
```

Following the transmission, we wait until data is available on the `Network-Stream`, polling on the `DataAvailable` property. When data is available, we again create a `byte` array to receive it. We then pass it to the `Read()` function, together with the size of the packet, and a beginning index. Finally, we convert the data received within the array into a string and display it on the console:

```
while( ! netstream.DataAvailable )
{
    byte[] packet = new byte[ max_packet ];
    int byteCnt = netstream.Read( packet, 0, max_packet );

    string dataRcd = Text.Encoding.ASCII.GetString( packet );
    Console.WriteLine( dataRcd );

    break;
}
```

5.10 System.Data

The `DataSet` class within the `System.Data` namespace is typically used for the in-memory storage of data within one or more `DataTable` class members. This data usually represents information retrieved from a database, the focus of this section, or stored within an XML document, the focus of the next section. A `DataTable` is represented by a collection of `DataRow` entries divided into a set of one or more `DataColumn` fields.

The sample database we'll use in this section is the USDA Nutrient Database maintained and freely distributed by the U.S. Department of Agriculture. This version, Release 13 (SR13), contains data on over 6,000 food items, such as cheese, potato chips, soft drinks, and so on. We'll be working with three tables of the relational database.

5.10.1 The Database Tables

The food description database table (FOOD_DES) has 6,210 rows of food entries with 11 columns of data. The primary key of the table is the NDB_NO column, which holds a unique number associated with each food entry. A second column of interest to us is DESC, which provides a brief description of the food item. For example, here are the NDB_NO and DESC entries for the first 11 rows of the FOOD_DES database table:

```
NDB_NO    DESC

01001 :: Butter, with salt
01002 :: Butter, whipped, with salt
01003 :: Butter oil, anhydrous
01004 :: Cheese, blue
01005 :: Cheese, brick
01006 :: Cheese, brie
01007 :: Cheese, camembert
01008 :: Cheese, caraway
01009 :: Cheese, cheddar
01010 :: Cheese, cheshire
01011 :: Cheese, colby
```

A second table in the database—the nutritional data table (NUT_DATA)—contains the nutritional values associated with each food. It has three columns of interest to us: (1) NDB_NO, which identifies the food item; (2) NUTR_NO, which uniquely identifies each nutritional element, such as protein, fat, carbohydrate, and so on; and (3) NUTR_VAL, which holds the nutritional value. Here's an example from the NUT_DATA table:

```
NDB_NO      NUTR_NO      NUTR_VAL

01001 ::    203 ::       0.85
01001 ::    204 ::       81.11
01001 ::    205 ::       0.06
```

```
01001 ::    207 ::      2.11
01001 ::    208 ::      717
01001 ::    255 ::      15.87
01001 ::    268 ::      3000
01001 ::    291 ::      0
01001 ::    301 ::      24
01001 ::    303 ::      0.16
01001 ::    304 ::      2
```

Each table by itself is incomplete. The food description table provides the name of each food but does not contain the nutritional values associated with the food. Those values are contained in the nutritional data table. The link between the two is the NDB_NO column. To navigate between the two tables, we'll need to define a data relationship between them. Within the .NET framework we do this by adding a DataRelation property to the DataSet. DataRelation defines a relationship between two tables based on a shared column.

Even taken together, these two tables are incomplete. We still have no way to identify the categories of the nutritional values represented by each entry. This information is available in a nutritional definition table (NUTR_DEF), which has two columns that interest us: (1) NUTR_NC, which provides us with the table's primary key; and (2) NUTRDESC, which holds a description of the nutritional element. The following example comes from the NUTR_DEF table:

```
NUTR_NO    NUTR_NO

203 ::     Protein
204 ::     Total lipid (fat)
205 ::     Carbohydrate, by difference
207 ::     Ash
208 ::     Energy
221 ::     Alcohol
255 ::     Water
262 ::     Caffeine
263 ::     Theobromine
268 ::     Energy
269 ::     Sugars, total
```

The link between the nutritional data table and the nutritional definition table is the NUTR_NO column. This link is also represented by a DataRelation object.

The complete in-memory representation of the nutritional database—in terms of the values we require—is made up of the three `DataTable` objects and the two `DataRelation` objects contained within a `DataSet` object. These classes and others found within the `System.Data` namespace make up the ADO.NET architecture.

5.10.2   Opening the Database: Selecting a Data Provider

All interactions with a database are carried out through a data provider. A *data provider* consists of four primary services, each represented by a class:

1. `Connection`, which handles the connection to a specific data source.
2. `Command`, which executes a command at the data source. There are select, update, insert, and delete categories of commands.
3. `DataReader`, which provides a forward-only, read-only stream of data from the data source.
4. `DataAdapter`, which populates a `DataSet` with an in-memory cache of the selected data. `DataAdapter` also handles updates to the data source.

Currently, the .NET framework provides two data providers: (1) a SQL Server .NET data provider (for Microsoft SQL Server 7.0 or later), defined in the `System.Data.SqlClient` namespace; and (2) the OLE DB .NET data provider, defined in the `System.Data.OleDb` namespace, for all other databases, such as Microsoft Access.

In this section we'll work with Microsoft Access and the OLE DB data provider. In Section 7.7 we'll look at using the SQL Server data provider in support of ASP.NET.

Here are the steps necessary, using the OLE DB data provider, first to connect to and select data from a database, and then to fill a `DataSet` object with the retrieved data:

1. Create a *connection* string. This string consists of two parts. The first part defines the database provider. *Microsoft.JET.OLEDB.4.0* is used for Microsoft Access, *MSDORA* for Oracle, and *SQLOLEDB* for SQL Server instances prior to version 7.0. The second part defines the source file and path—for example,

```
string connect = "Provider=Microsoft.JET.OLEDB.4.0;" +
        @"data source=C:\nutrition\database\FOOD_DES.mdb";
```

2. Create a *selection* command string. This minimally consists of a `SELECT` part and a `FROM` part. The `SELECT` part determines which columns are read from each row. The `FROM` part dentifies the table from which to read. In the first example we select all the columns of the `FOOD_DES` table. In the second, we select only the `NDB_NO` and `DESC` columns. We can optionally provide selection criteria through a `WHERE` part, a `GROUP` part, a `HAVING` part, and an `ORDER BY` part. In the third example, we select the `NUTR_NO` and `NUTRDESC` columns for only those entries whose units equal `'g'`:

```
string command1 = "SELECT * FROM FOOD_DES";
string command2 = "SELECT NDB_NO, DESC FROM FOOD_DES";
string command3 =
        "SELECT NUTR_NO, NUTRDESC FROM NUTR_DEF WHERE UNITS = 'g'";
```

3. Create an `OleDbConnection` object initialized with the connection string. We must be careful to explicitly close the connection when we are finished with it, through either `Close()` or `Dispose()`:

```
using System.Data.OleDb;
OleDbConnection db_conn = new OleDbConnection( connect );

// OK: access the data source ...
db_conn.Close();
```

4. Create an `OleDbDataAdapter` data adapter object. Then create an `OleDbCommand` object initialized with the command string and the connection object. `OleDbCommand` retrieves the data. Finally, assign the command object to the data adapter's `SelectCommand` property:

```
OleDbDataAdapter adapter = new OleDbDataAdapter();

string command = "SELECT * FROM FOOD_DES";
adapter.SelectCommand = new OleDbCommand( command, db_conn );
```

5. Create an instance of a `DataSet` object and pass it to the data adapter's `Fill()` method, together with a name for the table in which to place the data. `Fill()` executes the select command and places the data into the named `DataTable`. If the `DataTable` does not exist, it is created:

```
DataSet ds = new DataSet();
adapter.Fill( ds, "FOOD_DES" );
```

To add a second or subsequent table, we simply repeat the sequence of steps outlined here. Once within the `DataSet` object, all data is manipulated through that object.

5.10.3 Navigating the `DataTable`

The `Tables` property of the `DataSet` class returns a `DataTableCollection` object that holds the set of `DataTable` objects associated with the `DataSet`. We can index the collection either positionally:

```
DataTable food_des_tbl = ds.Tables[0];
```

or with a string representation of the table's name:

```
displayTableHeader( ds.Tables[ "NUT_DATA" ] );
```

Several different properties are associated with the `DataTable`, including `TableName`, `Rows`, `Columns`, and `PrimaryKey`:

```
public static void displayTableHeader( DataTable dt )
{
    Console.WriteLine("The DataTable is named {0}",dt.TableName);

    DataRowCollection    drows = dt.Rows;
    DataColumnCollection ccols = dt.Columns;

    Console.WriteLine( "It has {0} rows of {1} columns",
                       drows.Count, ccols.Count );

    Console.WriteLine( "The columns are as follows: " );
    foreach ( DataColumn dc in ccols )
            displayColumn( dc );

    DataColumn [] keys = dt.PrimaryKey;
    Console.WriteLine("It has {0} primary keys",keys.Length);
}
```

A *primary key* is a column that is guaranteed to contain a unique value for each record entry and that serves as the identity of the record within the table. (A primary key can also be a set of columns. This is why the `PrimaryKey` property returns an array of `DataColumn` objects rather than just a single `DataColumn` object.)

The `Rows` property of the `DataTable` returns a `DataRowCollection` object, which holds the set of rows associated with the table. A row is represented by a `DataRow` class object. The rows are indexed beginning at `0`. To retrieve the first row, we write

```
DataRow dr = drows[ 0 ]; // first row
```

To iterate across the entire `DataRowCollection,` we can use either a `foreach` statement:

```
foreach( DataRow row in dt.Rows )
```

or a `for` loop, incrementing the index with each iteration.

Each `DataRow` object contains data for one record of the table divided into one or more columns. The `ItemArray` property retrieves the column values as an array of type `object` with the first column at index `0`, the second at `1`, and so on:

```
object [] fieldValues = dr.ItemArray;
```

To access the value of an individual column, we can index by position, beginning with `0` for the first column:

```
int nutritionID = dr[ 0 ];
```

by a string representing the column name:

```
string nutritionDesc = dr["NUTRDESC" ];
```

or by the `DataColumn` object representing the column. That is, the `DataRow` class has defined a `DataColumn` indexer. Given a `DataColumn` object, the `DataColumn` indexer returns the associated value of the column as a generic value of type `object.`

```
public object this[ DataColumn index ]
        { get; set; }
```

For example, here is how we might use this indexer:

```
public static void displayTable( DataTable dt )
{
    displayTableHeader( dt );
```

```
foreach( DataRow row in dt.Rows)
{

    foreach ( DataColumn col in dt.Columns)
            Console.Write( "{0} ", row[ col ] );

    Console.WriteLine();


}
}
```

When this function is past the nutrition definition table NUTR_DEF, for example, it prints the contents of its four columns:

```
203 g PROCNT Protein
204 g FAT Total lipid (fat)
205 g CHOCDF Carbohydrate, by difference
207 g ASH Ash
208 kcal ENERC_KCAL Energy
221 g ALC Alcohol
255 g WATER Water
262 mg CAFFN Caffeine
263 mg THEBRN Theobromine
268 kj ENERC_KJ Energy
269 g SUGAR Sugars, total
291 g FIBTG Fiber, total dietary
301 mg CA Calcium, Ca
```

The DataColumn class represents a column in the DataTable. It does not itself hold data; rather it holds information describing the data that each row contains within that column. We retrieve a column through either a string or a numeric index, depending on whether we wish to retrieve the column by its name or ordinal position:

```
DataColumn primaryKey = ds.Tables[0].Columns[ "NDB_NO" ];
primaryKey.AllowDBNull = false;
primaryKey.Unique = true;
```

AllowDBNull specifies whether the user can enter a null value for that column. For a primary key, of course, a null value would be terrible. Unique stipulates that each row must contain a unique value for this column. This is essential for a primary key.

C# PRIMER

Other properties associated with a `DataColumn` are `DataType`, which returns the `Type` object associated with the stored value; `Table`, which returns the `DataTable` object to which the column belongs, and `ColumnName`.

5.10.4 Setting Up the `DataRelation`

The information we need is stored in the three separate tables that were introduced in Section 5.10.1: (1) the food description table (`FOOD_DESC`), (2) the nutritional data table (`NUT_DATA`), and (3) the nutritional definition table (`NUTR_DEF`).

Given a food identity value from the `FOOD_DES` table, we want to retrieve all the entries associated with that value. We do this by defining a `DataRelation` class object linking the columns of the two tables that hold the food identity value. We'll call the relationship `FoodID`:

```
DataRelation dr =
    new DataRelation("FoodID",
        ds.Tables["FOOD_DES"].Columns["NDB_NO"],
        ds.Tables["NUT_DATA"].Columns["NDB_NO"]);
```

The first column is referred to as the parent. Its value is used to retrieve the matching entries in the second column, which is referred to as the child. We add the relationship to the `DataSet`:

```
ds.Relations.Add(dr);
```

`DataRelation` provides a collection of links between columns of the various tables of the `DataSet`. These links allows for retrieval based on a column entry. For example, in the following code sequence we step through the food items in turn. So, for example, we retrieve the entry for *Butter, with salt*. Now we need all the nutritional values associated with this entry. Rather than explicitly searching each record of the `NUT_DATA` table for these values, we use the `DataRelation` object to retrieve an array of all the matching `DataRow` entries:

```
foreach ( DataRow dRow in ds.Tables["FOOD_DES"].Rows )
{
    // we retrieve all the matching entries
    DataRow [] food_desc = dRow.GetChildRows( dr );
```

```
Console.WriteLine ( " There are {0} food desc rows",
                        food_desc.Length );
```

Now that we have the array of DataRow objects, we can process it as we wish. For example, the following code sequence extracts the row values and prints out the string representation for each:

```
foreach ( DataRow ddr in food_desc )
{
    object [] row_values = ddr.ItemArray;

    foreach ( object o in row_values )
            Console.Write ( "{0} | ", o.ToString() );
}
```

The following is part of the output generated by this code:

```
There are 71 food desc rows
01001 | 203 | 0.85 | 16 | 0.074 | 1 |
01001 | 204 | 81.11 | 580 | 0.065 | 1 |
01001 | 205 | 0.06 | 0 |    | 4 |
```

5.10.5 Selection and Expressions

The DataTable supports an overloaded Select() method to retrieve all the DataRow entries that match an expression. Select() returns an array of DataRow objects. If the selection fails, the array is empty. For example, the following is a simple expression that searches the NUTR_NO column for the value 203:

```
DataRow [] datselect =
        ds.Tables ["NUTR_DEF"].Select ( "NUTR_NO = 203" );
```

Alternatively, we can build the string from an object:

```
DataRow [] datselect =
        ds.Tables ["NUTR_DEF"].Select ( "NUTR_NO = " + key );
```

where key is an integer representing a primary key, or

```
DataRow [] datselect =
    ds.Tables ["NUTR_DEF"].Select ("NUTR_VAL > " + someValue);
```

which returns all rows in which the NUTR_VAL column holds a value greater than someValue.

Expressions can also be associated with columns. In the following example found in the .NET documentation, we create a *calculated column:*

```
ds.Tables["Products"].Columns["tax"].Expression =
        "UnitPrice * 0.086";
```

where `0.086` represents a tax rate.

Unlike a calculated column, an *aggregate column* evaluates an expression based on an entire set of rows. The example in the .NET documentation shows an expression that counts the number of rows contained in the table:

```
ds.Tables["Orders"].Columns["OrderCount"].Expression =
        "Count(OrderID)";
```

where `OrderID` represents the primary key of the table and is therefore guaranteed to be unique.

5.11 `System.Xml`

The representation of relational table data can be poured like water back and forth between a `DataSet` object and an XML representation. In particular, the `XmlDataDocument` class, defined in the `System.Xml` namespace, has a special relationship to the `DataSet` class. It allows us to load relational data (or XML data, of course) and manipulate that data using the W3C Document Object Model (DOM). One way to do the binding is to pass the `DataSet` object to the `XmlDataDocument` constructor:

```
DataSet ds = new DataSet();
adapter.Fill( ds, "FOOD_DES" );

XmlDataDocument xmlDoc = new XmlDataDocument( ds );
```

Now we can manipulate the `XmlDataDocument` just as if we had directly loaded it with XML data. In this section we look at the DOM, its navigation using `XPath`, and its transformation using XSLT.

The sample XML file that is used throughout this section is a variant of our food nutrition database. The first four elements of the file consist of an XML declaration, a comment, a processing instruction, and the root element of the document:

```
<?xml version="1.0" encoding="utf-8" ?>
<!-- Place keywords in the PI below -->
<?calories diabetes?>
<food_composition>
```

Following the root element are four food element entries, each consisting of nine child elements. Each food element generally looks like this:

```
<food>
  <category>dairy</category>
  <family>cheese</family>
  <name>mozzarella</name>
  <calories weight="-1" diabetes="-1">281</calories>
  <fat>21.60</fat>
  <cholesterol>78</cholesterol>
  <carbohydrates>2.28</carbohydrates>
  <protein>19.42</protein>
  <fiber>0</fiber>
</food>
```

The file is named `food.xml`. If we wish, we can read it directly into a `DataSet` object:

```
DataSet ds = new DataSet();
ds.ReadXml( @"c:\C#Talks\food.xml" );
```

Then we can either manipulate it directly through the `DataSet` object, or we can construct an `XmlDataDocument` from the `DataSet`, as we did at the opening of this section.

The `DataSet` class also has a `WriteXml()` and `WriteXmlSchema()` pair of methods. With these methods we can generate an *.xml* file and an *.xsd* schema file for any `DataSet` object we manage to populate:

```
DataSet ds = new DataSet();
adapter.Fill( ds, "FOOD_DES" );
myDataSet.WriteXml( @"C:\C#Talks\northwind.xml" );
myDataSet.WriteXmlSchema(  @"C:\C#Talks\northwind.xsd" );
```

5.11.1 Getting XML Out of Our Programs

Let's say that we have gathered data on a meal that the user has recorded. We'd like to save that information as an XML document. We do this in two steps. In the first step we create our document out of the data we've gathered; we'll call the function registerMeal():

```
public static void
registerMeal( string client, MealTime mt, ArrayList foods )
{ ... }
```

The XML document is represented by an XmlDocument object. The Xml-Document is an in-memory representation of data under DOM. It is defined under the System.Xml namespace. First let's create an empty document:

```
XmlDocument theDoc = new XmlDocument();
```

Next we'll manually create the children, using a series of *Create* member functions of the document class. For example, here is how I create an XML declaration:

```
XmlNode theChild;
theChild = theDoc.CreateXmlDeclaration( "1.0", null, null );
theDoc.AppendChild( theChild );
```

XmlNode is the base class for all the node types that can occur within an XML document. The three string arguments to CreateXmlDeclaration() represent the version, standalone, and encoding attributes. If the second or third argument is null, the attribute is not printed. The AppendChild() method adds the specified node to the end of the list of children. The declaration generated looks like this:

```
<?xml version="1.0"?>
```

Here is how we might create a comment and a processing instruction node:

```
    theChild = theDoc.CreateComment( client + ":" +
                DateTime.Now.ToShortDateString());
    theDoc.AppendChild( theChild );

    theChild = theDoc.CreateProcessingInstruction(
                "nutrition", "diabetes heart" );
    theDoc.AppendChild( theChild );
```

If the client string is *Alice Emma Weeks*, then these two lines generate the following XML nodes:

```
<!--Alice Emma Weeks:8/17/2001-->
<?nutrition diabetes heart?>
```

Finally, we create the root element, and each of its children, as follows:

```
// create the root element ...
theChild = doc.CreateElement("k", "nutrition", "urn:nutrition");
doc.AppendChild(node);

// OK: let's populate this puppy
theChild = theDoc.CreateElement( "client" );
theChild.InnerText = client;

theDoc.DocumentElement.AppendChild( theChild );
theChild = theDoc.CreateElement( "meal" );
theChild.InnerText = mt.ToString();
theDoc.DocumentElement.AppendChild( theChild );

for( int ix = 0; ix < foods.Count; ++ix )
{
    theChild = theDoc.CreateElement( "item" + ix.ToString() );
    theChild.InnerText = (string) foods[ ix ];
    theDoc.DocumentElement.AppendChild( theChild );
}
```

Here is how we might invoke the function:

```
static public void Main()
{
    string client = "Alice Emma Weeks";
    ArrayList foods = new ArrayList();

    foods.Add( "banana' );
    foods.Add( "bread, whole wheat" );
    foods.Add( "Ben & Jerry, Quart, RockyRoad" );

    ClientMeal.registerMeal( client,
        ClientMeal.MealTime.SnackNight, foods );
}
```

And this is the output when it is executed:

```
<?xml version="1.0"?>
<!--Alice Emma Weeks:8/17/2001-->
<?nutrition diabetes heart?>
```

```
<k:nutrition xmlns:k="urn:nutrition">
  <client>Alice Emma Weeks</client>
  <meal>SnackNight</Meal>
  <item0>banana</item0>
  <item1>bread, whole wheat</item1>
  <item2>Ben &amp; Jerry, Quart, RockyRoad</item2>
</k:nutrition>
```

`MealTime` is an enumeration defined within the `ClientMeal` class. It looks like this:

```
class ClientMeal
{
    public enum MealTime
    {
        NotSure,
        Breakfast, Lunch, Dinner, SnackMorning,
        SnackAfternoon, SnackEvening, SnackNight
    };

    // ...
}
```

The second step—the code I haven't shown yet—is the generation of the XML document. For that we use `XmlTextWriter`, which is also defined within the `System.Xml` namespace. This, too, is a two-step process. First we create an `XmlTextWriter`, binding it to where we wish to direct our XML document, and adjusting the formatting. Second, we invoke the `Save()` method of the document, passing it our `XmlTextWriter` objects—for example,

```
XmlTextWriter theWriter = new XmlTextWriter(Console.Out);

theWriter.Formatting = Formatting.Indented;
theDoc.Save( theWriter );
```

The `XmlSerializer` class, also defined within the `System.Xml` namespace, allows us to *serialize* and *deserialize* objects back and forth from XML document instances. XML serialization is the process of converting an object's *public* properties and fields to a serial format (in this case, XML) for storage or transport. Deserialization re-creates the object—in its original state—from the XML output. Here is a `Point` class that we wish to serialize:

```
[XmlRoot( "rootElement" )]
public struct Point
{
    public float   m_x, m_y, m_z;
    public string m_now;

    public Point( float x, float y, float z )
    {
        m_x = x; m_y = y; m_z = z;
        m_now = DateTime.Now.ToString();
    }
}
```

The strange bracketed item atop the `Point` class definition:

```
[XmlRoot( "rootElement" )]
```

is called an *attribute.* It attaches metadata to objects. This metadata can then be queried for and retrieved at runtime. The `XmlRoot` attribute identifies the name that should be associated with the root element of the document.

We create the `XmlSerializer` object by passing it the `Type` node of the class we wish to serialize. The `Type` class is referred to as the *runtime reflection gateway* in the .NET framework—for example,

```
XmlSerializer xs = new XmlSerializer( typeof( Point ) );
```

The two pieces necessary for serialization are the object to be serialized and the destination to which to direct the data stream. So let's serialize the `Point` class now:

```
Point pt = new Point( 0.5f, 1.5f, 4.5f );
FileStream fs =
        new FileStream( @"C:\temp\xs.xml", FileMode.Create );
```

For the `Point` class, that's all we need to do. The rest is done for us by the `XmlSerializer` object. We invoke its `Serialize()` member function, passing it the `Point` class object and the file stream—for example,

```
xs.Serialize( fs, pt );
fs.Close();

xs.Serialize( Console.Out, pt );
fs.Close();
```

When this code is compiled and executed, it generates the following output:

```
<?xml version="1.0" encoding="IBM437"?>
<rootElement xmlns:xsi="http://www.w3.org/2001/XMLSchema-
instance" xmlns:xsd="http://www.w3.org/2001/XMLSchema">
  <m_x>0.5</m_x>
  <m_y>1.5</m_y>
  <m_z>4.5</m_z>
  <m_now>8/17/2001 3:22:25 AM</m_now>
</rootElement>
```

5.11.2 `XmlTextReader`: The Firehose

One way to process our XML document is to read it one node at a time. We grab the node, process it, maintain the necessary state context, and proceed to the next node. We do that under .NET with the `XmlTextReader` class. In addition, the `XmlTextReader` class allows us to skip nodes that are not of interest to us. The `XmlTextReader` is defined within the `System.Xml` namespace. Here is the general engine to pump through each node:

```
public static void Main()
{
   string      fname = @"C:\c#primer\Food.xml";
   FileStream fs = new FileStream( fname, FileMode.Open );

   XmlTextReader xrd = new XmlTextReader( fs );

   while ( xrd.Read() == true )
   {
       // OK: process each node ...
   }
}
```

The `FileStream` object reads the text. The `XmlTextReader` provides the capability to understand and structure what it all means. Each invocation of `Read()` reads the next node from the `FileStream`. It returns `true` for a successful read, `false` when it reaches the end of the stream. We access the content of the node through the reader object. Some of the properties available for the current node include `Name`, `HasValue`, `HasAttributes`, `Attribute-Count`, `NodeType`, `Prefix`, `AttributeCount`, `Value`, and `NamespaceURI`:

```
while ( xrd.Read() == true )
{
    Console.WriteLine("node type is {0}", xrd.NodeType);

    if ( xrd.Name != String.Empty )
        Console.WriteLine( "\tname is {0}", xrd.Name);
    else
        Console.WriteLine("\tThis node has no name");

    if ( xrd.HasValue )
        Console.WriteLine("\tvalue is {0}", xrd.Value );

    if ( xrd.NodeType == XmlNodeType.Element )
        if ( xrd.HasAttributes )
        {
            Console.Write( "\thas {0} attributes: ",
                            xrd.AttributeCount );

            while ( xrd.MoveToNextAttribute() )
                Console.Write( "{0} = {1} ",
                            xrd.Name, xrd.Value );

            Console.WriteLine();
        }
        else Console.WriteLine( "\thas no attributes" );
}
```

Attributes are not treated as children of an element. Rather we must explicitly access them. `MoveToAttribute()` moves to a specified attribute, using one of the following overloaded instances:

```
// move to the index attribute
void MoveToAttribute(int index)

// move to the name attribute
bool MoveToAttribute(string name)

// move to the attribute with these characteristics
bool MoveToAttribute( string localName, string namespaceURI )
```

To iterate across all the attributes of an element, we can also use the `MoveToNextAttribute()` method. If the current node is an element node, this method moves to the first attribute. Each subsequent invocation moves to the next attribute in turn until there are no more attributes. `MoveToElement()` returns us to the element node containing the attributes. Although this represents a forward-only, noncached reading of the document, we are afforded some flexibility, as the following fragment of our XML file shows:

```
<?xml version="1.0" encoding="utf-8" ?>
<!-- Place the analysis keywords in the PI below -->
<? calories diabetes ?>
<food_composition>
// ...
<carbohydrates diabetes="-1">15</carbohydrates>
```

Here is the output generated by the `Read()` sequence. Notice that the `version` and `encoding` attributes of the XML declaration are stored as its value properties, while the attribute of the element `carbohydrates` is stored as a separate attribute node; its value property is empty:

```
node type is XmlDeclaration
        name is xml
        value is version="1.0" encoding="utf-8"
node type is Comment
        This node has no name
        value is  Place keywords in the ...
node type is ProcessingInstruction
        name is calories
        value is diabetes
node type is Element
        name is food_composition
        has no attributes
node type is Element
        name is carbohydrates
            has 1 attributes: diabetes = -1
node type is Text
        This node has no name
        value is 15
node type is EndElement
        name is carbohydrates
```

By default, `XmlTextReader` returns a `Whitespace` node to represent the new-line character that is present at the end of each entry. For example, here is a trace of reading the first two lines of the XML file with the default treatment of white space:

```
node type is XmlDeclaration
node type is Whitespace
node type is Comment
node type is Whitespace
```

To remove the nonsignificant `Whitespace` node, we can set the `WhitespaceHandling` property of the reader. White space comes in two flavors: `Whitespace`, such as a new-line character, and `Significant-Whitespace`. Significant white space represents actual content of an element or attribute. By default, both flavors of white space are returned. We can request that neither be returned by setting the property to `None`. To turn off the return of nonsignificant whitespace only, we set the `WhitespaceHandling` property to `Significant`—for example,

```
xrd.WhitespaceHandling = WhitespaceHandling.Significant;
```

The result is the following simplified sequence:

```
node type is XmlDeclaration
node type is Comment
```

To discover the type of the current node, we examine the `NodeType` property—for example,

```
if ( x.NodeType == XmlNodeType.Whitespace )
    continue;
```

The `XmlNodeType` enum serves as a kind of flag to identify the type of the current node, such as in the following examples:

- `enum XmlNodeType{ Element, EndElement, ... }`

  An `Element` node can have the following child node types: `Text`, `EntityReference`, `ProcessingInstruction`, `Element`, `Comment`, and `CData`. The `Element` node can be the child of a `Document`, `DocumentFragment`, `Element`, or `EntityReference` node. `EndElement` is returned to signal the end of an element.

- `enum XmlNodeType{ Attribute, ... }`

  An `Attribute` node cannot appear as a child node of any other node type; in particular, it is not considered a child node of an `Element`. It can have a `Text` or `EntityReference` node as a child node.

- `enum XmlNodeType{ XmlDeclaration, ... }`

  The `XmlDeclaration` node has to be the first node in the document. It can have no children. It is a child of the root node. It can have attributes that provide version and encoding information.

- `enum XmlNodeType{ ProcessingInstruction, ... }`

  A `ProcessingInstruction` node cannot have any child nodes. It can appear as the child of a `DocumentFragment`, `EntityReference`, `Element`, or `Document` node. The first word of a processing instruction is interpreted as its name; the remaining text is treated as its value—for example,

  ```
  <?SQLQuery SELECT * FROM Food_Des?>
  ```

  `SQLQuery` represents the name, and the select statement represents the value content.

- `enum XmlNodeType{ Comment, ... }`

  A `Comment` node cannot have any child nodes. It can appear as the child of a `DocumentFragment`, `EntityReference`, `Element`, or `Document` node.

- `enum XmlNodeType{ Text, ... }`

  A `Text` node cannot have any child nodes. It can appear as the child of a `DocumentFragment`, `EntityReference`, `Element`, or `Document` node.

Determining the node type held in the `XmlTextReader` after each `Read()` is typically programmed using a `switch` statement in which each `case` label represents an `XmlNodeType` enumeration. As an example, let's calculate the total value of an element identified in the processing instruction. In addition, let's look for attributes of the health category also identified in the processing instruction. Our output is a list of the matching elements, with any health concerns, plus the total value of those elements. First, here is the handling of the processing instruction to extract the element name and health attribute of interest:

```
string filter = null;
string health = null;
XmlTextReader xrd = new XmlTextReader( fs );

while ( xrd.Read() == true ){
```

```
switch( xrd.NodeType )
{
        case XmlNodeType.ProcessingInstruction:
                filter = xrd.Name;
                health = xrd.Value;
        break;

        case XmlNodeType.Element:
                // ...
        break;
    }
}
```

Within an element, we first need to discover if the element matches the one indicated by the processing instruction:

```
case XmlNodeType.Element:
{
    if ( xrd.Name.Equals( filter ))
    {
            // ... ok, found it
    }
```

If there is a match, we need to walk through the element's attributes, if any, searching for one that matches the health concern indicated in the value portion of the processing instruction:

```
if ( xrd.HasAttributes )
{
    while ( xrd.MoveToNextAttribute() )
        if ( xrd.Name.Equals( health ))
        {
            suffix = "\t*** " + health + " : " + xrd.Value;
            break;
        }
}
```

We also need to retrieve the value associated with the element. Oops. The reader is currently positioned on the element's attributes. First we need to reset the reader back to the element:

```
// restore reader to element, from attribute
xrd.MoveToElement();
```

Now we retrieve the value and convert it to an `int` in order to add it to the running total:

```
// this is the value to compute
text = xrd.ReadString();

// convert and total
total += Convert.ToInt32( text );
```

`ReadString()` concatenates all text, significant white space, white space, and `CData` section node types and returns the concatenated data as a string. This works in our case, and saves us from having to explicitly walk through the element's child text node.

For each matched element, we'll create a string holding the name of the food, the category to filter, and any associated health attributes. For example, we'd like our output to look like this:

```
whole milk      calories : 150
mozzarella      calories : 281   *** diabetes : -1
muenster        calories : 368   *** diabetes : -1
provolone       calories : 351   *** diabetes : -1

*** Total calories : 1150
```

We have a problem, however. The element holding the name of the food has already been read and discarded. And there is no way to move backward to retrieve it in this firehose parse model. Rather we'll have to add a test for the name element, and tuck its value away—for example,

```
// need to tuck away the food's name
if ( xrd.Name.Equals( "name" ))
{
    food = xrd.ReadString();
    break;
}
```

Now we can generate our string, adding it to an `ArrayList` object of matching elements:

```
// tuck it away in a container
elements.Add( food + "\t" + xrd.Name + " : " + text + suffix );
```

This *switch-on-a-node-type-and-process* coding style is essentially typeless in terms of the individual nodes. In the next section we look at the Document Object Model (DOM), in which the entire document is stored in memory as a hierarchy of class node types that we can randomly navigate.

5.11.3 Document Object Model

In this section we look at the classes that provide support for the W3C Document Object Model (DOM). Under this model, an entire XML document is stored in memory in a tree representation, and we are able to navigate and edit its branches. An XML document is represented by the XmlDocument class. The individual node types are represented by the XmlNode class hierarchy, which contains such derived classes as XmlElement and XmlAttribute.

We still use a FileStream and XmlTextReader pair to read and structure the XML. The difference is in what we do with the XmlTextReader object. Rather than manipulate it directly, we pass it to the Load() method of the XmlDocument class. Load() builds an in-memory tree representation of the document. (The XmlTextReader feeds it the node information.) Once the document has been loaded, we can randomly navigate, query, and edit it:

```
using System;
using System.Xml;
using System.IO;
class testXML
{
    public static void Main()
    {
            string xfile = @"C:\c#primer\food.xml";
            FileStream fs =
                    new FileStream( xfile, FileMode.Open );

            // so far, same as before ...
            XmlTextReader xr = new XmlTextReader( xmlfile );

            // OK: here is the difference
            XmlDocument xd = new XmlDocument();

            // build the in-memory representation
            xd.Load( xr );
```

```
            // this is our program logic
            processDom( xd );
        }
    }
```

The `XmlDocument` class provides a set of properties that support queries about the in-memory representation of the document, including the following:

- `Attributes`, which returns a collection of this node's attributes.
- `ParentNode`, which returns the parent of this node.
- `HasChildNodes`, which returns `true` if node has children. (`ChildNodes` returns all the children of this node.)
- `FirstChild`, which returns this node's first child.
- `LastChild`, which returns this node's last child.
- `NextSibling`, which returns the node immediately following this node.
- `PreviousSibling`, which returns the node immediately preceding this node.
- `DocumentElement`, which returns the root `XmlElement` for the document.
- `DocumentType`, which returns the node containing the *DOCTYPE* declaration.
- `OwnerDocument`, which returns the `XmlDocument` to which this node belongs.
- `InnerText`, which gets or sets the values of this node and its children.
- `InnerXml`, which gets or sets the markup representing the children of this node.
- `OuterXml`, which returns the markup representing this node and all its children.
- `Name`, which returns the qualified name of this node.
- `LocalName`, which returns the local name of this node.
- `NamespaceURI`, which returns the namespace Uniform Resource Identifier (URI) of this node.
- `NodeType`, which returns the type of the current node.
- `Value`, which gets or sets the value of the node.

For example, here is the `processDom()` function invoked as the last statement of our earlier example. The interior nodes of the document are each represented by a class object, all of which are rooted in the abstract `XmlNode` base
class. In fact, the `XmlDocument` class itself inherits from `XmlNode`. (We look at
these classes briefly at the end of this section.):

```csharp
static public bool processDom( XmlDocument xd )
{
    Console.WriteLine( "XmlDocument {0} :: {1} ",
                        xd.Name, xd.Value );

    XmlAttributeCollection xac = xd.Attributes;
    if ( xac.Count != 0 ) // ...

    Console.WriteLine(
            "Retrieving the {0} XmlDocument  Children\n",
            xd.ChildNodes.Count );

    XmlNodeList children = xd.ChildNodes;
    foreach ( XmlNode node in children )
    {
        Console.WriteLine( "Child node: {0} of type {1}",
                            node.Name, node.NodeType );
        Console.WriteLine(
            "Child has children? {0} :: Node's parent: {1}",
                node.HasChildNodes, node.ParentNode.Name );
    }

    XmlElement root_elem = xd.DocumentElement;
    Console.WriteLine( "OK: {0} is the root element: ",
                        root_elem.Name );

    if ( root_elem.HasChildNodes )
        Console.WriteLine(
            "OK: {1}'s first child: {0}\n",
            root_elem.FirstChild.Name, root_elem.Name );

    XmlNodeList foodElem =
                root_elem.GetElementsByTagName( "food" );

    return true;
}
```

When we execute the program, it generates the following output from our food.xml file:

```
XmlDocument #document ::
        Document has no attributes.


Retrieving the 4 XmlDocument  Children

Child node: xml of type XmlDeclaration
    Child has children? False :: Node's parent: #document

Child node: #comment of type Comment
    Child has children? False :: Node's parent: #document

Child node: calories of type ProcessingInstruction
    Child has children? False :: Node's parent: #document

Child node: food_composition of type Element
    Child has children? True :: Node's parent: #document


OK: grabbing root element using DocumentElement
OK: food_composition is the root element:
OK: food_composition's first child: food
```

Each of the node types is represented by a class derived from the abstract XmlNode base class. XmlElement represents an element; XmlAttribute, an attribute; XmlComment, a comment; and so on. The ChildNodes property returns the node's children maintained within an XmlNodeList object.

The GetElementsByTagName() method allows us to retrieve all child elements matching the tag name. For example, the following invocation retrieves all the food elements within the document:

```
XmlNodeList foodElem = xelem.GetElementsByTagName( "food" );
```

The returned XmlNodeList object lists each of the retrieved elements in the order in which they occur within the document.

The LoadXml() method of the XmlDocument class allows us to load an in-memory XML document from a string—for example,

```
XmlDocument doc = new XmlDocument();

// OK: let's explicitly load the elements ...

doc.LoadXml(
    "<food id=\"123\">" +
    "    <category>dairy</category>" +
    "    <family>cheese</family>" +
    "    <name>mozzarella</name>" +
    "    <calories>281</calories>" +
    "    <fat>21.60</fat>" +
    "    <isEmtpy/>" +
    "    <cholestrol>78</cholestrol>" +
    "    <carbohydrates>2.28</carbohydrates>" +
    "    <protein>19.42</protein>" +
    "    <fiber>0</fiber>" +
    "</food>"
);
```

Although the firehose `XmlTextReader` and the DOM `XmlDocument` representations of individual nodes are quite different, moving between the two is not difficult. The `ReadNode()` method of the `XmlDocument` class takes as its argument an `XmlTextReader` object. It returns an equivalent node element, such as `XmlElement` or `XmlAttribute`. Because it must be able to return any of the node elements, however, it returns the node itself through an abstract `XmlNode` base-class object:

```
XmlTextReader xrd;
// ...

// position reader on a node or attribute
xrd.Read();

XmlDocument xdoc = new XmlDocument();

// OK: convert reader data into equivalent node
//     returned through an abstract base-class object

XmlNode xn = xdoc.ReadNode( xrd );
```

A downcast to the node type, such as `XmlElement`, is necessary only if the generic `XmlNode` interface is not adequate for handling the node.

Finally, we can traverse either an entire `XmlDocument` tree or a subtree rooted at a particular `XmlNode` using an `XmlNodeReader` class object. Both this reader and the `XmlTextReader` are derived from the abstract `XmlReader`. Both provide a forward-only, firehose read strategy.

5.11.4 `System.Xml.Xsl`

XSLT stands for Extensible Stylesheet Language (XSL) Transformations. A *transformation* consists of three parts:

1. An XML document, the source document to be transformed
2. An XSLT style sheet
3. The transformation engine (an `XslTransform` class object)

The `XslTransform` class is an XSLT processor implementing the XSL Transformations (XSLT) Version 1.0 recommendation. `Load()`, which loads the style sheet to use for the transformation, and `Transform()`, which carries out the transformation, are the `XslTransform` methods. Both are overloaded to support multiple parameter sets—for example,

```
using System;
using System.IO;
using System.Xml;
using System.Xml.Xsl;
using System.Xml.XPath;

public static void
Transform( string xmldoc, string xsltdoc )
{
    // get a processor object
    XslTransform xslt = new XslTransform();

    // OK: load the .xslt style sheet
    xslt.Load( xsltdoc );

    // OK: load the source .xml document
    XPathDocument xdoc = new XPathDocument( xmldoc );

    // OK: we need an output target
    TextWriter writer = Console.Out;
```

```
        // OK: let's transform this puppy ...
          xslt.Transform( xmldocument, null, writer );
    }
```

The goal of our transformation is to extract the `name` and `calories` elements of `food.xml`. Our new `meal.xml` document should look like this:

```
<meal>
    <item>
      <name> xxx </name>
      <calories> xxx </calories>
    </item>
```

The XSLT file consists of two parts, conceptually at least. The declaration portion provides version identification in the required `xsl:stylesheet` entry and optionally modifies the output of the result tree in an `xsl:output` entry:

```
<?xml version="1.0" encoding="UTF-8" ?>
  <xsl:stylesheet version="1.0"
        xmlns:xsl="http://www.w3.org/1999/XSL/Transform">

  <xsl:output method="xml" indent="yes" encoding= ="UTF-8" />
    // ... template definitions go here
</xsl:stylesheet>
```

The template portion, indicated by each `xsl:template` entry, selects the `name` and `calories` portions for each food element, outputting them into the result tree:

```
<xsl:template match="/">
  <meal>
  <xsl:for-each select="/food_composition/food">
    <item>
      <name>
        <xsl:value-of select="name"/>
      </name>
      <calories>
        <xsl:value-of select="calories"/>
      </calories>
    </item>
  </xsl:for-each>
  </meal>
</xsl:template>
```

The invocation of `Transform()` generates the following output:

```xml
<?xml version="1.0" encoding="IBM437"?>
<meal>
  <item>
    <name>whole milk</name>
    <calories>150</calories>
  </item>
  <item>
    <name>mozzarella</name>
    <calories>281</calories>
  </item>
  <item>
    <name>muenster</name>
    <calories>368</calories>
  </item>
  <item>
    <name>provolone</name>
    <calories>351</calories>
  </item>
</meal>
```

5.11.5 `System.Xml.XPath`

`XPath` expressions allow us to randomly reach any branch of an XML document tree. The two parts to an `XPath` expression are

- the *location path,* which identifies our intended destination in the document.
- the *context node,* which represents the node where we are currently positioned in the document.

The movement across nodes within the document tree is carried out through an `XPathNavigator` object through a collection of `Select()` methods. The `XPathNavigator` can navigate an `XmlDocument`, an `XmlDataDocument`, or an `XPathDocument`. The `XPathDocument` is optimized for random traversal. For example, here is how we create an `XPathNavigator` object bound to an `XPathDocument`:

```csharp
XPathDocument xpdoc =
    new XPathDocument( @"C:\C#Talks\Food.xml" );

XPathNavigator navi = xpdoc.CreateNavigator();
```

Next we invoke `Select()` on the element across which we wish to iterate. For example, here is a selection that captures the four food elements of our `food.xml` sample file:

```
XPathNodeIterator iter =
        navi.Select( "/food_composition/food" );
```

`Select()` returns an `XPathNodeIterator`. The `XPathNodeIterator` class implements the `IEnumerator` interface, allowing us to access the individual node through the `Current` property and advance to the next node with an invocation of `MoveNext()`:

```
while ( iter.MoveNext() )
{
    Console.WriteLine( iter.Current.Name );
    if ( iter.Current.HasChildren )
    {
            iter.Current.MoveToFirstChild();
            Console.WriteLine( iter.Current.Name );

            while ( iter.Current.MoveToNext() )
                    Console.WriteLine( iter.Current.Name );

    }
}
```

`Current` represents an `XPathNavigator` object positioned on the current node. The `HasChildren` property and the `MoveToFirstChild()` and `MoveToNext()` methods are members of `XPathNavigator`. The outer `while` loop moves through the selected food elements. The inner `while` loop iterates across the nine child nodes of each food element.

An interesting selection method is `SelectChildren()`, which accepts an `XPathNodeType` enumerator:

```
enum XPathNodeType
{
    All,
    Attribute, Comment, Element, Namespace,
    ProcessingInstruction, Root, SignificantWhitespace,
    Text, Whitespace
}
```

In the following example, we pass in `All`, thereby retrieving all the child nodes of the document itself. In our `food.xml` sample document, there are three child nodes: the comment, the processing instruction, and the root `food_composition` element. (The `food` elements are children of `food_composition`):

```
iter = navi.SelectChildren( XPathNodeType.All );
int icnt = 0;
while ( iter.MoveNext() )
    Console.WriteLine( (++icnt).ToString() + ". " +
                            iter.Current.Name + " ==> " +
                            iter.Current.ToString());
```

This code generates the following three lines. Notice that the `ToString()` method of the `XPathNavigator` class concatenates all the values of the current node and its children:

```
1. ==>  Place keywords in the PI below
2. calories ==> diabetes
3.
food_composition==>dairymilkwholenilk150801580dairycheesemozzar
ella28121.60782.2819.420dairycheesemuenster36830.04961.1223.410da
irycheeseprovolone35126.62692.1425.580
```

The remaining two primary areas of XML support (which, for space reasons, I do not cover here) are the schema support under the `System.Xml.Schema` namespace, and Simple Object Access Protocol (SOAP) support under the `System.Xml.Serialization` namespace.

Chapter 6

Windows Forms Designer

In a real-world program, our interactions with users are expected to be through a graphical user interface (GUI). Under .NET we do that through a collection of classes defined within the `System.Windows.Forms` namespace. Although we can program these classes directly, by defining an instance of a radio button—specifying its location, the text to display, and so on—in practice that approach is simply too tedious and error-prone.

Rather we use the Windows Forms *drag-and-drop designer,* a rapid application development (RAD) tool that is part of Visual Studio.NET. Visual Basic programmers have been doing RAD development for many years with impressive results. Under .NET, RAD support has been extended to C# as well. This chapter provides a tour of Windows Forms programming. Because of its visual nature, many screen shots are included to illustrate what is being discussed.

6.1 Our First Windows Forms Program

For our first Windows Forms program, we'll again greet the user, as we did in Chapter 1, except that this time we'll do it interactively through a graphical user interface (GUI). The initial window is pictured in Figure 6.1.

The window is represented as a `Form` class object. The title bar has been set to the string *Hello, Windows Forms!* As the user enters his or her name in the text box, we update the title bar to the text entered by the user. We do this through an event handler associated with the text box. The event is triggered whenever the content of the text box is altered. Within the form, we have placed the following controls.

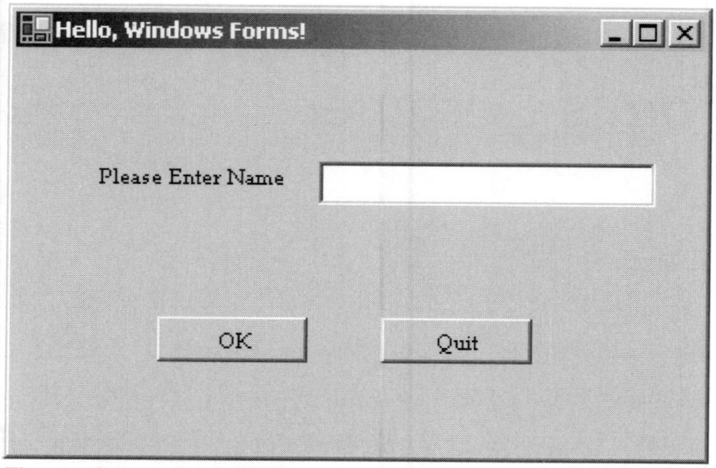

Figure 6.1   Initial Window

- A `Label` object with the associated text *Please Enter Name*.
- A `TextBox` object to the right of the label, where the user enters her name.
- Two `Button` objects—one labeled *OK* and the other labeled *Quit*.

When the user clicks **OK,** a dialog window pops up to formally greet him or her. This window displays not only the user's name, but the current date and time as well, as pictured in Figure 6.2.

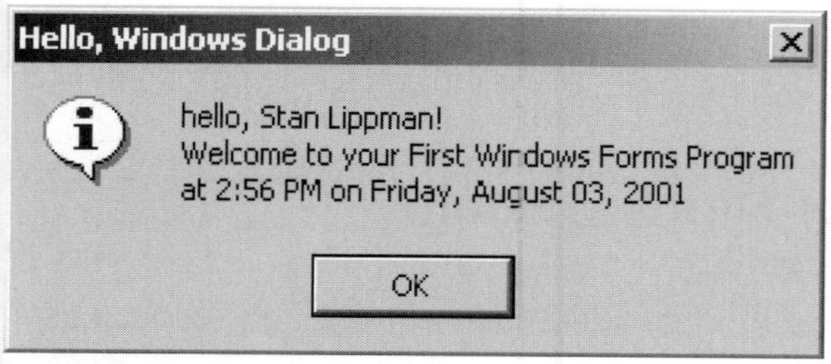

Figure 6.2   Greeting Dialog

If the user clicks **OK** without having filled in the text box, a dialog window pops up requesting the user to fill in the text box (see Figure 6.3).

If the user presses **Quit,** a dialog box pops up asking the user to confirm (see Figure 6.4). Notice that the icon and the number of available buttons change for each dialog box. (We look at how to program events such as button clicks in Section 6.4.)

Figure 6.3   Bad Data Dialog

If the user presses **OK,** we pop up a final goodbye dialog box without an icon (see Figure 6.5.).

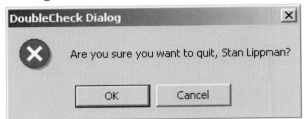

Figure 6.4   Are You Sure? Dialog

And that's our first Windows Forms application. In the next sections we'll look at how it's implemented—through control widget drag-and-drop GUI design for the look of the form and event callback programming for its behavior.

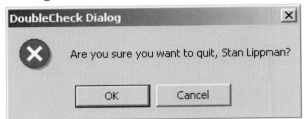

Figure 6.5   Ok, Bye Dialog

6.2   Building the GUI

To build a Windows Forms application using Visual Studio.Net, bring up the **New Project** window (see Figure 6.6). Choose **Visual C# Projects** in the **Project Types** window on the left. Choose the **Windows Application** icon in the **Templates** window to the right. By default, the project is given the generic name WindowsApplication1 (the trailing digit is incremented by one with each default project name).

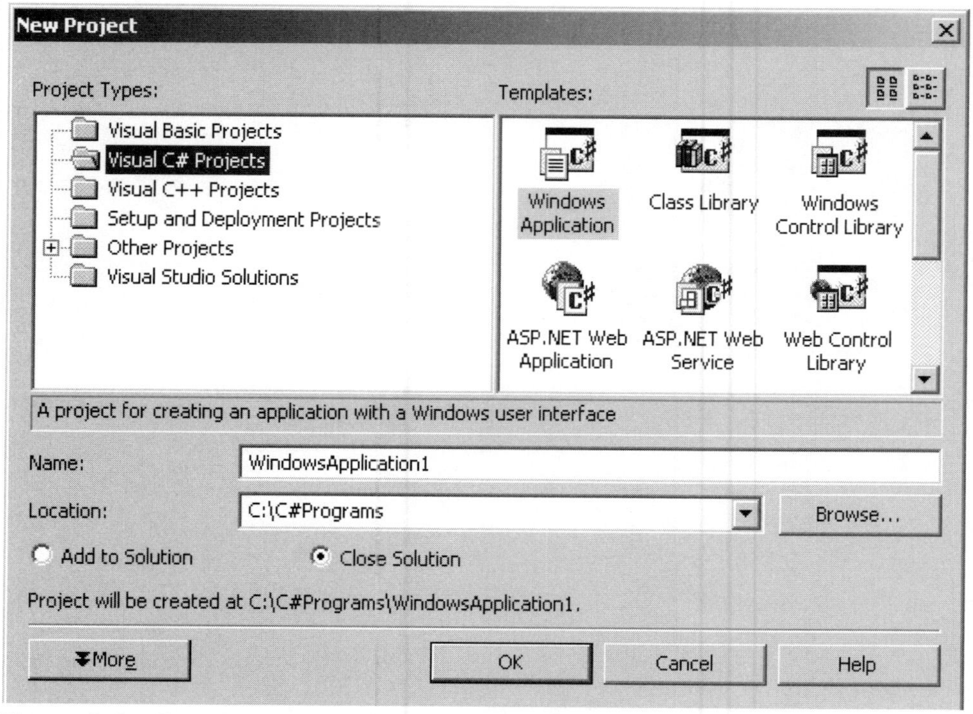

Figure 6.6 Creating a Windows Forms C# Project

The project opens in the graphical Windows Forms designer view—a blank square form with dotted grid lines and a title bar. By default, the `Form` control and title bar are named *Form1*. This is the main window of our application.

The **Properties** window on the right (see Figure 6.7) displays the attributes of the active control within the form designer. When you click on a property, an explanation of its functionality is displayed at the bottom of the **Properties** window. For example, if you want to turn off the grid lines, set the `DrawGrid` property to `false`. Figure 6.7 represents the default designer view, but with the `BackgroundImage` property set to a `JPEG` image.

Take some time now to click on the properties that interest you. Modify the associated values, and then reexecute the program to see what happens. For example, try changing the `Location`, `Size`, and `Opacity` properties. `Size` changes the form within the designer. `Location` and `Opacity` modify the window displayed when you rebuild and run the application.

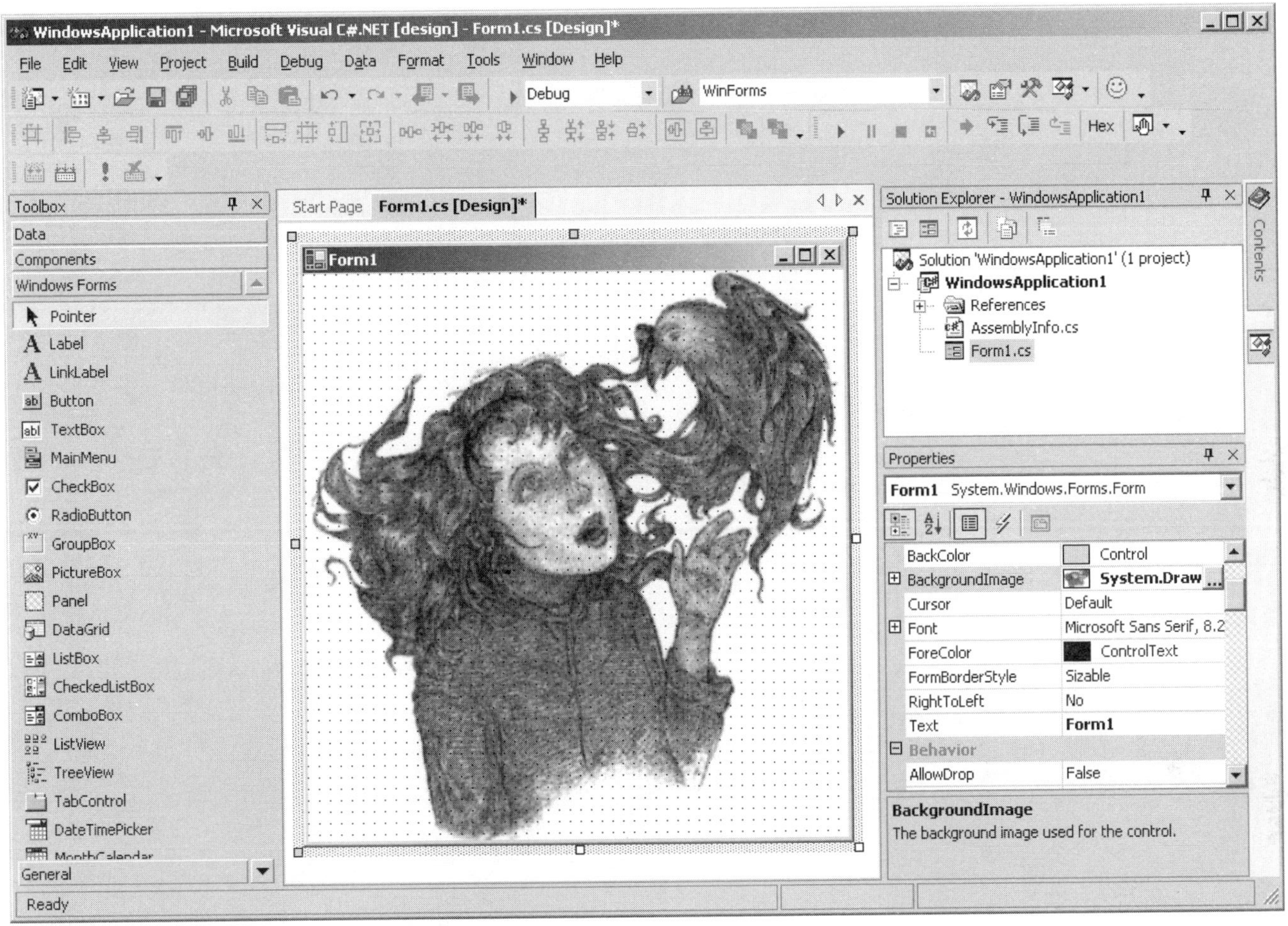

Figure 6.7 Designer View of a Windows Forms Project

The Windows Forms **Toolbox** window on the left-hand side (see Figure 6.7) provides a palette of controls that we drag and drop onto our form. For our first application we need a label with the associated text *Please Enter Name.* To the right of that, we need a text box. Under that, we need two buttons—one that says *OK* and one that says *Quit.* Try to drag and drop the associated controls onto your form. When you're done, your designer form should look like the one pictured in Figure 6.8.

To see how it looks when presented to the user, build and execute the application. Of course, if you press either of the two buttons or enter your name in the text box, nothing happens. All we've done so far is design the form; the next step is to add to it the capability to interact with the user.

6.3   Implementing the Event Callback Routines

Our implementation is driven by three user-initiated events:

1. The entry of text into the text box.
2. The clicking of the **OK** button signaling that entry is complete.
3. The clicking of the **Quit** button to terminate the application.

The methods we implement to respond to these events are referred to as *callbacks* or *event handlers.* There are two steps to implementing event handlers: Writing the code, of course, is the first step. The second step is registering the callback function with the control widget through which the event occurs. For our program, the three controls are the text box and the two buttons.

When we double-click on the control—for example, the text box—the designer generates the skeleton of a callback method for that control (and generates the code necessary to register the event handler with the control). The view changes to the code view, and our cursor is placed between the curly braces of the empty function body (see Figure 6.9).

Notice that the designer and code views share the same name (Form1.cs, by default). The designer view is distinguished by the [Design] attribute to the right of its name. We can toggle between the two views of the form by clicking either on the name or on the **Code (F7)** or **Design (Shift+F7)** menu item under **View.**

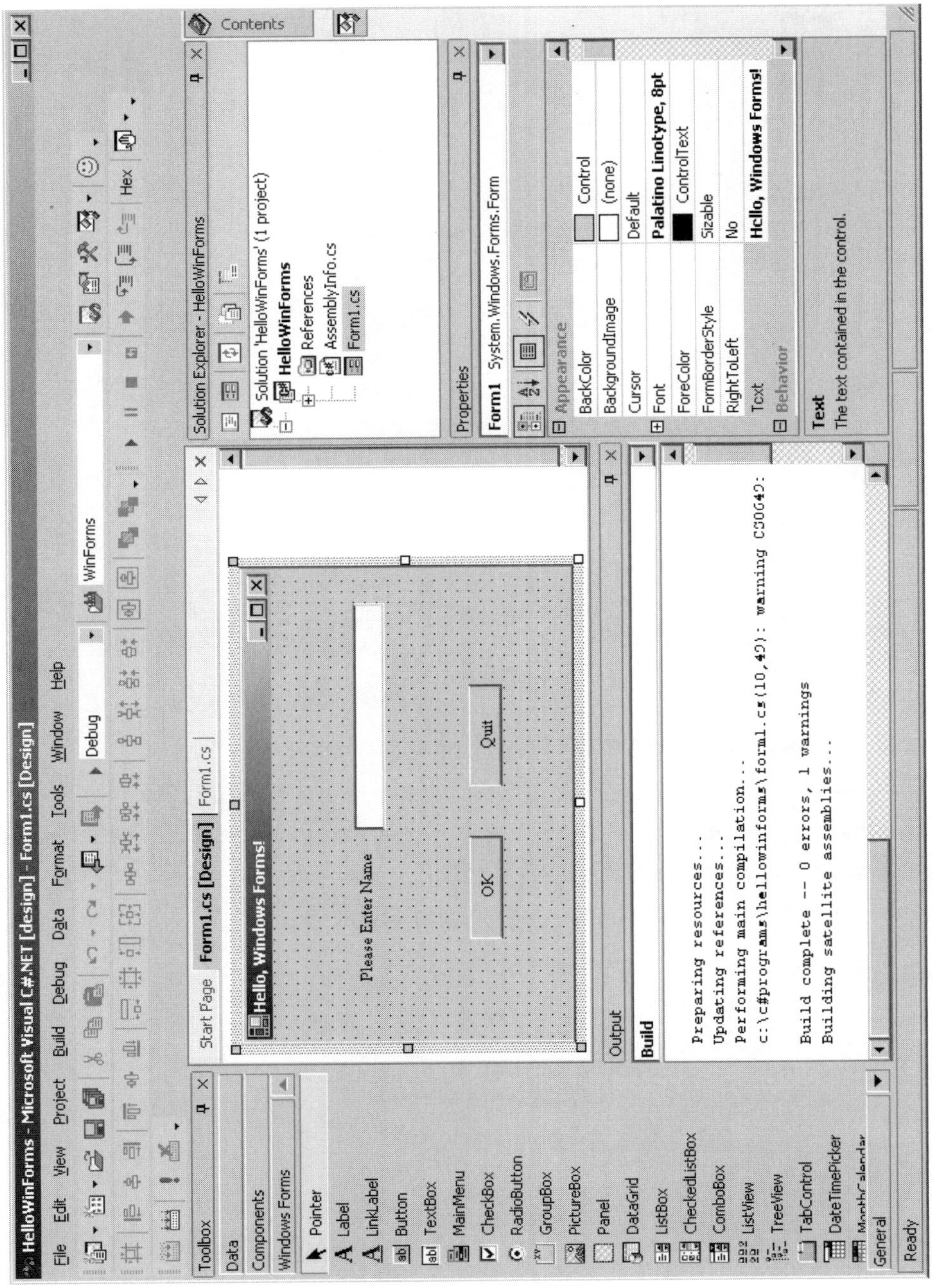

Figure 6.8 Completed Designer View

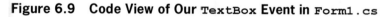

```
textBox1.TextChanged += new System.EventHandler (textBox1_TextChanged);
Text = "Hello, WinForms";

Controls.Add (button2);
Controls.Add (button1);
Controls.Add (label1);
Controls.Add (textBox1);
}

protected void textBox1_TextChanged (object sender, System.EventArgs e)
{

}

public static void Main(string[] args)
{
    Application.Run(new Form1());
}
```

Figure 6.9 **Code View of Our** `TextBox` **Event in** `Form1.cs`

The object representing our window is automatically inherited from the `Form` class defined within the `System.Windows.Forms` namespace. Each of the controls we drag and drop onto the design form is added to the class as a private member. For example, here is the data portion of the generated class definition:

```
public class Form1 : System.Windows.Forms.Form
{
    private System.Windows.Forms.Button   button2;
    private System.Windows.Forms.Button   button1;
    private System.Windows.Forms.Label    label1;
    private System.Windows.Forms.TextBox  textBox1;

    // ...
}
```

By default, when we add a control using the designer, the name of the object is the name of the control, but with a lowercase first letter, and a number suffix

C# PRIMER

representing the count of instances of that type of control that our `Form` object currently contains. For our `TextBox` control, the associated object is named `textBox1`. For our two `Button` controls, the objects are named `button1` and `button2`. The `Label` object, not surprisingly, is named `label1`.

`button1` and `button2` are particularly uninformative as names. In a form with many controls, these generic names quickly become confusing. It is much more helpful to rename the button objects to something meaningful—perhaps `buttonOK` and `buttonQuit`.

In general, we change the name of a control by modifying the `Name` entry of the control's **Properties** window. (By the way, I recommend that you do this before you add your own code. The form designer updates code that it has generated; it does not modify code that you have added.)

`Controls` is a property of the `Form` class. It represents an initially empty collection of the child controls associated with the window. As we drag and drop each control into our form, the designer generates code to define the control and insert it into the `Controls` property. `Add()` is the collection's insertion method. For example, if you look at Figure 6.9, you'll see the code generated by the designer to associate the four controls with our window:[1]

```
Controls.Add( button2 );
Controls.Add( button1 );
Controls.Add( label1 );
Controls.Add( textBox1 );
```

Our job at this point is to implement the associated event handlers for these controls. The name of the first event we wish to handle is `TextChanged`. This event is triggered whenever the content of the text box changes—literally as soon as we lift a finger from the key we've pressed.

The default name for the event handler is the combination of the control name and the event name, joined by an underscore. The event handler always has a return value of `void` and a two-parameter signature. The first parameter refers to the control through which the event occurs. For our event, the control is

---

1. The strategy for the designer has changed since the version of code reflected in Figure 6.9. An `AddRange()` method is now used to add all the controls within one statement rather than each control being added individually.

the `TextBox` object whose text string is being modified. The second parameter holds additional event data, if any. For the `TextChanged` event, this parameter is empty.

Code to register the callback method is generated automatically by the form designer. It appears as the first line of code in Figure 6.9:

```
textBox1.TextChanged +=
    new System.EventHandler(textBox1_TextChanged);
```

`TextChanged` is an *event* property of the `TextBox` control. Each time the content of the text box changes, the callback methods currently registered with `TextChanged` are invoked.

`EventHandler` is a *delegate* type. A delegate serves as a reference to a static or nonstatic class member function. In this example the designer creates an `EventHandler` object that is bound to the event handler. (See Section 2.12 for a discussion of the `delegate` type.)

The compound assignment operator (+=) does the registration. It adds this new event handler to the list maintained by the `TextChanged` property.

6.3.1 Implementing a `TextBox` Event

What we want to do within this callback method is modify the title bar, which begins the application as **Hello, Windows Forms,** to reflect the entry as the user types in his or her name. So, for example, as the user enters *Stan,* the title bar becomes in turn **Hello, S; Hello, St; Hello, Sta;** and finally **Hello, Stan.**

How can we do that? The text associated with `textBox1` is stored in its `Text` property. For example, to test if the text box is empty, we write

```
if ( textBox1.Text == string.Empty )
        return;
```

The title bar is part of our `Form1` class, and it is represented by its associated `Text` property. If you look at Figure 6.9, you'll see it assigned its initial string value on line 2 of the code:

```
Text = "Hello, Windows Forms";
```

(Outside a `Form1` member function, we would write `Form1.Text`.)

To modify the title bar within our callback method, we'll reset the title bar `Text` property with the `Text` property of the text box:

```
protected void
textBox1_TextChanged( object sender, EventArgs e )
{
    if ( textBox1.Text != String.Empty )
         Text = "Hello, " + textBox1.Text;
}
```

6.3.2 Implementing the `Button` Events: OK

By clicking on the **OK** button, the user indicates that she has completed entering her name. The first thing we need to do in response to the click event, then, is confirm that the text box is not empty. If it is empty, we pop up a message box indicating that the entry in the text box is invalid. Otherwise, we pop up a message box containing our greeting. Our greeting includes not only the user's name, but the current date and time as well. OK, let's see how we do that.

The event we wish to respond to is the `Click` property of the `Button` class. The **OK** button object is by default named `button1`, just because it is the first button we designed. Here is the code generated by the form designer to register the `button1_Click` callback method:

```
button1.Click +=
     new System.EventHandler( button1_Click );
```

First we check whether the `textBox1.Text` property is empty. If it is, we display a bad-data pop-up dialog and return (see Figure 6.3 for an illustration). In the following code segment, the dialog messages, titles, and style attributes for the dialog are factored into individual arrays:

```
protected void
button1_Click( object sender, System.EventArgs e )
{

    string [] messages =
    {
        "Please enter your name before pressing OK",
        "Welcome to your first Windows form"
    };
```

```
string [] titles =
{
    "Bad Data Dialog",
    "Hello, Windows Dialog"
};

if ( textBox1.Text == string.Empty )
{
    MessageBox.Show( messages[0], titles[0],
                    MessageBoxButtons.OK,
                    MessageBoxIcon.Warning );
    return;
}
```

Let's defer discussing the `MessageBox` pop-up dialog class until later (it is covered in Section 6.5). Everything else in the code segment should be familiar at this point. Finally, we compose our *Hello* message string to greet the user, and we invoke the `MessageBox.Show()` method to generate the corresponding pop-up dialog (see Figure 6.2):

```
string helloMessage = "hello, " +
    textBox1.Text + "!\n" +
    messages[1] + '\nat " +
    current.ToShortTimeString() + " on " +
    current.ToLongDateString();

MessageBox.Show( helloMessage, titles[1],
                MessageBoxButtons.OK,
                MessageBoxIcon.Information );
}
```

That completes the callback method to be invoked when the user clicks on the **OK** button.

6.3.3   Implementing the `Button` Events: Quit

When the user clicks on the **Quit** button, we'll spawn one of those annoying *Are you sure?* pop-up dialogs (see Figure 6.4). If the user responds by clicking **OK,** we generate an *OK: bye!* pop-up dialog (see Figure 6.5) and close the application using the `Close()` method of our `Form1` class. The callback method is implemented as follows:

```
protected void
button2_Click( object sender, System.EventArgs e )
{
    string message =
            "Are you sure you want to quit, "
            + textBox1.Text + "?";

    string title = "DoubleCheck Dialog";

    DialogResult dr =
            MessageBox.Show(
                    message,
                    title,
                    MessageBoxButtons.OKCancel,
                    MessageBoxIcon.Error
            );

    if ( dr == DialogResult.OK )
    {
            MessageBox.Show(
                    "OK: "
                    + textBox1.Text + " -- bye!"
            );

            Close();
    }
}
```

That's the full implementation of our first Windows Forms application. In the next section we look in more detail at the events associated with the various controls.

6.4   Inspecting and Generating Control Events

What additional events are associated with a `TextBox` control? More generally, how can we discover the set of events associated with a control?

To inspect the set of events associated with a control, we do the following: (1) click on the control to display its **Properties** window, and (2) in the **Properties** window, click on the yellow jagged lightning icon. The **Properties** window now displays the set of events associated with the current control (as Figure 6.10 shows).

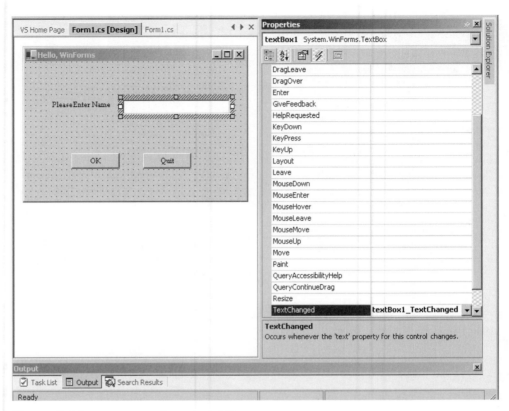

Figure 6.10 `TextBox`-**Supported Events**

The entries on the left in the **Properties** window represent each of the events supported by the control. The entries on the right, if present, represent registered callback methods. (In Figure 6.10, only `TextChanged` displays an associated callback method.) To see a summary description of the event's meaning, click on the event once. At the bottom of the **Properties** window, a summary description is displayed. To generate the stub callback method for the event and the code to register it, double-click on the event.

6.4.1 Labels Are Programmable

At first glance, labels look like one of the more uninteresting controls. Typically, we drag a label to its position, set its text, and that's all. However, because we are able to set and unset its text during program execution, a label serves double duty as an attractive target for setting text dynamically.

C# PRIMER

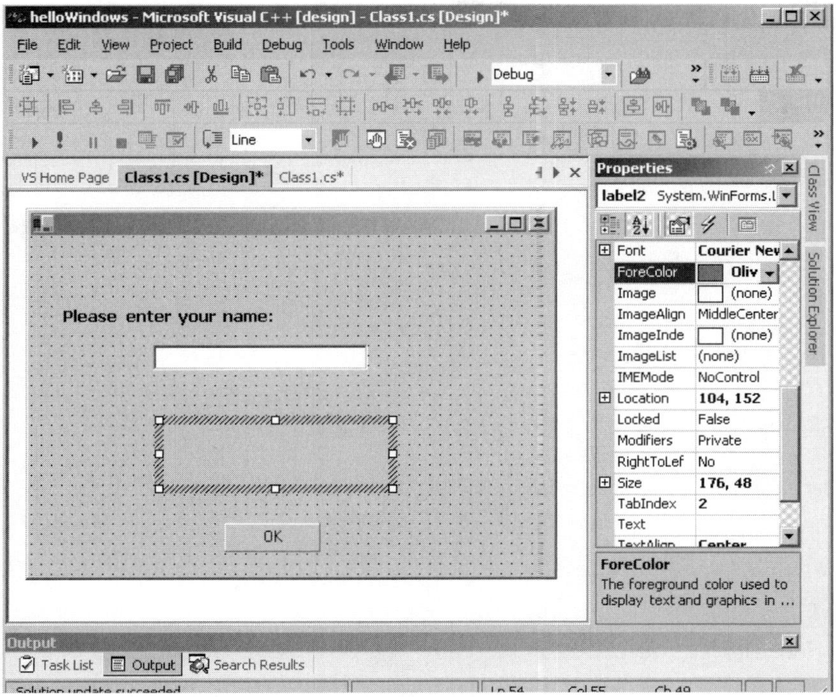

Figure 6.11 Targeting a Label at Runtime

For example, let's redo our first program to respond by writing into a blank label in the form rather than popping up a message box. The initial form is pictured in Figure 6.11. Note that `label2` has its `Text` field set to an empty string (we'll set this field in response to the **OK** button event).

When this program is executed, the form pops up with the second label (which is not visible because we have set its `Text` property to empty). Alternatively, we can ignore the `Text` property. Rather we initialize the label's `Visible` property to `false`. Whenever a control's `Visible` property is `false`, that control is not displayed to the user. The **OK** button click event would then set both the `Text` property to the greeting and the `Visible` property to `true`. Here is how that might look:

```csharp
protected void button1_Click (object sender, EventArgs e)
{
     label2.Text = "Hello," + "\n" + textBox1.Text;
     label2.Visible = true;
}
```

6.5 Implementing the `MessageBox` Pop-Up Dialog

The `MessageBox` class allows for the easy generation of a pop-up dialog box. Typically it consists of message text, one or more buttons, and an optional icon such as the information icon pictured in Figure 6.2.

To display the `MessageBox` dialog, we invoke an instance of its static member function `Show()`. For example, the following invocation generated the **Bad Data Dialog** pictured in Figure 6.3:

```
string messages = "Please enter your name before pressing OK";
string title    = "Bad Data Dialog";

if ( textBox1.Text == string.Empty )
    MessageBox.Show( message, title,
                     MessageBoxButtons.OK,
                     MessageBoxIcon.Warning );
```

We invoke a four-parameter instance of `Show()`. The first parameter is the string displayed within the dialog box. The second parameter is the string displayed in the title bar of the dialog box. The third parameter represents one of the `enum MessageBoxButtons` values. This value determines the number and text of buttons displayed in the message. The following six enumerators are currently defined:

1. `AbortRetryIgnore` creates **Abort, Retry,** and **Ignore** buttons.
2. `OK` creates an **OK** button.
3. `OKCancel` creates **OK** and **Cancel** buttons.
4. `RetryCancel` creates **Retry** and **Cancel** buttons.
5. `YesNo` creates **Yes** and **No** buttons.
6. `YesNoCancel` creates **Yes, No,** and **Cancel** buttons.

The fourth parameter represents one of the `enum MessageBoxIcon` values. This value determines the icon displayed in the message box. For example, `Warning` is represented by a black exclamation point nested in a yellow triangle. Other icon values include the following:

- `Asterisk` is represented by a lowercase *i* in a circle.
- `Error` is represented by a white *x* in a red circle (pictured in Figure 6.4).

- `Information` is represented by a blue *i* in a white dialog bubble (pictured in Figure 6.2).
- `Question` is represented by a blue question mark, also in a white dialog bubble.

`Show()` can be invoked with simply a string to be displayed:

```
MessageBox.Show( "OK: bye!" );
```

The resulting display box in this case is pictured in Figure 6.5.

6.6 The List Box for Unformatted Output

Up to this point we have been directing our text to a console window. A somewhat more visually appealing alternative is to direct our output to the list box of a Windows Forms window. For example, Figure 6.12 displays the content of a text file directed into a simple form containing only a list box. As configured, the vertical and horizontal scrolling is added as needed. The program is virtually unchanged, although factored out into an independent function:

```
private void
process_file( string file_name )
{
      StreamReader ifile = File.OpenText( file_name );

      string textline;
      int    lineCnt = 0;

      while (( textline = ifile.ReadLine()) != null )
      {
            thisForm.TheListBox.Items.Add( textline );
            if ( lineCnt++ == 0 )
                  thisForm.Text = textline;
      }
}
```

`thisForm` is the `Form` object representing our window. `TheListBox` is the `ListBox` control. I dragged the `ListBox` control onto the form, then resized both. `Items` represents the container in which elements of the list box are stored. `Add()` inserts an item at the end of the container. (The `Text` property of the form, recall, represents the title bar.)

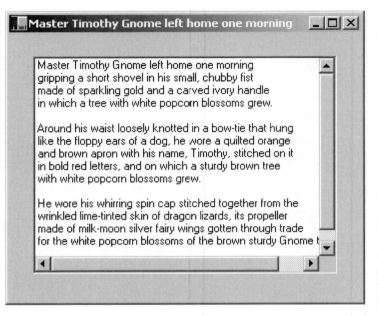

Figure 6.12 The Windows Forms List Box Window

Because we are using the window only as a display area rather than to capture and respond to events, I factored the processing of the file into a separate class. Inside the form constructor, I created an instance of the class, passing it a reference to the form. This is how the `thisForm` object is initialized.

When the designer generates its C# code, it creates the following general constructor for our `Form1` object:

```
public Form1()
{
    //
    // required for Windows Forms designer support
    //
    InitializeComponent();

    //
    // TODO: add any constructor code after InitializeComponent()
    //
}
```

After changing the generic `Form1` class name to `ListboxForm` and adding the creation and invocation of our class, the revised constructor looks like this:

C# PRIMER

```
public ListboxForm()
{
    InitializeComponent();

    processListbox proc = new processListbox( this );
    proc.process_file( @"c:\fictions\word.txt" );
}
```

Of course, hard-coding the file name is not very flexible. One possible program extension to provide more flexibility is to add a text box for the user to enter the path of the file to display. An **OK** button event handler reads the text box text and invokes `process_file()`, passing in the file name:

```
protected void button1_Click (object sender, EventArgs e)
{
    if ( textBox1.Text.Length != 0 )
        proc.process_file( textBox1.Text );
}
```

Let's add a **Clear** button just to show how to empty the list box. To count how many items it holds, we invoke `Count()`. If it is not empty, we clear the items by invoking `Clear()`:

```
protected void button3_Click (object sender, System.EventArgs e)
{
    if ( TheListBox.Items.Count != 0 )
        TheListBox.Items.Clear();
}
```

The other design change has to do with the idea of the lifetime of an object. Originally we defined `proc` within the form constructor:

```
public ListboxForm()
{
    InitializeComponent();

    processListbox proc = new processListbox( this );
    proc.process_file( @"c:\fictions\word.txt" );
}
```

Recall from the code example earlier in this section that `proc` is a reference to the `processListbox` object allocated through the `new` expression. The lifetime of `proc`—that is, the extent of time it exists as a handle to a `process-`

```
```

Listbox class object—is the duration of the constructor invocation, during which time the list box is filled with items. Moreover, proc is visible only within that constructor. (We say that proc has *scope* local to the constructor.) There is no direct way to access proc from outside the constructor, as we attempt to do inside our button click event handler. Oops!

We have to extend both proc's accessibility and its lifetime. Minimally, our click event handler must be able to access proc. Potentially any method of the Form class may wish access to proc. To make it visible to any class method and to provide it with a lifetime coincident with that of the Form class, we simply declare proc to be a member of that class.

To introduce our own members within the Form class, we open up the C# text file generated by the designer. We then scroll down to find the control definitions generated by the form designer, and, following them, introduce our own—for example,

```csharp
public class ListboxForm : Form
{
// these are generated by Windows Forms designer
    private System.ComponentModel.Container components;
    private System.Windows.Forms.Button button3;
    private System.Windows.Forms.Button button2;
    private System.Windows.Forms.Button button1;
    private System.Windows.Forms.TextBox textBox1;
    private System.Windows.Forms.Label label1;

// also generated by Windows Forms, but I renamed it
    private ListBox theListbox;

// OK: this is our member
    private processListbox proc;
```

6.7 Exploring the File Dialog

Nobody really wants to type in a file name, let alone a file name and path. What users want is a directory tree dialog window to pop up that they can navigate and select from. The first step, as always, is to drag the control onto the form. Unlike the other controls so far, OpenFileDialog is not a visible control. It does not display in the form. Rather we need to associate it with a visible control. The usual suspect is an **Open** menu item.

When the user clicks the menu item, we need to respond by invoking the openFileDialog1 object's ShowDialog() member function. The menu item event handler looks like this:

```
private void menuItem2_Click(object sender, System.EventArgs e)
{
      Text = "Open Menu Item Clicked";
      openFileDialog1.ShowDialog();
}
```

The ShowDialog() method launches the file dialog window and handles everything until the user clicks **Open.** At that point, a FileOk event is raised associated with openFileDialog1. (If **Cancel** is clicked, no event is raised.) Our event handler retrieves the selected file from the openFileDialog1 object. It then reads the file and places the text in a list box. It also writes the path and file names into an adjacent text box. It looks like this:

```
protected void openFileDialog1_FileOk( object sender,
                  ComponentModel.CancelEventArgs e)
{
      // get file name selected by user ...
      textBox.Text =  openFileDialog1.FileName;

      // open the file ...
      StreamReader strmInput =
              new StreamReader(openFileDialog1.FileName );

      // read through and add each line to the list box
      string item;
      while (( item = strmInput.ReadLine() ) != null )
              listBox1.Items.Add( item );

      // close the StreamReader
      strmInput.Close();

      // repaint the list box and
      // have no item be treated as selected ...
      listBox1.Invalidate();
      listBox1.SelectedIndex = -1;
}
```

There is also a SaveFileDialog control.

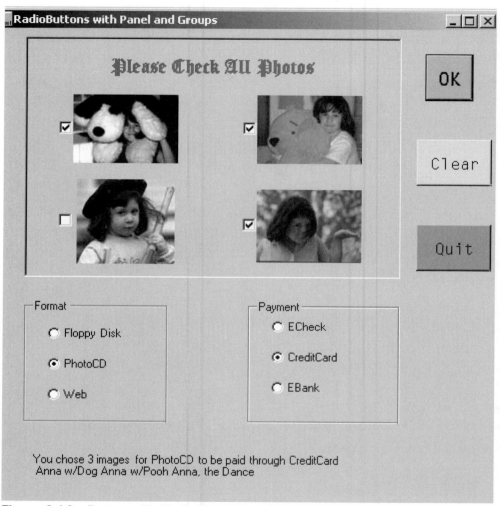

Figure 6.13   Buttons, Radio Buttons, and Check Boxes

6.8 A Pocketful of Buttons

There are three primary button controls—conventional click event buttons, radio buttons, and check box buttons—as pictured in Figure 6.13:

1. **The `Button` control.** Buttons are used to signal that a particular action should now occur. In Figure 6.13, we provide three buttons: **OK, Clear,** and **Quit.** The primary `Button` event is a user's *click*. For example,

```
protected void button1_Click( object sender, EventArgs e )
{
    int cnt = 0;

    // figure out which images were selected
    for ( int ix = 0; ix < imageSet.Count; ++ix )
        if ( imageSet[ ix ] )
            { image += imageTitle[ ix ]; cnt++; }

    // make sure all necessary items were selected
    if ( payment == null || format == null || cnt == 0 )
    {
        string msg =
          "Please Select Photo(s), Format, and Payment";
        MessageBox.Show( msg );
        Clear();
        return;
    }

    string message = "You chose " + cnt +
                " images for " + format +
                " to be paid through " + payment;

    label2.Text = message + "\n" + image;
}
```

2. **The `RadioButton` control.** Radio buttons are used primarily for mutually exclusive selection. When the user selects one radio button within a group, the others clear automatically. In Figure 6.13 we provide two groups of radio buttons: **Format** and **Payment.** We design this setup in two steps: First we drop a `GroupBox` control into the form; second, we drop each `RadioButton` control into the group box. The primary radio button event is `CheckChanged`, which occurs whenever the *checked* status of the button changes. For example, here is our event handler for one of the radio buttons:

```
protected void
radioButton7_CheckedChanged( object sender, EventArgs e )
   { if ( radioButton7.Checked ) format = radioButton7.Text; }
```

`Checked` is the property that indicates whether the button has been selected. To clear a selection, we set that property to `false`. `format` is a `string` member introduced to hold the selection.

3. **The `CheckBox` control.** Check boxes are used to support multiple selections. In Figure 6.13 we provide a panel of four check boxes; the user can select any combination of the four. As with the `RadioButton` control, the primary check box event is `CheckChanged`, which occurs whenever the *checked* status of the box changes. In the following example, `imageSet` is a `BitArray` class object used to keep track of which images the user has selected:

```
protected void
checkBox4_CheckedChanged( object sender, EventArgs e )
{
    // Anna with Dog
    imageSet[ 0 ] = checkBox4.Checked ? true : false;
}
```

6.9 Serving Up Menus

Menus are very simple to insert into a form. Figure 6.14 illustrates the design of a three-level hierarchy of menu items under the title **Edit.** The steps to create such a menu are as follows:

1. Click on **MainMenu** in the Windows Forms **Toolbox** window (on the left in Figure 6.14) and drag it onto the form. The menu is a nonvisible control, so the icon appears below the form. (In Figure 6.14, there are four nonvisible controls.)

2. Click on the **mainMenu1** icon; a **Type Here** box appears on the second line of the form.

3. Click on the box. Two additional **Type Here** boxes appear—one below the current item and the other to its right.

4. Enter the name of the menu item. Modify any additional characteristics of the item using its **Properties** box (on the right in Figure 6.14).

5. Double-click on the menu item to add a click event handler. For example, here is the handler for the case in which a user clicks on the `ForeColor` menu item for the **TextBox** menu item; this example illustrates the use of the `ColorDialog` control:

```
protected void menuItem10_Click( object sender, EventArgs e )
{
    // instantiate a new ColorDialog object
    ColorDialog diag   = new ColorDialog();
```

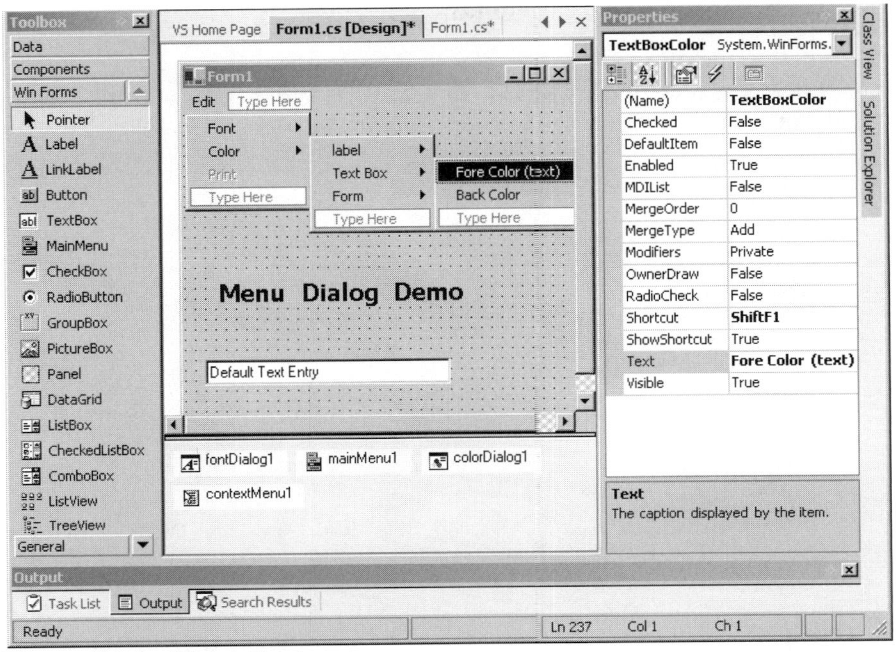

Figure 6.14 Menu Design

```
              // don't allow user the custom color option
              diag.AllowFullOpen = false;

              // set the current text colcr as default for dialog
              diag.Color = textBox1.ForeCclor ;

              // OK: show the dialog box and let the user select
              diag.ShowDialog();

              // set the new text color tc what the user chose
              textBox1.ForeColor = diag.Cclor;
          }
```

A context menu pops up when the user left-clicks over the control. It is created pretty much the same way as a main menu. Once completed, we need to attach it to the control. This is simple to do: Click on the **ContextMenu** entry of the control's **Properties** box. A down arrcw appears to the right of the entry. Clicking on that arrow lists all the context menus currently defined. Click on the one you want to attach. That's it.

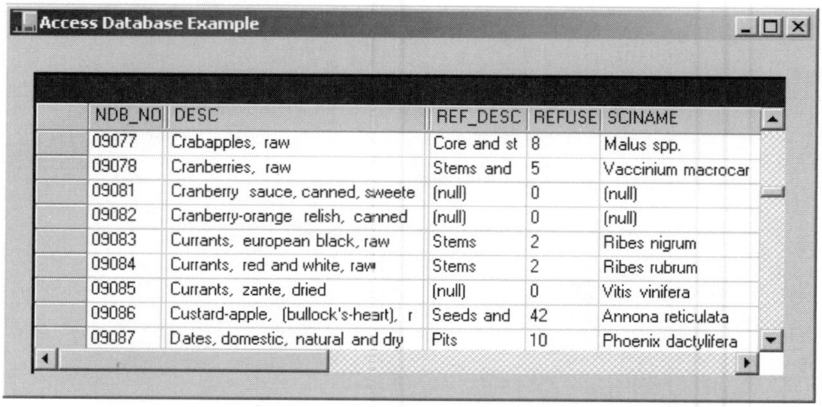

Figure 6.15 The Default `DataGrid` View of an Access Database File

6.10 The `DataGrid` Control

The `DataGrid` control supports the display, entry, and selection of data in table format, with row and column access. This section shows a simple use of `Data-Grid` to display database and XML data. In Figure 6.15, for example, a data grid is used to display the Access database food description table we worked with in Section 5.10.

`DataGrid` is a drag-and-drop control of the Windows Forms designer. We simply drop the grid on the form, then position and size it. Our work involves getting the data into the grid. Typically, this is a two-step process:

1. We retrieve the data from its storage location, copying it into a `DataSet` object. We'll look at two examples: selecting data from an Access database and reading data from an XML file.

2. We set the `DataSource` property of our grid to the `DataSet` table we wish to display. The formatting of the data within the grid is automatic.

The data grid needs to be populated before the form is displayed to the user. I chose to do that within the `Form1` constructor, encapsulated within a member function I called `initDataGrid()`—for example,

```
public Form1()
{
    InitializeComponent();
    initDataGrid();
}
```

C# PRIMER

`InitializeComponent()` is a function generated by the Windows Forms designer. It allocates and sets the properties of both the form and the controls dropped on it through our design session. Our code, if any, is placed after that call.

The opening, selection, and retrieval of data within `initDataGrid()` is implemented by the same code sequence as that covered in Section 5.10, up to the filling of the `DataSet` object:

```
private void initDataGrid()
{
    string connect = "Provider=Microsoft.JET.OLEDB.4.0;" +
        @"data source=C:\nutrition\database\FOOD_DES.mdb";

    OleDbConnection db_conn  = new OleDbConnection(connect);
    OleDbDataAdapter adapter = new OleDbDataAdapter();

    string command = "SELECT * FROM FOOD_DES";
    adapter.SelectCommand = new OleDbCommand(command, db_conn);

    DataSet ds = new DataSet();
    adapter.Fill( ds, "FOOD_DES" );

    dataGrid1.DataSource = ds.Tables["FOOD_DES"].DefaultView;
    db_conn.Close();
}
```

To display the data as rows and columns within the `DataGrid` object, we must set `DataGrid`'s `DataSource` property to our `DataSet` object, and its `DataMember` property to the table within the `DataSet` that we wish to display. The following two lines do that explicitly:

```
dataGrid1.DataSource = ds;
dataGrid1.DataMember = "Food_DES";
```

Two shortcuts accomplish the same in a single assignment:

```
dataGrid1.DataSource = ds.Tables["Food_DES"].DefaultView;
dataGrid1.SetDataBinding( ds, "Food_DES" );
```

The following code fragment illustrates a second common data source for our control: an XML file (see Section 5.11 for a discussion of XML processing).

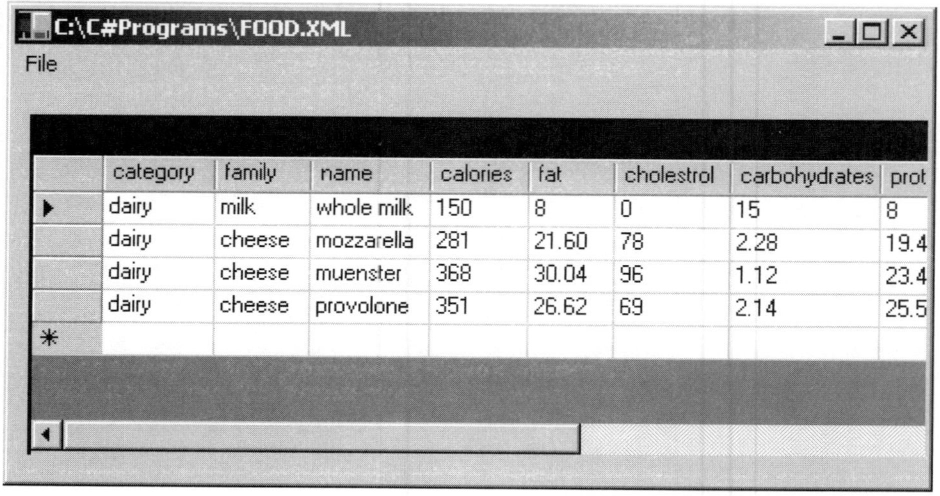

	category	family	name	calories	fat	cholestrol	carbohydrates	prot
▶	dairy	milk	whole milk	150	8	0	15	8
	dairy	cheese	mozzarella	281	21.60	78	2.28	19.4
	dairy	cheese	muenster	368	30.04	96	1.12	23.4
	dairy	cheese	provolone	351	26.62	69	2.14	25.5
✳								

Figure 6.16   The Default `DataGrid` View of an XML File

The two-step process is the same: We retrieve our data into one or more table formats, then set the `DataGrid`'s `DataSource` to the table we wish to display. Figure 6.16 illustrates the resulting form:

```
DataSet ds = new DataSet();
ds.ReadXml( @"C:\C#Programs\food.xml"; );
dataGrid1.DataSource = ds.Tables[0].DefaultView;
```

We look at the `DataGrid` control again in Chapter 7, which focuses on ASP.NET.

6.11   Adding a `PictureBox` Control

The simplest way of displaying an image is through the `PictureBox` control. The steps to do this are as follows:

1. Click on **PictureBox** in the Windows Forms **Toolbox** window and drag it onto the form.

2. In the **Properties** box, in the **Image** entry, click on the right-hand gray box.

3. An open-file dialog box pops up. Select an image for the dialog to open. When you click **Open,** the image is displayed within the picture box as, for example, in Figure 6.17.

4. Resize the picture box to best display the image.

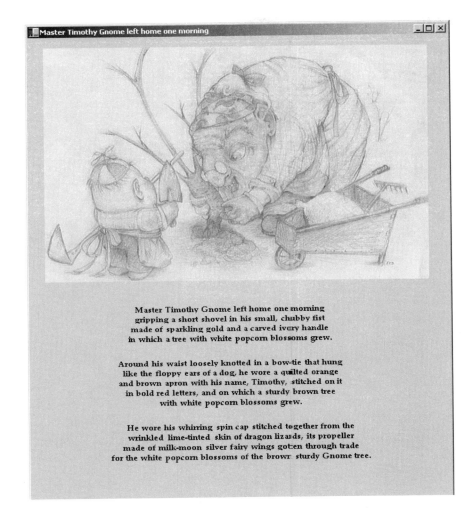

Figure 6.17   A Simple Use of the `PictureBox` Control

As a somewhat more complex example, let's add event handling to `PictureBox`. We'll display several small images. If the user clicks on an image, a new window pops up displaying the larger image. In addition to handling the click event, this example illustrates opening a new window, dynamically creating and drawing a `Bitmap` image using a `Graphics` object, and handling an `OnPaint` window event.

The primary form consists of six `PictureBox` controls and a label (see Figure 6.18). Each picture box supports a click event handler—for example,

```
protected void pictureBox4_Click( object sender, EventArgs e )
{
    Form2 f2 = new Form2( @"c:\C#Primer\bigAnnaPooh.JPG" );
    f2.Show();

    label1.Text = "You last selected " +
                @"c:\C#Primer\bigAnnaPooh.JPG";
}
```

Form2 represents a second window that we've designed; you can see it listed to the right of our primary Form1 window in Figure 6.18. We create a new instance of a Form2 object, passing in the full path of the image file. The form's Show() method displays the form by setting its Visible property to true. We then reset the Text property of the label to display the path of the image last selected.

Form2 represents a blank form. It does not contain a picture box. Rather we've added a Bitmap class member to it:

```
public class Form2 : System.Windows.Forms.Form
{
    // this will hold our image
    public Bitmap theImage;
```

The Bitmap class is part of the System.Drawing namespace. It allows us to query the image about its characteristics, to set or inspect individual pixels, and so on. We create the Bitmap object within the Form2 constructor (for simplicity, I have left out all error checking):

```
public Form2( string theFile )
{
    InitializeComponent();

    // we should do some error checking here
    theImage = new Bitmap( theFile );
    Text = theFile;

    AutoScroll = true;
    AutoScrollMinSize = theImage.Size;

    ClientSize = new Drawing.Size( theImage.Width+5,
                                    theImage.Height+5 );
}
```

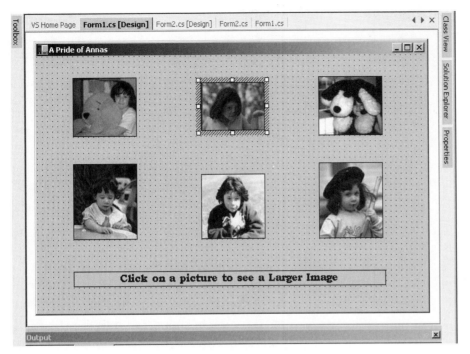

Figure 6.18 A More Complex `PictureBox` Example

We invoke the version of the `Bitmap` constructor that takes a `string` parameter representing the image file. We then set the title bar of the `Form2` window by assigning `Text` the path and file name of the image.

If `AutoScroll` is set to `true`, scroll bars are automatically provided if the image extends outside the form's client region. `AutoScrollMinSize` represents the minimum height and width of the scroll bars in pixels. `ClientSize` represents the size of the form's client area where controls or graphics can be placed. It does not include the borders and title bar.

All that's left to do is draw the image to the client area of the form. We'll do that by providing the form with its own instance of the `OnPaint()` handler:

```
protected override void OnPaint( PaintEventArgs e ){
    if ( theImage != null ){
        Graphics g = e.Graphics;
        g.DrawImage( theImage, ClientRectangle );
    }
}
```

The `PaintEventArgs` object passed to `OnPaint()` contains the `Graphics` object that we'll use to draw the image. A paint event occurs when a control is redrawn. The `Graphics` class, defined within `System.Drawing`, represents the drawing surface to use to paint the control. `DrawImage()` draws the image passed to it within the client area of the control, the second parameter passed to the method.

IThe Windows Forms designer greatly simplifies the design and implementation of interactive graphical front ends for our programs. This tour has been necessarily brief. It has focused on the most commonly used controls, such as buttons, list boxes, labels, menus, the data grid, and so on. Additional prebuilt controls include `Splitter`, `ProgressBar`, `Font`, `Color`, and `Print` dialog controls, as well as `TrackBar`, `MonthCalendar`, `DatePicker`, and others. Several of these controls are illustrated in the programs that accompany this text. In addition to using the prebuilt controls, we can create controls of our own—either those we've built or those we've acquired from third parties. In the next chapter we look at the Web Forms designer in support of ASP.NET. Many of the prebuilt Windows Forms controls are also available within the Web Forms designer.

Chapter 7

ASP.NET and Web Forms Designer

During a slow period in the making of the *FireBird* segment of *Fantasia 2000*, I was asked to develop a set of internal Web pages for the segment. To do that, I wrote raw HTML using a editor under UNIX called vi. To see what the stuff looked like, I concurrently opened the HTML file within the Netscape Web browser. I positioned the two windows side by side. I would modify the HTML in the editor, save it, then hit the Netscape **Refresh** button to see the effect of the change.

This was not very sophisticated—okay, it was downright primitive—but the result was nice enough that I was asked to extend the pages to include the other *Fantasia 2000* segments. Wanting to jazz it up somewhat, I added a bit of Java-Script to dynamically compute a *days-until-opening* countdown. Unfortunately, several executives felt that a prominent display of the release date was tempting fate, and they requested that I remove it.[1] There was the end to the dynamic aspect of my Web pages.

This chapter is about how different Web page development is today, in particular with ASP.NET and the Web Forms designer. It is organized as follows: First we step through the development of a reasonably complex Web page using the Web Forms designer. Next we broadly review the Web page abstraction: What is the life cycle of a page, where in that cycle can we insert our code hooks, how are events triggered, when do round-trips occur between the client and server, and so on? The chapter ends with a review of the Web Forms server and validation controls.

---

1. They were needlessly concerned, as it turned out. *Fantasia 2000* was screened as planned on New Year's Eve, 1999.

7.1 Our First Web Forms Program

Our first Web page represents an employee phone directory. It is pictured in Figure 7.1. The employee data is pulled out of a SQL database and displayed within a `DataGrid` control.[2] To illustrate selection within the data grid, our page pretends to dial the selected employee. To illustrate the use of a check box, the page optionally initiates a video stream as well. (The dial-up and video stream support are generously left as exercises for the reader.) The selected employee is highlighted within the data grid. In addition, the person selected, the associated phone number, and whether the video option has been checked are displayed within the text of a label—for example,

```
OK. Dialing: Andrew Fuller at (206) 555-9482 with video on.
```

The page also displays the current time and provides two links: one to a second Web Forms page built within the project (the *Author* link), and one to a URL on the Web (the *Recital* image).

The Web Forms page design and supporting C# code are implemented in much the same way as in Windows Forms. The **Toolbox** window contains controls that we can drag and drop onto our Web Forms page. Each control has its own **Properties** window, and there is a **Properties** window for the page as well.

Although the Web Forms development experience mirrors that of Windows Forms, the Web Forms processing model is much different. The browser through which the user views and interacts with the page represents the *client* side of the application. Our code executes on the *server* side. The handling of an event, such as a button click, represents a round-trip to the server and back.

7.2 Opening an ASP.NET Web Application Project

We'll open a new ASP.NET Web application project.[3] By default the project title is WebApplication1. The default location is displayed as *http://localhost*. Physically, the project is divided between the server's Web content root (`inetpub/wwwroot`) and the `Visual Studio Projects` directory under `MyDocuments`.

---

2. The database is the NorthWind sample SQL Server database supplied by Microsoft.
3. ASP.NET requires both Internet Information Services (IIS) and FrontPage Server Extensions to be installed.

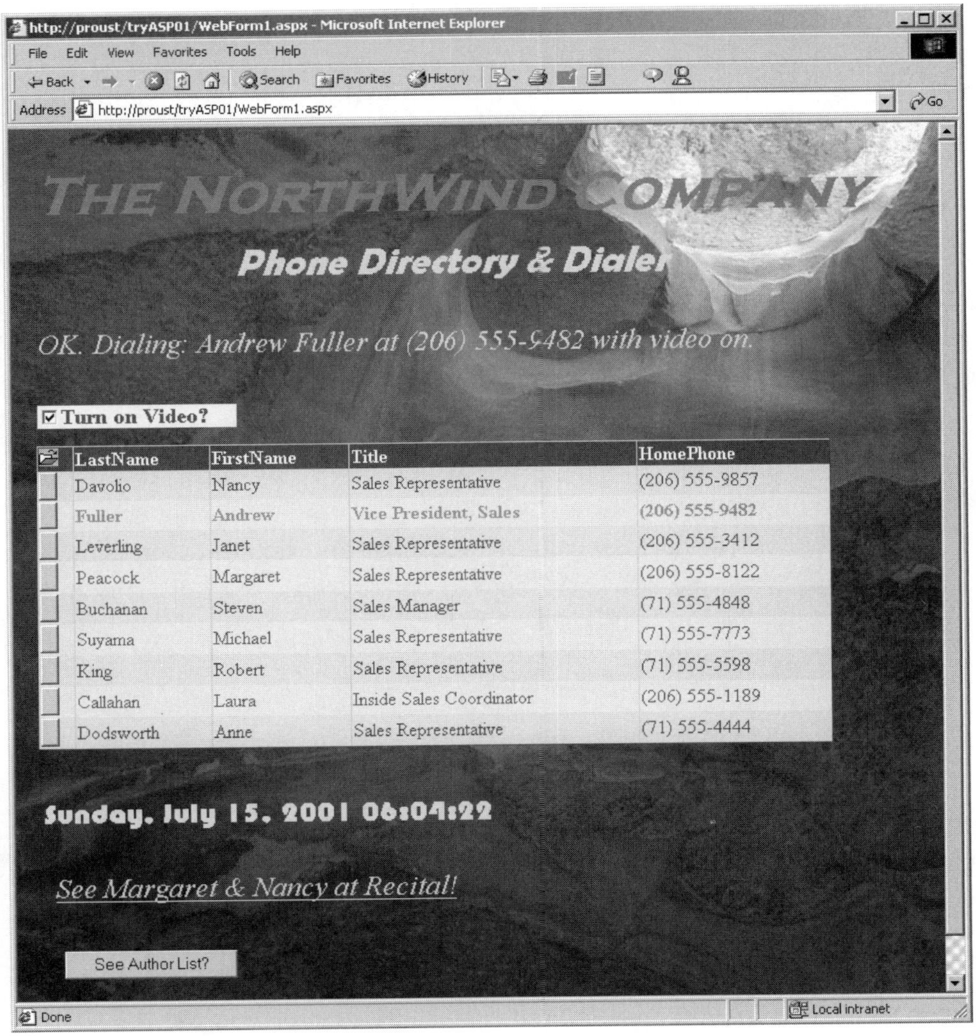

Figure 7.1   A Client Browser Web Forms Page Display

Visual Studio opens the project in the **Design** view of the ASP.NET page. This is the drag-and-drop designer view. Alternatively, we can display the page within the HTML editor. We can toggle between the two views by clicking the **Design** or **HTML** button at the left-hand bottom corner of the page display.

By default, the page is named `WebForm1.aspx`. (An ASP.NET page ends in `.aspx`; the pages of its ASP predecessor end in `.asp`.) To change its name, open the **Properties** window, click on **WebForm1** in the drop-down control menu, and change the `Name` property entry. (Similarly, to change the default name of a control, click on its entry in the **Properties** drop-down control menu and change the control's `ID` property entry.[4])

By default, the **Solution Explorer** window does not show the *code-behind* C# file associated with each page. To see these files, we need to first click on the **Show All Files** icon of the Explorer. A directory expansion symbol (+) now appears beside the `WebForm1.aspx` and `Global.asax` files. Clicking on the + sign displays the C# files `WebForm1.aspx.cs` and `Global.asax.cs`. Double-clicking either file, of course, opens it within the text display window.

Before we begin our implementation, let's execute the empty project. Your browser should pop up with a blank page. The browser's title bar should print the page's URL path, which is what we start with.

In Windows Forms, the `Form` class represents the window abstraction. We add controls to it, we give it a title, and so on. Our class is derived from the `Form` class. By default, it is called `Form1`—for example,

```
public class Form1 : System.Windows.Forms.Form
```

Added controls and callbacks become members of the `Form1` class. Web Forms works on a very similar model. For example, the `Page` class represents the page we design. Our class is derived from the `Page` class. By default, it is called `WebForm1`—for example,

```
public class WebForm1 : System.Web.UI.Page
```

The controls and callbacks we introduce become members of the `WebForm1` class. The public and protected `Page` class members are available as well.

7.2.1 Modifying the Document Properties

The **Properties** window of the general document, referred to as `DOCUMENT` within the **Properties** window, allows us to set up the display characteristics of

---

4. The smoothest approach is to change the default names of the page and its controls before introducing code. Otherwise you may need to go into either the the HTML or the C# code and manually change one or another name that was not automatically updated.

the page, such as its background color (`bgColor`) or whether to tile a background image (`background`). The text of the browser's title bar is set through the `title` property. The color of any text appearing on the page is set through the `text` property. The color of page links is set through the `link` (unvisited links), `vLink` (visited links), and `aLink` (active links) properties.

One of the important decisions is whether to set the `pageLayout` property to `GridLayout` (the location of the controls are at fixed x/y coordinates) or `FlowLayout` (the controls' location flows from the top to the bottom of the page according to the relative sizes and shapes of the objects).

Over 30 properties are associated with the document. Clicking on a property displays a short description of it at the bottom of the **Properties** page, the same as under Windows Forms. Each time we set a property, the underlying HTML text is modified to reflect our change. To incrementally view the changes, toggle between the design and HTML views of the page as you set or reset a property, add a control, and so on.[5]

7.2.2 Adding Controls to the Document: `Label`

The **Toolbox** window supports a collection of Web Forms controls that we can double-click or click and drag onto the page. Each control has an associated **Properties** window. The two static headings on the page in Figure 7.1—that is, *The NorthWind Company* and *Phone Directory & Dialer*—are both `Label` controls. The `Text` property holds the text of the `Label`. `ForeColor` allows us to set the color in which the text is displayed. A series of `Font` properties—such as `Name`, `Bold`, `Italic`, and `Size`—allows us to set specific features of the font.

The `ToolTip` property allows us to display additional text when the mouse rests over the link. Whether this text displays, however, depends on the browser. (The `ToolTip` property is generally available across all the controls. You simply associate it with a line of text.)

The dynamic display of the user's selection:

---

5. Alternatively, you can hand-code the page within the HTML editor, adding controls using a special ASP.NET syntax. The only motivation for doing this is to convert existing ASP pages. The underlying HTML contains the new syntax and should be self-explanatory.

```
OK. Dialing: Andrew Fuller at (206) 555-9482 with video on.
```

is also a `Label` control. It is set programmatically when the label's `Text` property is assigned in the selection event associated with the `DataGrid` control. The other `Label` properties are also available at runtime, of course, if we wish to modify other aspects of `Label`'s display, such as the color or aspects of the font.

7.3 Adding Pages to a Project

We can add a new Web Forms page to our project through the **Add Web Form** or **Add New Item** menu item under **Project.** (There is an **Add New Item** icon as well.) By default, each new page is called `WebFormi.aspx`, where *i* is a digit. This is why our second NorthWind page is called `WebForm2.aspx`.

By default, the first Web Forms page of the project is treated as the project start page. We can specify an alternative start page by setting the start-up page property of the project. To do this, click on the **Properties** menu item under **Project.** A **Property Pages** window displays as pictured in Figure 7.2. Enter the name of the page you wish to have displayed at start-up. (Note that you'll need to explicitly override the default for each configuration property—for example, both the `Debug` and `Release` configurations.)

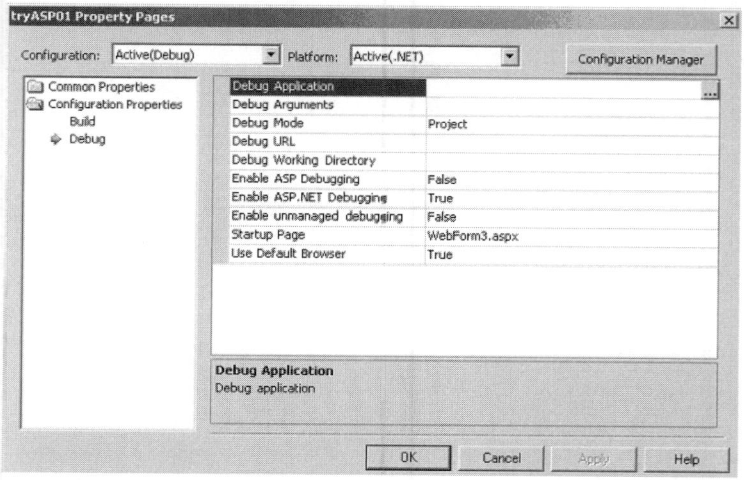

Figure 7.2   Changing the Project Start-up Page

For example, if we wished to add a first page asking the user for a login name and password, we would add the new Web Forms page to the project, design it, and then change the start-up page entry to use that page.

7.4 The `HyperLink` Control: Linking to Other Pages

One common task we need to provide for is that of navigating links to other pages, both third-party Web links, such as http://www.amazon.com, and other ASP.NET pages in our project. We do this with the `HyperLink` control, setting its `NavigateUrl` property to either a URL or another page. The `Text` property displays the description of the link—for example, *See Margaret & Nancy at Recital!* is the text of a `HyperLink` control in Figure 7.1.

The `NavigateUrl` string can be any valid Web location. For example, the NorthWind link displays a Renoir painting of a piano recital currently available at

```
http://www.ibiblio.org/wm/paint/auth/renoir/renoir.filles-piano.jpg
```

Alternatively, if we click to the right of the `NavigateUrl` property, a file dialog box pops open displaying the contents of our project directory. We can select any of the project Web pages—for example,

```
NavigateUrl        WebForm2.aspx
```

We can represent the `HyperLink` control by an image rather than through its `Text` property by setting the `ImageUrl` property. If both are set, the `ImageUrl` property takes precedence and the text is not displayed. If the image is unavailable, the text in the `Text` property is displayed. If the `ToolTip` property is left blank, the `Text` property is treated as the text of the tool tip as well.

The `Target` property specifies the target window within which to display the page. If we leave it blank, the currently active window is the target. To display the page in a new browser window, we select `_blank` from the drop-down menu.

7.5 The `DataGrid` Control

To allow the user to select an employee row of the `DataGrid`, we must provide a *button column*. A button column can be any of three types: **Select; Edit, Update, Cancel;** or **Delete.** Clicking on a specific button column raises its associated event. For example, the blank push-button in the leftmost `DataGrid` column is a button column of type **Select.** When the user clicks on it, a select event is raised. Here is the associated handler:

```
public void
DataGrid1_SelectedIndexChanged (object sender, EventArgs e)
{
   Label5.Text = "OK. Dialing: " +
         DataGrid1.SelectedItem.Cells[2].Text + " " +
         DataGrid1.SelectedItem.Cells[1].Text + " at " +
         DataGrid1.SelectedItem.Cells[4].Text + " with video ";
   Label5.Text += CheckBox1.Checked ? "on." : "off.";
}
```

To insert a button column in a data grid, click on the `Columns` property of a `ButtonColumn` object. Click the push-button. A window pops open. Click the + sign to the right of the **Button Column** entry. Click on **Select,** and then click the arrow push-button (**>**) between the **Available columns** and **Selected columns** elements. Fill in the text boxes as appropriate. Figure 7.3 provides a snapshot of a completed `Columns` property window.

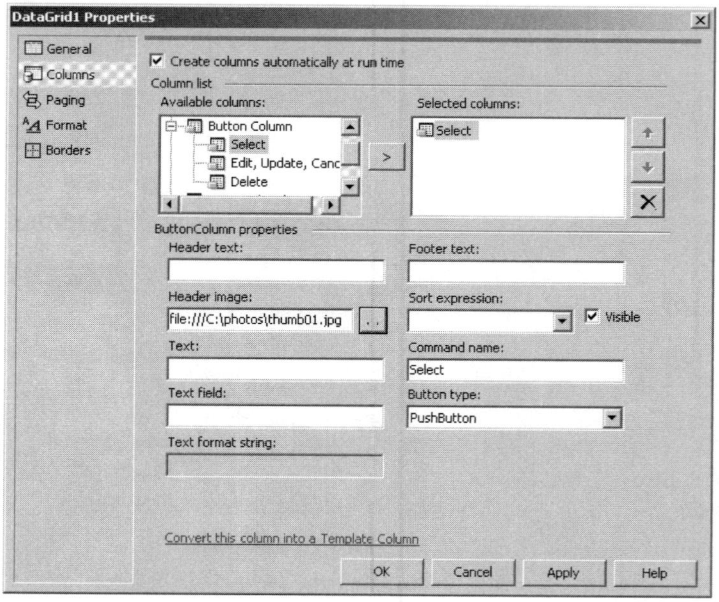

Figure 7.3   Adding a Button Column to a Data Grid

7.6 Understanding the Page Event Life Cycle

Events are raised on the client side as the user interacts with the form. The event information is captured and either immediately transmitted to the Web server through an HTTP post or cached until a post is triggered. The actual event handling is carried out on the server. When done, the modified page is then rendered into HTML and streamed back to the client for display.

Because event handling requires a round-trip, events that occur frequently and that can be raised without the user ever being aware, such as a *mouse-over*, are not supported. In fact, by default only *click events* cause the page to be posted back to the server. *Change events,* such as the filling in of a text box or the selection of a radio button, are captured but do not cause an immediate post. When a post does occur, these captured events are raised and processed before the event that triggered the post; the order of processing the pending events, however, is undefined. (To force the immediate posting of a change event, we can set the control's `AutoPostBack` property to `true`.)

A Web Forms page goes through a complete life cycle on the Web server following the initial page request and with each subsequent round-trip. In the life cycle's first phase, the compiled page is retrieved and loaded. The page and control *view states* are initialized (or restored if this represents a post back). A `Load` event is then raised and the associated callback is invoked.

In our application we need to populate a `DataGrid` control with the North-Wind employee records from our SQL database before displaying the page to the user. The `Page_Load()` event handler is where this kind of one-time page initialization is placed.

Here are the three steps in binding data to a Web control. First, we populate a `DataSet` object with the SQL database records. We then set the `DataGrid` object's `DataSource` property to the first table within the data set. Under Windows Forms, this would be sufficient for the successful display of the data grid. Under Web Forms we must then explicitly invoke the `DataBind()` method of the `DataGrid` object; otherwise neither the data nor the grid displays.[6]

---

6. This example captures something of the nature of learning a new technology. If we do not invoke `DataBind()`, no warning is generated. Nothing seems wrong, but nothing is working. In this case, what you don't know can drive you up the wall.

```
protected void Page_Load(object sender, EventArgs e)
{
    DateTime theDate = DateTime.Now;
    Label3.Text = theDate.ToLongDateString() + " " +
                  theDate.ToLongTimeString();

    string cs = "server=localhost;uid=sa;pwd=;database=northwind";
    SqlConnection conn = new SqlConnection( cs );

    string cmd =
        "select LastName,FirstName,Title,HomePhone from Employees";

    SqlCommand scmd = new SqlCommand( cmd, conn );
    DataSet ds = new DataSet();

    SqlDataAdapter sda = new SqlDataAdapter();
    sda.SelectCommand = scmd;

    sda.Fill( ds, "Employees" );
    conn.Close();

    // OK: fill the DataGrid
    DataGrid1.DataSource = ds.Tables[0].DefaultView;

    // now bind the data ...
    DataGrid1.DataBind();
}
```

This implementation is *almost* correct. The problem is that `Page_Load()` is invoked with each post back. Because the database does not change between round-trips, there is no benefit in executing the database code more than once, although we would like to update the `DateTime` object with each round-trip.

We need to execute code conditionally, on the basis of whether the `Page_Load()` invocation is in response to a page request or a subsequent post back. We do this through a test of the `IsPostBack` property of the page. When it evaluates to `false`, `Page_Load()` is handling the initial page request:

```
protected void Page_Load(object sender, EventArgs e)
{
    // always evaluate this
    DateTime theDate = DateTime.Now;
    Label3.Text = theDate.ToLongDateString() + " " +
                  theDate.ToLongTimeString();
```

```
    // evaluate this once at the initial page request
    if ( ! IsPostBack )
    {
        // the database code goes here
    }
}
```

At the other end of the life cycle the page is disposed of following the HTML rendering of its content back to the client. An `Unload` event is raised. We can add our code to the event handler to perform any necessary cleanup.

7.7   The Data Provider

All interactions with a database are carried out through a *data provider*. In Section 5.10 we walked through the OLE DB data provider. This section steps through the analogous use of the SQL Server data provider defined within the `System.Data.SqlClient` namespace. It can be used with Microsoft SQL Server 7.0 or later versions.

Here are the steps necessary, using the SQL Server data provider, first to connect to and select data from a database, and then to fill a `DataSet` object with the retrieved data:

1. Create a *connection* string. The string must identify the server, user ID, password, and database—for `example`,

   ```
   string cs = "server=localhost;uid=sa,pwd=;database=northwind";
   ```

2. Create a *selection* command string. This minimally consists of a `SELECT` part and a `FROM` part. The `SELECT` part determines which columns are read from each row. The `FROM` part identifies the table from which to read—for `example`,

   ```
   "SELECT LastName,FirstName,Title,HomePhone FROM Employees";
   ```

3. Create a `SqlConnection` object init alized with the connection string. We must be careful to explicitly close the connection when we are finished with it through either `Close()` or `Dispose()`:

   ```
   using System.Data.SqlClient;
   SqlConnection db_conn = new SqlConnection( cs );
   // OK: access the data source ...
   db_conn.Close();
   ```

4. Create a `SqlDataAdapter` data adapter object. Next create a `SqlCom-mand` object initialized with the command string and the connection object. `SqlCommand` retrieves the data. Finally, assign the command object to the data adapter's `SelectCommand` property:

```
SqlDataAdapter adapter = new SqlDataAdapter();
adapter.SelectCommand  = new SqlCommand( cmd, conn );
```

5. Create an instance of a `DataSet` object and pass it to the data adapter's `Fill()` method, together with a name for the table within which to place the data. This executes the select command and places the data retrieved into the named `DataTable`. If the `DataTable` does not exist, it is created:

```
DataSet ds = new DataSet();
adapter.Fill( ds, "Employees" );
```

Once the data is within the `DataSet` object, we manipulate all of the data through that object. In our case we choose to display the data within a Web Forms `DataGrid` control.

7.8   Web State Management

A Web Forms page is re-created from scratch with each server round-trip. Information associated with the page's view states is saved automatically and restored during the page's load phase. This includes the state of the page and its current properties, as well as the state and base properties of the controls of the page. For example, the `Text` properties of controls, the `Checked` property of boxes and radio buttons, the `Items` object associated with a data list, and so on, are maintained across round-trips without our having to do anything. Values not associated with controls, however, are lost between round-trips, unless we explicitly preserve them. Let's look at an example that both illustrates Web state management and introduces us to a handful of additional controls.

The application is simple. We present the user with an `ImageButton` control that displays two figures: my daughter Anna and Winnie-the-Pooh. The user is asked to click on the button. If the user clicks on Winnie's face, it's considered a *Pooh* hit. If the user clicks on Anna's face, it's considered an *Anna* hit. Otherwise, it is considered a miss. The hit count is updated with each user click. In addition, we populate a `ListBox` control with the *x/y* coordinates of each user click, together with whether it is an *Anna* or a *Pooh* hit, or represents a miss.

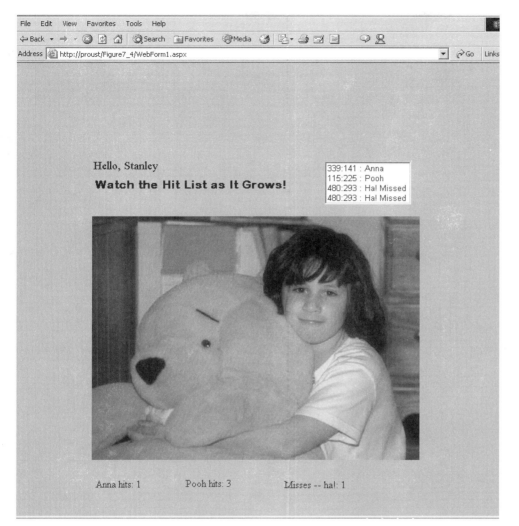

Figure 7.4　Session 2 of HitOrMissPooh

In addition, we request that the user enter his or her name in a `TextBox`. We display the name in a `Label` object, then turn to `false` the `Visible` property of both the `TextBox` and the `Label` requesting the user name. A snapshot of the application is presented in Figure 7.4.

What's hard about this? Recall that each click represents a round-trip. The page and control properties, together with the data placed in the `ListBox`, `TextBox`, and `Label` objects, are saved and restored automatically in the page and control view states. The three hit count values, however, represent data that we have to manage ourselves.

The four instances recorded in the `ListBox` object represent the four clicks of the current session. The count below the picture records six hits, however. Although we see that two misses occurred, the miss count shows only one. The reason is that our representation doesn't persist across round-trips. The *Pooh* count lists four hits, but there was only one this session. The other three occurred in an earlier session. Our representation of this value persists not only across round-trips, but across page sessions as well. This is a bit too robust! The *Anna* count is the only correct hit count. In addition, the hit count across sessions is correctly persisted.

In the following sections we'll look at each of the state management solutions in turn. First let's briefly look at the `TextBox`, `ImageButton`, and `List-Box` controls.

7.8.1   Adding a `TextBox` Control

The `TextBox` control should be familiar from our use of it under Windows Forms. We can set the `TextMode` property to `SingleLine`, `MultiLine`, or `Password`. `SingleLine` accepts as many characters as specified by `Max-Length` or ends when the user hits **Enter.** Setting `MaxLength` to `0` allows an unlimited number of characters.

`MultiLine` causes one or two scroll bars to be inserted within the `Text-Box`, which can now accept an unlimited number of text lines. If the `Wrap` property is set to `true`, a new line is generated whenever the text extends past the length of the `TextBox`. Only a single north-south scroll bar is present. If the `Wrap` property is set to `false`, each line extends until the user enters a new line. A second east-west scroll bar is added. `Password` causes the entry to be displayed as asterisks.

The `TextBox` event handler in the example sets the `Text` property of a `La-bel` to a greet-the-user string. It then sets to `false` the `Visible` property of both the `Label` requesting the user's name and the `TextBox` holding the user's response, essentially wiping them from the display at the same time the greeting appears:

```
private void TextBox1_TextChanged(object sender, EventArgs e)
{
    Label1.Text = "Hello, " + TextBox1.Text;

    TextBox1.Visible = false;
    Label3.Visible = false;
}
```

7.8.2   Adding an `ImageButton` Control

What makes the `ImageButton` control interesting is that the event argument passed to the event handler contains the x and y coordinate properties of the mouse click. This is how I determine the hit or miss characteristic of the click:

```
private void ImageButton1_Click( object sender,
                           System.Web.UI.ImageClickEventArgs e)
{
    // x and y hot zones for the image
    int [] AnnaZone = { 302, 388, 75, 194 };
    int [] PoohZone = { 62, 196, 108, 301 };

    // OK: simple test of hit or miss ...
    if ( e.X >= AnnaZone[0] && e.X <= AnnaZone[1] &&
         e.Y >= AnnaZone[2] && e.Y <= AnnaZone[3] )
    { ... }
    else
    if ( e.X >= PoohZone[0] && e.X <= PoohZone[1] &&
         e.Y >= PoohZone[2] && e.Y <= PoohZone[3] )
    { ... }
    else { ... } // miss ...
}
```

The `ImageUrl` property specifies the image to display. It can be either local or remote. The `ToolTip` property is useful because there is no `Text` property to provide instruction to the user. The ability to determine the mouse click location allows us to support different behaviors within the same button.

7.8.3   Adding a `ListBox` Control

The `ListBox` control in this example is being used only to display each mouse click. It does not support user selection of an item, so I have not associated an event handler with it. The code to add an item to the `ListBox` looks like this:

```
private void
ImageButton1_Click( object sender,
                     System.Web.UI.ImageClickEventArgs e)
{
    string coords =
        e.X.ToString() + ":" + e.Y.ToString();

    if ( e.X >= AnnaZone[0] && e.X <= AnnaZone[1] &&
         e.Y >= AnnaZone[2] && e.Y <= AnnaZone[3] )
    {
        coords += " : Anna";
        // ...
    }

    // same for Pooh and for a miss ...

    ListBox1.Items.Add( coords );
}
```

`Items` is the collection object in which the elements are stored. It is a specialized class named `ListItemCollection`. It supports both `Capacity` and `Count` properties, and provides an indexer for element access, as well as methods for adding, searching, and removing elements.

The `ListBox` can have its `SelectionMode` property set for either `Single` or `Multiple` selection. Under `Single` selection, `SelectedIndex` holds the index of the selected item, or −1 to indicate that no selection has been made. Under `Multiple` selection, `SelectedIndex` holds the index of the lowest item selected. To find the remaining items selected, we iterate across each item, testing its `Selected` property. `SelectedItem` holds a reference either to the selected item in `Single` mode, or to the lowest indexed selected item in `Multiple` mode. For example, here is an event handler for `ListBox` selection events that handles both `Single` and `Multiple` modes:

```
private void
ListBox1_SelectedIndexChanged( object sender, EventArgs e)
{
    int ix = ListBox1.SelectedIndex;

    if ( ix == -1 ) // shouldn't happen
        return;
```

```
        if ( ListBox1.SelectionMode == ListSelectionMode.Single )
        {
            // OK: one item; let's get it and do something ...
            ListItem li = ListBox1.SelectedItem;

            // the something goes here ...
            return;
        }

        // maximum required capacity
        ArrayList select_elems = new ArrayList(ListBox1.Items.Count);
        select_elems.Add( ListBox1.Items[ ix++ ] );

        // this could also have been
        // select_elems.Add( ListBox1.SelectedItem );

        // now we need to collect the other selections ...
        while ( ix < ListBox1.Items.Count )
                if ( ListBox1.Items[ ix ].Selected )
                    select_elems.Add( ListBox1.Items[ ix++ ] );
                else break;

        // OK: now we do something with them
    }
```

7.9   Managing State: Class Members

How do we store the mouse click count? My first thought was to introduce instance members within the `WebForm1` class that represents the page:

```
public class WebForm1 : System.Web.UI.Page
{
    // generated by Web Forms designer ...
    protected System.Web.UI.WebControls.TextBox TextBox1;
    protected System.Web.UI.WebControls.Label Label1;
    protected System.Web.UI.WebControls.Label Label2;
    protected System.Web.UI.WebControls.ListBox ListBox1;
    protected System.Web.UI.WebControls.Label Label3;
    protected System.Web.UI.WebControls.ImageButton ImageButton1;

    // OK: my guys ...
    protected int AnnaCount;
    protected int PoohCount;
    protected int MissCount;
```

Unfortunately, this fails miserably. The page is reloaded with each post back, and each instance member is initialized to its default value. The control view state is then restored before the `Load` event is invoked. This means that with each post back, class instance variables are always initialized back to `0`. If an instance is set to `1` within the on-click event handler, that value is lost.

Turning the three instance members into static members appears to work correctly, but only for a session of a single page. The value associated with each static member of the page persists across posts back, and therefore reflects the running hit count. Unfortunately, the value also persists across sessions running either concurrently or following one another. This is why the *Pooh* count in Figure 7.4 is too large. It reflects the mouse clicks of the current session and a previous session.

7.10 Managing State: The `Session` Object

How do we correctly maintain values across posts back of a page? An `HttpSessionState` class object is maintained for each user that requests a page from an ASP.NET application. We store and retrieve values within this session object that we wish to persist across posts back. This object can be accessed through the page's `Session` property.

To initialize the values within the `Session` object, we need a hook into its initialization. The `Session_Start()` event handler provides just that hook. It is invoked once just prior to the start of a session. This is where we will insert our *Anna, Pooh,* and *Miss* count values that we increment with each appropriate user mouse click—for example,

```
protected void Session_Start(Object sender, EventArgs e)
{
    // OK: for curiosity's sake, let's announce ourselves …
    Response.Write( "<B>Inside Session_Start()</B> <br>" );
    Response.Write( "<B>Session_ID: "   +
                        Session.SessionID + "</B> <br>" );

    Session.Add( "AnnaCount", 0 );
    Session.Add( "PoohCount", 0 );
    Session.Add( "MissCount", 0 );
}
```

`Session_Start()` is found inside the project-generated `Global.asax.cs` file. (If you don't see it, click the **Show All Files** icon in the **Solution Explorer** window. It is displayed as though it were a subdirectory of the `Global.asax` file.) Inside the file the project has defined a class named `Global` with several event handlers, including `Session_Start()`:

```
public class Global : System.Web.HttpApplication { ... }
```

The `HttpApplication` class encapsulates properties common to all application objects within ASP.NET. These include the `Session` object, a `Response` object that supports transmission of HTTP response data to a client, a `Request` object that provides access to incoming HTTP request data, as well as a `Server`, a `User`, and an `Application` object.

Inside of our `WebForm1` event handler, we access the `Session` values by a name index just as we do for a `Hashtable`—for example,

```
private void
ImageButton1_Click(object sender, ImageClickEventArgs e)
{
    if ( e.X >= AnnaZone[0] && e.X <= AnnaZone[1] &&
        e.Y >= AnnaZone[2] && e.Y <= AnnaZone[3] )
    {
        Session[ "AnnaCount" ] =
                (int)Session[ "AnnaCount" ] + 1;

        Label5.Text = Session[ "AnnaCount" ].ToString() +
                " Anna Hits!";
    }
}
```

7.11 Managing State: The `Application` Object

There is analogous support for maintaining values across sessions within the `Application` object. The `Global` class provides a skeletal definition of an `Application_Start()` event handler. It is invoked once at the start of the application. This is where we initialize global data for our application. For example, let's provide values to hold total mouse clicks across all sessions:

```
protected void
Application_Start(Object sender, EventArgs e)
{
        Application.Add( "TotalAnnaCount", 0 );
```

```
        Application.Add( "TotalPoohCount", 0 );
        Application.Add( "TotalMissCount", 0 );
}
```

These values can be accessed concurrently through multiple sessions, so we need to be more careful when writing them. For example, the following read and write operation of the `AnnaCount` value:

```
Application[ "AnnaCount" ] =
        (int) Application[ "AnnaCount" ] + 1;
```

is potentially unsafe because a concurrent access may occur between the read and assignment of the value. A safer implementation provides a lock to ensure an atomic read/write operation:

```
Application.Lock(); // locks entire Application object
Application[ "AnnaCount" ] =
        (int) Application[ "AnnaCount" ] + 1;
Application.Unlock();
```

We might access this variable as follows within `Page_Load()`:

```
private void Page_Load(object sender, System.EventArgs e)
{
    if ( ! this.IsPostBack )
        Label7.Text =
            "Total Anna Hits Prior to This Session: " +
            Application[ "AnnaCount" ].ToString();
}
```

7.12 Validation Controls

Whenever we solicit user input, the possibility exists that the user will make an error. If possible, we'd like to catch as many errors as possible before we process the form. For example, if we are accepting credit card information, we can verify that the user has entered a credit card number and expiration date. The credit card number should be all digits, of course, and for Visa and Mastercard it should be 16 digits in length. Beyond that, we can't determine if it represents a valid credit card number. Similarly, the expiration date's month should be between 1 and 12, the year should be equal to or greater than the current year, and so on.

Figure 7.5   An Appointment Schedule Form

Web Forms provides validation controls to simplify the checking of user input. One or more validation controls are associated with an input control. We can specify error messages to display in case of invalid input, either next to the control or in a separate summary control.

In the following sections we'll look at each of the validation controls in turn. The page we'll use as an example prompts the user to make a fitness appointment with one of three trainers; it is pictured in Figure 7.5. This gives me the opportunity to briefly introduce some additional controls: `DropDownList`, `RadioButton`, `CheckBox`, `Image`, and `Calendar`.

7.13   Adding a `DropDownList` Control

The `DropDownList` control allows the user to select one of any number of items. In our case we wish to present the user with the available appointment times. Unlike a list box, a drop-down list displays only one item—the item currently selected. To see the entire item list, the user clicks on the right-hand down arrow. We can either add each item individually to the list:

```
DropDownList1.Items.Add( "7:00 AM" );
```

or else assign a collection of items to the control's `DataSource` property—for example,

```
private void
Page_Load( object sender, System.EventArgs e )
{
    if ( ! IsPostBack )
    {
        string [] times = {
                "7:00 AM",   "8:00 AM",   "9:00 AM",
                "10:00 AM", "11:00 AM", "12:00 Noon",
                "2:00 PM",   "3:00 PM",   "4:00PM"
        };

        DropDownList1.DataSource = times;
        DropDownList1.DataBind();
    }
}
```

By default, the first item of the item list is displayed prior to the user selection. If we wish to initially display a different item, we must set the `Selected-Index` property. For example, to have *12:00 Noon* display, we would write the following:

```
DropDownList1.SelectedIndex = 5;
```

Typically we access the selected item through the `SelectedItem` property rather than using the `SelectedIndex` as a subscript to `Items`. The event handler is triggered not by a selection, but by a *change* in the selection. If the user selected **8:00 AM** five times, only the first selection invokes our event handler.

```
private void
DropDownList1_SelectedIndexChanged( object sender, EventArgs e )
{
    Label3.Text = DropDownList1.SelectedItem.Text;
}
```

7.14 Adding a Group of `RadioButton` Controls

The `RadioButton` of Web Forms is similar to that of Windows Forms, except that by default the event is cached rather than immediately handled. In the following example I've used a `RadioButtonList` control instead, binding to its `DataSource` property in a manner similar to that of `DropDownList`:

```
private void Page_Load( object sender, System.EventArgs e )
{
    if ( ! IsPostBack )
    {
        string [] trainers = {
                    "Jennifer Juniper",
                    "Brian Bradley",
                    "Anita Anastasia"
            };

        RadioButtonList1.DataSource = trainers;
        RadioButtonList1.DataBind();
    }
}
```

`SelectedIndexChanged()` is also the event handler for this control. The `SelectedIndex` property identifies the selected radio button by its position within the item list. `SelectedItem` is a handle to the actual item. The implementation looks the same:

```
private void
RadioButtonList1_SelectedIndexChanged( object s, EventArgs e )
    { Label4.Text = RadioButtonList1.SelectedItem.Text; }
```

We can control the layout of the radio buttons through the `RepeatColumns` and `RepeatDirection` properties of the control. For example, rather than displaying the buttons from top to bottom, we can display them horizontally in three columns as follows:

```
RadioButtonList1.RepeatColumns = 3;
RadioButtonList1.RepeatDirection = RepeatDirection.Horizontal;
```

The radio button items in the list are mutually exclusive. If we wish to provide the user with a choice of multiple selections, we must provide a group of check boxes instead.

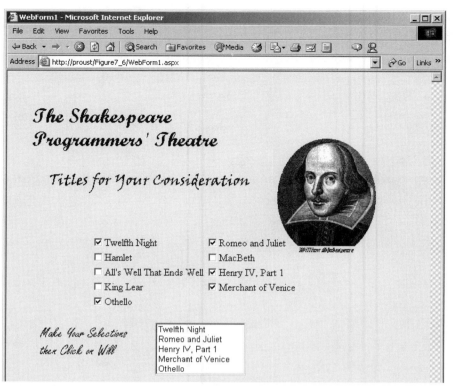

Figure 7.6 A `CheckBoxList` Control Example

7.15   Adding a CheckBoxList Control

This section adds a `CheckBoxList` control. The motivation is to allow the user to vote for multiple items by clicking on them. The page is pictured in Figure 7.6.

The initialization of the `CheckBoxList` control is similar to that of the previous two list controls, except that we specify that the check boxes should be displayed in columns of two items per line:

```
private void Page_Load(object sender, System.EventArgs e)
{
    if ( ! IsPostBack )
    {
        string [] selections = {
            "Twelfth Night", "Romeo and Juliet", "Hamlet",
            "MacBeth", "All\'s Well That Ends Well",
            "Henry IV, Part 1", "King Lear",
            "Merchant cf Venice", "Othello"
        };
```

```
CheckBoxList1.DataSource = selections;
CheckBoxList1.DataBind();

// display two items per line

CheckBoxList1.RepeatColumns = 2;
CheckBoxList1.RepeatDirection =
            RepeatDirection.Horizontal;
    }
}
```

The event handler is invoked when the selection of one or more of the boxes is changed. The `SelectedItem` property holds the position of the selected item with the lowest index (or `-1` if no boxes are checked). Unfortunately, we need to iterate across the remainder of the items, checking the `Selected` property of each to determine whether it, too, is selected—for example,

```
private void
CheckBoxList1_SelectedIndexChanged(object s, EventArgs e)
{
    // check if no item is selected ...
    if ( CheckBoxList1.SelectedIndex == -1 )
        return;

    for( int ix = CheckBoxList1.SelectedIndex;
            ix < CheckBoxList1.Items.Count; ++ix  )
    {
        if ( CheckBoxList1.Items[ ix ].Selected )
            ListBox1.Items.Add( CheckBoxList1.Items[ix].Text );
    }
}
```

One aspect of the page that displayed poorly with the original implementation is the situation in which a user votes, changes the selected check boxes, and votes again. My original implementation appended the selected items to those already present in the `ListBox`. This was not really correct.

One solution is to check if the `ListBox` is nonempty and, if so, to clear it by invoking `Clear()`:

```
if ( CheckBoxList1.Items.Count != 0 )
    CheckBoxList1.Items.Clear();
```

Alternatively, we can set the `Vote` button's `Enable` property to `false`. This grays out the display; the user is no longer able to activate the control. In effect, we are not allowing a user to vote more than once within a session.

A second alternative is to set the `EnableViewState` property of the `ListBox` to `false`. The control view state, remember, is what is saved and restored automatically with each round-trip. By disabling the view state associated with the `ListBox`, each time the user clicks **VOTE,** the earlier data inserted within the `ListBox` is lost. Not only is this exactly what we want, but it also illustrates another aspect of state management within ASP.NET.

7.16 Adding Validators to a Control

If you look back at Figure 7.5, you'll see that we must have two input fields to set up an appointment for the user: the user's name and the date of the appointment. A phone number is optional. If submitted, however, we want to confirm whether it is a seven-digit or a ten-digit U.S. phone number. If the user does not select a time, we'll assume that the default time on display is intended. If the user does not select a trainer, we'll make that assignment ourselves.

Web Forms provides the following validation controls (an icon for each is available in the Web Forms section of the **Toolbox** window):

- `RequiredFieldValidator`, which prevents an entry from being skipped. For example, we will attach this to the `TextBox` in which the user enters his or her name. We cannot associate it with the `Calendar`.

- `RangeValidator`, which confirms that an entry falls between a lower and an upper boundary. For example, a month entry might be checked to be a digit between 1 and 12. The values to be compared can be constant values or values from other controls. The types supported are numbers, characters, and the `DateTime` type.

- `CompareValidator`, which compares an entry against a particular value using a specified relational operator. For example, we might compare the selected appointment date to see if it is less than or equal to the current date. The value being compared, as with `RangeValidator`, can be either a constant value or a value from another control. For example, if the user were changing her password, we might have `CompareValidator` check a second entry of the password against the first.

- `RegularExpressionValidator` which verifies that the input matches a regular-expression pattern. This control provides some useful predefined regular expressions, such as phone number, Internet URL, and zip code.

- `CustomValidator`, which checks the input entry using validation logic that we code explicitly.

When we drop a validator control on the form, by default it takes up the amount of space required to display its `ErrorMessage`. Multiple validators associated with a control can end up taking up a lot of real estate on the page.

If we change the validator's `Display` property to `Dynamic`, the validation control takes up no space on the page until its error message is displayed. This approach allows us to stack multiple validators associated with a control. The drawback is that when an error message is displayed, the page layout may abruptly shift to accommodate the message.

Because these validations are performed on the server, error messages do not appear until the page is rendered back to the client.

A validator does not need to be placed next to the control it validates. Rather its placement determines where the error message, if triggered, is displayed on the page.

A common practice is to have all the validator error messages appear in a single location as a list. We do this by dropping a `ValidationSummary` control onto the form in the location where we wish the summary to appear. We set the `HeaderText` property to the string we wish displayed as the summary header. If we wish (and if the client's browser supports it), we can set the `ShowMessageBox` property to `true`. Doing this generates a pop-up summary of the error messages, as well as a display on the page.

The `ErrorMessage` entry of each triggered validator is now directed to the `ValidationSummary` control. What happens at the location of each validator? We have a choice. If we wish, we can set its `Text` property to an alternative text display—maybe an asterisk or an exclamation point. For example, these are my `Text` and `ErrorMessage` entries for our `RequiredFieldValidator` control associated with the `TextBox` that accepts the user's name:

```
ErrorMessage      Please Enter Your Name
Text              <B>****</B>
```

Figure 7.7 Sample `ValidationSummary` Display

Figure 7.7 shows the result, where both the user name and the phone entry are flagged as invalid.

The binding of a validator to a control is accomplished through the `ControlToValidate` property. When we click on it in the **Properties** window of the validator control, a drop-down menu lists the available controls to which we can bind the validator. A validator can be bound to only one control at a time.

The `RegularExpressionValidator` provides a predefined set of regular expressions, such as phone number, Social Security number, zip code, Internet URL, and Internet e-mail address. There is support for phone and postal conventions as well for countries such as Japan, France, and Germany. Alternatively, we can provide our own regular expression against which to match the user's input.

To support multiple valid patterns, we separate the patterns with a bar (|). (Regular expressions are covered in Section 5.6.)

C# PRIMER

In comparing a user entry against a value or range of values, the user input is also validated against the `Type` property—one of `string`, `int`, `double`, `Date`, or `Currency`. If the data type of the entry does not match the validator's `Type` property, the validation fails and the comparison is not carried out.

If the user skips the input field, however, the validation control to compare the data does not fail. For example, if we set up a `RangeValidator` control to check that a `TextBox` entry is between a `MinimumValue` of 1 and a `MaximumValue` of 12, an entry of 13 triggers an error but a blank entry is treated as valid.

If we require field entry, we must associate a `RequiredFieldValidator` control with the control in addition to any explicit testing of that input. Multiple validators associated with a control are evaluated until either all succeed or one fails.

To compare the user input against a constant value, we specify that value in the `ValueToCompare` property of the `CompareValidator` control. By default, `CompareValidator` does an equality comparison. Alternatively, we can set the `Operator` property to one of the following: `NotEqual`, `GreaterThan`, `GreaterThanEqual`, `LessThan`, or `LessThanEqual`.

If we wish, we can compare the user input against the value of another control by setting the `ControlToCompare` property. (It's a drop-down menu of the available controls.) If both the `ValueToCompare` and `ControlToCompare` properties are set, the latter takes precedence—for example,

```
ControlToValidate   DepartureDateEntry
ControlToCompare    ArrivalDateEntry
Type                DateTime
Operator            GreaterThanEqual
```

`CustomValidator` requires that we provide an event handler associated with the control's `ServerValidate` event. It returns a `true` or `false` value. Server-side validation is performed when the page is submitted, but before our code is invoked. Each validation control is invoked in turn. If a validation fails, the `IsValid` property of the validation control is set to `false`. If one or more validation controls fail, the `IsValid` property of the page itself is set to `false`.

7.17 Adding a `Calendar` Control

The `Calendar` control is the most visually elegant of the Web Forms controls. The `SelectionMode` property can be set in one of four modes:

1. `None`: The user can page through the `Calendar` by month but cannot make a selection.

2. `Day`: The user can page through and select any day of the `Calendar` by month.

3. `DayWeek`: The user can page through the `Calendar` by month. The user can either click on an individual day or select a week by clicking on an arrow placed in the leftmost column of the week.

4. `DayWeekMonth`: The same as `DayWeek`, except that the user can also select the entire month by clicking on the double array in the leftmost column of the row holding the days of the week.

Clicking on a day, a week arrow, or a month double arrow (see Figure 7.7) raises the `SelectionChanged` event—unless the item is already marked as selected. The `SelectedDate` property refers to a `DateTime` object that is either the date selected in `Day` mode or the first date in the range of either the week or the month. For example, here is our event handler for the `Calendar` control when the user is able to select only a day:

```
private void
Calendar1_SelectionChanged(object s, EventArgs e)
{
    Label2.Text = Calendar1.SelectedDate.ToLongDateString();
}
```

The `SelectedDates` property contains the collection of the dates for the selected week or month. For example, to display the first and last dates selected, we would use either `SelectedDate` or `SelectedDates[0]` for the first date, and the last `SelectedDates` element for the last date in the selected range. Here is the code to do that, with the values placed in a pair of labels:

```
private void Calendar1_SelectionChanged(object s, EventArgs e)
{
    // really should go in Page_Load()
    Label1.Text =
            Calendar1.TodaysDate.ToLongDateString();
```

```
if ( Calendar1.SelectedDates.Count > 1 )
{
    int last = Calendar1.SelectedDates.Count-1;
    Label3.Text =
         Calendar1.SelectedDates[last].ToLongDateString();
}
else Label3.Text = null;

Label2.Text = Calendar1.SelectedDate.ToLongDateString();
}
```

The `TodaysDate` property of the `Calendar` control represents the current calendar date. By default, it is set to the date of the server on which the page runs. Alternatively, we can assign it any `DateTime` object.

Nearly every aspect of the appearance of the `Calendar` control can be modified through the appearance and style categories of `Calendar` properties. In addition, a set of predefined calendar formats is available. Click on the **Auto-Format** link at the very bottom of the `Calendar` **Properties** window to select from among them.

7.18 Adding an `Image` Control

The `Image` control is largely self-explanatory. The `ImageUrl` property holds the local or remote path of the image. The `AlternateText` property is displayed if the image cannot be found. Under some browsers, `AlternateText` serves as a tool tip if the `ToolTip` property is not set.

7.19 Programming Web Server Controls

All the control properties we've set interactively in the **Properties** window while using the Web Forms designer, such as `ForeColor` or input `Mode` for a `Text-Box`, can also be set within our program. For example, to dynamically reset the `Mode`, `Width`, and `ForeColor` of a `TextBox`, we would write the following,

```
TextBox1.Mode = TextBoxMode.SingleLine;
TextBox1.Width = new Unit( 200, UnitType.Pixel );
TextBox1.ForeColor = Color.Red;
```

where `TextBoxMode` and `UnitType` are enumeration types of alternative property values, and `Red` is a static property of the `Color` class.

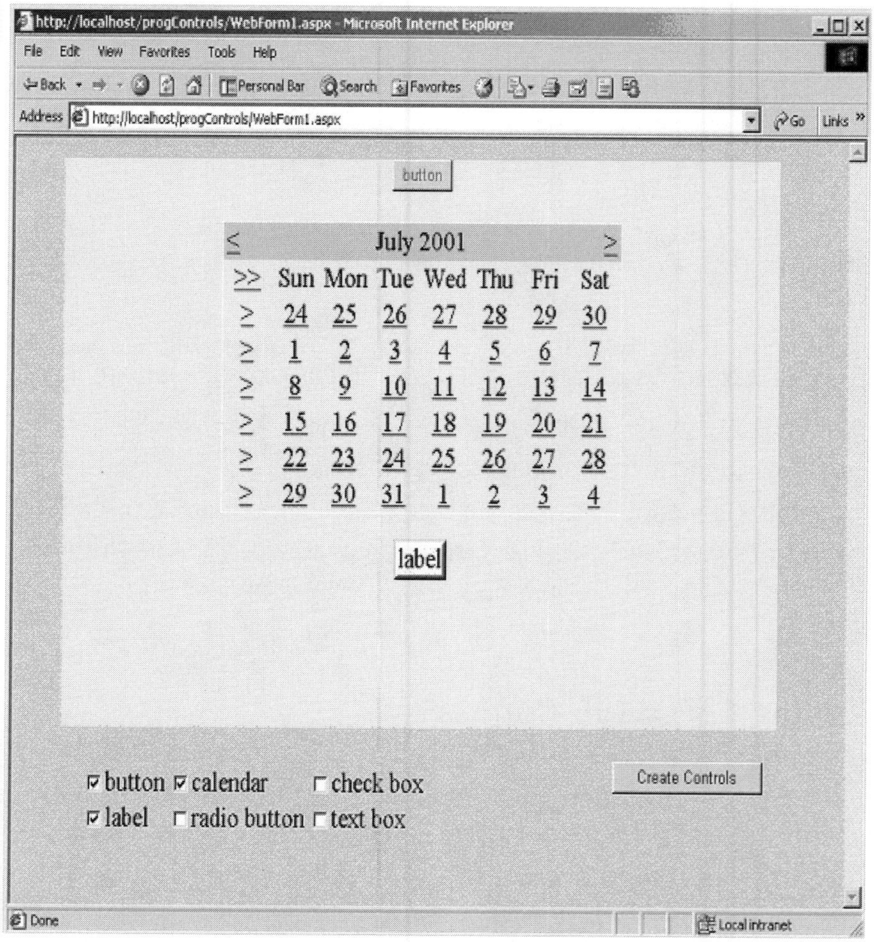

Figure 7.8 Adding Controls to a Page at Runtime

`Color` provides many named colors, such as `Black`, `Blue`, `BlanchedAlmond`, and `BurlyWood`.

In addition to changing the properties of an existing control, we can create controls during the execution of our program. Figure 7.8 pictures an application in which the user selects controls to be added to the page dynamically.

There must be a container into which to add a control created from within the program. The `Panel` control can serve as a container. We add the new control to the `Controls` collection property of the `Panel` class. For example, here is how we add the `Calendar` control:

```
case controlTypes.calendar:
{
    Calendar newCal = new Calendar();
    newCal.SelectionMode = CalendarSelectionMode.DayWeekMonth;
    newCal.ID = controls[ ix ] + id++.ToString();

    Panel1.Controls.Add( newCal );
    Panel1.Controls.Add( new LiteralControl( "<br>" ) );

    break;
}
```

`LiteralControl` allows us to create static text. In this example we are inserting a line break to keep the controls from butting up against one another.

`controlTypes` is an enumeration identifying the control types the user can ask to have created. `controls` is an array of strings identifying those controls; it serves as the `CheckBoxList` data source. `id` is a static integer that allows us to set a unique ID for each control. The event handler for the check box list looks like this:

```
private void
CheckBoxList1_SelectedIndexChanged(object s, EventArgs e)
{
    // check if no item is selected ...
    if ( CheckBoxList1.SelectedIndex == -1 )
        return;

    for( int ix = CheckBoxList1.SelectedIndex;
            ix < CheckBoxList1.Items.Count; ++ix   )
    {
        if ( CheckBoxList1.Items[ ix ].Selected )
            switch( (controlTypes)ix )
            {
                case controlTypes.button:
                    { ... }

                case controlTypes.calendar:
                    { ... }

                // and so on ...
    }
}
```

Dynamically added controls are not automatically saved as part of the view state of the page. Rather we must manage them ourselves or lose them after a round-trip. (For example, make a selection on the Calendar control within the Panel. The controls do not reappear following the post back.)

Typically, then, dynamic controls are created within the Page_Load() event handler in order to be restored with each round-trip. If program data within the controls needs to be restored as well, we'll have to manage that within the Session object.

Chapter 8

The Common Language Runtime

The Common Language Runtime (CLR) provides a runtime environment that manages the execution of code and provides services such as security, versioning, and garbage collection. Metadata about our programs is generated during compilation. The runtime environment uses this metadata to locate and load classes, lay out objects in memory, and so on.

When we build our programs or components, both metadata and code are stored in self-contained units called *assemblies*. An assembly stores information about the components and resources against which it is compiled, as well as the types defined within it. The CLR accesses this information to guarantee that the application has the correct versions of its dependencies. We can access this metadata information as well.

The primary focus of this chapter is runtime access to the metadata information available through the CLR. We begin by looking at the `Assembly` class. From there we turn to two programming topics:

1. The runtime support for *type reflection* made possible by the metadata

2. Introducing custom metadata in the form of `Attribute` classes

We conclude this chapter with a brief look at the machine-independent intermediate language (IL) representation of not just C# but all .NET languages and the `ildasm` tool for exploring the assembly metadata and code.

8.1 Assemblies

A namespace allows us to neatly package the types defined within our component, ensuring that others can safely include our component within their program without any existing code breaking because of unexpected name conflicts. This is a very important guarantee.

Under Visual Studio.NET, the unit of program deployment is the assembly. An assembly serves as a kind of component DNA. It is a self-contained, versionable, self-describing unit of a .NET application. It contains all the executable code we've written, of course. This code is stored in an intermediate language. We'll talk about that a bit later. In addition, it holds metadata about the types within our program, and the environment in which the program was built. This information is generated during the compilation and build of our code. It also contains a *manifest*. The manifest describes the content of the assembly—what is necessary for execution: dependencies, versioning, and security.

Assemblies are loaded on demand. That is, the runtime environment loads the assembly only when our program makes use of a type or associated metadata about the type contained within the assembly. This is when the type's static constructor is executed.

We can access a runtime representation of both our executing assembly and each assembly associated with our program. There are several different ways to do this, depending on how general or specific our retrieval needs are.

What if we need access to all the assemblies associated with our application? First we need to gain access to a representation of the currently executing thread. We access it through the `CurrentDomain` property of the `AppDomain` class. An app domain acts as the container for a process. Assemblies are loaded into an app domain. The following code sequence retrieves all the assemblies associated with the current thread as an array of `Assembly` class objects:

```
AppDomain theApp = AppDomain.CurrentDomain;
Assembly [] currAssemblies = theApp.GetAssemblies();

Console.WriteLine( "The current AppDomain has {0} Assemblies",
                   currAssemblies.Length );
```

In order for this code to compile, we must use the `System.Reflection` namespace, which is where the `Assembly` class is defined (we'll come back to the `Reflection` namespace in Section 8.2):

```
using System.Reflection
```

To retrieve only the `Assembly` object from which our code is executing, we invoke the static `GetExecutingAssembly()` method of the `Assembly` class:

```
Assembly myAssembly = Assembly.GetExecutingAssembly();
```

Alternatively, to retrieve the `Assembly` object within which a particular type is defined, we invoke the static `GetAssembly()` method of the `Assembly` class, passing it the `Type` object associated with the type.

There are two ways to retrieve a `Type` object. If we have an object of the type, we simply invoke its inherited `GetType()` method. Alternatively, we can invoke the static `GetType()` method of the `Type` class, passing it a string holding the name of the type:

```
Object o = new Fibonacci();
Assembly fibAssem = Assembly.GetAssembly( o.GetType() );


Type     calType = Type.GetType( "JulianCalendar" );
Assembly calAssem = Assembly.GetAssembly( calType );
```

We can learn nearly everything that we might wish to know about our component through the `Assembly` class. To retrieve information about the entry point of the `Assembly` object, if it has one, we query the `EntryPoint` property of the `Assembly` class:

```
MethodInfo ep = fibAssem.EntryPoint;
```

The `MethodInfo` class contains detailed information about the method to which it refers, such as its name, access level, return type, parameter list, and so on. It is defined within the `System.Reflection` namespace. We'll look at it further in Section 8.2.

To retrieve all the types defined within the assembly, we invoke the `GetTypes()` method:

```
Type [] types = fibAssem.GetTypes();
```

Alternatively, we can request a specific type by name through the `GetType()` method:

```
Type fibType = fibAssem.GetType( "Fibonacci" );
```

If the type is not found, `GetType()` returns `null`. If we prefer that it throw an exception, we pass in a literal `true` value as a second argument:

```
Type fibType = fibAssem.GetType( "Fibonacci", true );
```

For example, the following output:

```
The current AppDomain has 2 Assemblies

The Assembly FullName Property:
    mscorlib, Ver=1.0.2204.21, Loc="", SN=03689116d3a4ae33

assembly name:    mscorlib
manifest loc:     C:/WINNT/Microsoft.NET/Framework/v1.0.2204/
mscorlib.dll
entry point:      Not Defined
number of types:  1205

The Assembly FullName Property:
    Assemblies, Ver=1.0.471.38017, Loc=""

assembly name:    Assemblies
manifest loc:     C:/C#Programs/Assemblies/bin/Debug/
Assemblies.exe
entry point:      Void Main()
number of types:  2
The types contained within the assembly are:
        type name:  AssemblyEntryPoint
        type name:  AssemblyExplore
```

is generated from the following method:

```
public static void getAssemblies()
{
    AppDomain theApp = AppDomain.CurrentDomain;
    Assembly [] currAssemblies = theApp.GetAssemblies();

    Console.WriteLine( "The current AppDomain has {0} Assemblies",
                          currAssemblies.Length );

    foreach ( Assembly a in currAssemblies )
    {
      message( "\nThe Assembly FullName Property: \n\t",
               a.FullName );
```

```
    int     pos  = a.FullName.IndexOf( ',' );
    string  name = a.FullName.Substring(0, pos);
    Type [] t    = a.GetTypes();

    string     manifestLocation = a.Location;
    MethodInfo theEntry         = a.EntryPoint;

    message( "assembly name:   ", name );
    message( "manifest loc:    ", manifestLocation );
    message( "entry point:     ",
                theEntry != null
                    ? theEntry.ToString():"Not Defined");

    message( "number of types: ", t.Length );

    if ( t.Length < 10 )
    {
        Console.WriteLine(
            "The types contained within the assembly are:");

        foreach ( Type tt in t )
            message( "\ttype name: ", tt.Name );
    }
}
```

We can use the static `Load()` or `LoadFrom()` method of the `Assembly` class to explicitly load an assembly. To create an instance of a type defined within the `Assembly` object, we can use the `CreateInstance()` method. We'll see an example in our discussion of reflection in the next section.

There are quite a number of administrative issues with assemblies that I won't cover, such as whether to package the assembly in a single module or in multiple modules, whether the assembly should be private or shared, and versioning and security issues. By default, Visual Studio generates a private assembly in a single module.

8.2 Runtime Type Reflection

The `System.Reflection` namespace defines a set of special *Info* classes, such as the `MethodInfo` class we saw in the previous section, that provide access to the attributes and metadata of constructors, events, fields, methods, parameters, properties, and so on. These classes are listed in Table 8.1.

Table 8.1 Info Classes within the `System.Reflection` Namespace

class	Description
MemberInfo	Discovers the attributes of a member and provides access to member metadata. Abstract base class.
MethodInfo	Discovers the attributes of a method and provides access to methoc metadata.
ParameterInfo	Discovers the attributes of a parameter and provides access to parameter metadata.
ConstructorInfo	Discovers the attributes of a class constructor and provides access to constructor metadata.
PropertyInfo	Discovers the attributes of a property and provides access to property metadata.
FieldInfo	Discovers the attributes of a field and provides access to field metadata.
EventInfo	Discovers the attributes of an event and provides access to event metadata.

All reflection operations are rooted in the abstract `Type` class. Access of the reflection *Info* classes goes through the associated `Type` object of a type. The `Type` class is the key to accessing type information of objects at runtime.

There are three primary methods of retrieving a `Type` object. If we have an arbitrary object, its associated `Type` object is retrieved by an invocation of the inherited nonvirtual `GetType()` method of the `Object` class:

```
public static
void TypeDisplay( object o )
{
    Type t = o.GetType();

    // ... OK: now we have metadata access
}

// example of TypeDisplay() invocation

TextQuery tq = new TextQuery();
TypeDisplay( tq );
```

We can explicitly request the associated `Type` object by passing the static `GetType()` method of `Type` a string containing the name of the type:

```
public static void TypeDisplay( string t_name )
{
        Type t = Type.GetType( t_name );

        if ( t == null )
            // couldn't find it ...
            return;

        // ... OK: now we have metadata access
}

// an unqualified name ... note that it won't be found
// if the type is defined within a namespace
t.TypeDisplay( "Math" );

// a fully qualified name
t.TypeDisplay( "System.Math" );

// a fully qualified name and assembly
t.TypeDisplay( "System.Math, mscorlib" );
```

We can get all `Type` instances or a specific instance of a `Type` from an `Assembly` object. We saw an example of how to do this in the previous section.

The next step, once we have the `Type` object, is to retrieve the associated *Info* class objects. For example, imagine that we were curious about the type and the get or set accessibility of the `Length` property of the `string` class. How might we obtain that information?

First we grab the `Type` object of a `string` instance:

```
string s = "a simple string";
Type t = s.GetType();
```

Next we invoke the `GetProperty()` method of the `Type` class, specifying the `Length` property by name:

```
PropertyInfo pi = t.GetProperty( "Length" );
```

Now that we have the `PropertyInfo` object for the `Length` property, we can probe it as deeply as we wish. For example, the following output:

```
Length is of type Int32
Can Read? True
```

```
Can Write? False
Actual value is 15
```

is generated by the following code sequence:

```
Console.WriteLine( "{0} is of type {1}",
                    pi.Name, pi.PropertyType );

Console.WriteLine( "Can Read? {0}\nCan Write? {1}",
                    pi.CanRead, pi.CanWrite );

Console.WriteLine( "Actual value is {0}",
                    pi.GetValue( s, null ));
```

What if we had no idea which and how many properties the `string` class contained? How would we obtain that information? The `Type` class provides a pair of *Get* methods. One instance of the pair returns the *Info* object associated with a specified member; this is what we did with `GetProperty()`. The second instance by default retrieves all *public* members of the particular type as an array of *Info* objects. (If the invocation fails to retrieve any members, an empty array, not `null`, is returned.) To obtain the information for all properties, we use a method called `GetProperties()`:

```
PropertyInfo [] parray = t.GetProperties();
Console.WriteLine( "{0} has {1} properties",
                    t.FullName, parray.Length );
```

We can then iterate through the array, examining each element in turn:

```
foreach ( PropertyInfo pinfo in parray )
{
  // same Console.WriteLine as above ...
  Console.WriteLine("Actual value is {0}",
                    pi.GetValue(s,null));
}
```

Unfortunately, this last invocation of `GetValue()` results in an exception. The reason is that the `GetProperties()` method retrieves both properties *and* indexers. The second argument passed to `GetValue()` needs to be `null` for a property. For an indexer, however, the second argument must be an array holding the same number of values as the number of dimensions supported by the indexer. The value placed in the array represents the position from which to get the value. So for our code to work in general, we must do the following:

First we need to determine whether the `PropertyInfo` object addresses a property or an indexer. We do that by a call to `GetIndexParameters()`:

```
ParameterInfo [] pif = pinfo.GetIndexParameters();
```

If `pif` is `null`, the member addressed by `pinfo` is a property. Things are simple: We pass in a `null` second argument. Otherwise, `GetValue()` expects an array of type `object` for its second argument, with each element holding an appropriate value of each index type. How do we determine both the number and the type of the indexer parameters?

The length of the returned array represents the number of indices supported by the indexer. `ParameterInfo` provides the `ParameterType` property that returns a `Type` object for the parameter. The `Position` property indicates the position of the parameter. The position is zero-based. The first parameter, that is, is associated with a position value of 0.

```
ParameterInfo [] pif = pinfo.GetIndexParameters();

if ( pif.Length != 0 )
{
    Console.WriteLine( "{0} is an indexer of {1} indices",
                       pinfo.Name, pif.Length );

    foreach ( ParameterInfo parm in pif )
               Console.WriteLine( "index {0} is of type {1}",
                       parm.Position+1,
                       parm.ParameterType );
}
```

It turns out that the `string` class has two public properties: a `char` indexer of one dimension named `Chars`, and the `Length` property of type `int`. Here is the result of our query:

```
System.String has 2 properties

Chars is an indexer of 1 indices
index 1 is of type Int32
Chars is of type Char
```

```
Can Read? True
Can Write? False
First index value is A

Length is of type Int32
Can Read? True Can Write? False
The Property value is 15
```

Hopefully this discussion has illustrated at least in part how conceptually different runtime programming is from the compile-time programming that we have been doing throughout the rest of the text. Runtime programming requires greater attention to the implementation details of the type system. It provides a great deal of flexibility, but because of its interaction with the runtime environment, it is significantly slower in performance.

8.3   Modifying the Retrieval through `BindingFlags`

As it happens, the string class has five properties, only two of which are public. By default, the *Get* methods retrieve only public instance members—both inherited members and those declared in the class. We can use a `BindingFlags` `enum` object to override the default retrieval policy to retrieve both static and nonpublic members or to suppress retrieval of inherited members.

The `BindingFlags` enumerators provide instructions to the retrieval algorithm as to what members to consider. The default pair of `BindingFlags` enumerators consists of `Public` and `Instance`. If we want to retrieve the nonpublic members as well, we pass in the `NonPublic` enumerator.[1] The following, however, does not work:

```
PropertyInfo[] parray = t.GetProperties(BindingFlags.NonPublic);
```

This invocation always returns `null`, failing to retrieve anything. For this to work, we must also tell the algorithm which members to consider. To find all the nonpublic instance members, we apply the bitwise OR operator on the values:

```
BindingFlags f=BindingFlags.NonPublic | BindingFlags.Instance;
PropertyInfo[] parray = t.GetProperties( myFlags );
```

---

1. Provided that the `ReflectionPermission` security code permits access to nonpublic members. If it does not, an exception of type `SecurityException` is thrown.

To find all the static and instance properties—both public and nonpublic—we write the following:

```
// OK: retrieve all static and instance members
// that are public and nonpublic

BindingFlags bitmap = BindingFlags.Public|
                            BindingFlags.NonPublic;

// consider all static members
bitmap |= BindingFlags.Static;

// consider all instance members
bitmap |= BindingFlags.Instance;

PropertyInfo [] parray = t.GetProperties( bitmap );
```

The `LookupAll` enumerator provides a shorthand notation for the retrieval of all public and nonpublic static and instance members. The following call is the equivalent of the one we just made:

```
// OK: this is a shorthand notation:
// it also retrieves all public
// and nonpublic static and instance members

PropertyInfo[] parray = t.GetProperties(BindingFlags.LookupAll);
```

Generally we apply bitwise OR on the individual enumerators only when we wish to fine-tune our retrieval between the default of public instance members only and the all-inclusive retrieval of `LookupAll`.

The `NonPublic` and `LookupAll` values retrieve protected members of the base class. They do not retrieve the base-class private members.

Let's query the `String` class regarding its data members both with and without the `BindingFlags` argument.

The `FieldInfo` class holds information about a data member. By default, `GetFields()` is not likely to retrieve most class members; typically we define data members as private. For example, here is the result of invoking `Get-Fields()` on a string:

```
number of public string fields: 1
```

That's surprising. We would expect more than one field to be associated with the `String` class. When we invoke `GetFields()` with the `LookupAll` value as its argument:

```
fi = t.GetFields(BindingFlags.LookupAll);
Console.WriteLine( "total number of string fields: {0}",
                      fi.Length );
```

our retrieval is considerably more successful:

```
total number of string fields: 13
```

Some of the properties associated with the `FieldInfo` class include `Name`, `IsPublic`, `IsPrivate`, and `IsStatic`. (For some reason there is currently no property for protected access.) The following `foreach` loop reads each of these members:

```
foreach ( FieldInfo f in fi )
{
    Console.Write( "\t{0} :: ", f.Name );
    Console.Write( "{0} ",
            f.IsPublic
                    ? "public"
                    : f.IsPrivate
                    ? "private" : "property?" );

    Console.Write( "{0} ", f.IsStatic ? "static" : "" );
}
```

This loop generates the following output:

```
The 13 fields are as follows:
      m_arrayLength :: private
      m_stringLength :: private
      m_firstChar :: private
      Empty :: public static
      WhitespaceChars :: private static
      MASK_LENGTH :: private static
      MASK_CHARS :: private static
      HAS_NO_HIGH_CHARS :: private static
      HAS_HIGH_CHARS :: private static
      HIGH_CHARS_UNDETERMINED :: private static
      TrimHead :: private static
```

```
TrimTail :: private static
TrimBoth :: private static
```

Twenty enumerator values are defined within `BindingFlags`. Two others of interest are `DeclaredOnly`, which limits the retrieval to members defined in the class (no inherited members are retrieved), and `IgnoreCase`, which we optionally pass when retrieving a member by name. Each *Get* method supports an overloaded second instance, taking a second argument of type `BindingFlags`.

The `GetConstructors()` method retrieves public instance constructors only. To retrieve the static constructor as well, we must explicitly request the static instance, as follows:

```
// retrieves public constructors and
// the static constructor, if present
BindingFlags f = BindingFlags.Instance;
f |= BingingFlags.Static;
f |= BindingFlags.Public;

ConstructorInfo[] ci = t.GetConstructors(f);
```

To retrieve the nonpublic constructors as well, either we explicitly add the `Private` enumerator through a bitwise OR or we can use `LookupAll`. Because base-class constructors are not inherited, they are not retrieved.

How do we select an individual constructor? We can't just give its name; all constructors share the same name. What distinguishes a constructor is its signature. That's what we must pass in. To retrieve an individual constructor, we create and pass in an array of `Type` objects representing the type of each parameter of the constructor. The following code shows two examples. The first retrieves a constructor that takes no arguments, or `null` if this constructor is not present. The second retrieves a constructor that takes a `string` first argument and an `int` second argument:

```
// first we define the two arrays
static Type [] nullSignature = new Type[0];

static Type [] stringIntSignature = new Type[]{
        Type.GetType("System.String", true ),
        Type.GetType("System.Int32" )
};
```

```
ConstructorInfo ctor = t.GetConstructor( nullSignature );
if ( ctor != null ){ ... }

ctor = t.GetConstructor( stringIntSignature );
if ( ctor != null ){ ... }
```

This is also true of overloaded functions. We cannot distinguish between two overloaded instances of a function named `Print()` by the name alone. Rather we must pass in a second argument identifying the signature of the instance we wish to retrieve. This second argument is an array of `Type` objects representing each parameter in turn—for example,

```
MethodInfo mi = t.GetMethod( "Print", stringIntSignature );
```

To get all the class methods (but *not* constructors), we use `GetMethods()`. This method returns an array of `MethodInfo` objects. If the type has no methods, an empty array is returned.

So far we have retrieved members of only a certain kind—all properties, for example, or all constructors. If we want to retrieve every member unconditionally, we use the `GetMembers()` method. By default, `GetMembers()` returns only public static and instance members. We can override the default, of course, by passing in a second argument of type `BindingFlags`.

There is also a `GetMember(string)` method. If a member with the specified name is found, `GetMember()` returns a `MemberInfo` array rather than a single object. The reason is that a method's name may be overloaded. If no member with the name is found, `null` is returned rather than an empty array.

8.4   Invoking a Method during Runtime

The overloaded `Invoke()` method of the `MethodInfo` and `ConstructorInfo` classes allows us to execute the member reflected by the object of either class. To do this, we must build up an object array with the parameters to pass into the method. If it is an instance method, we must also provide an object of that type. Let's look at an example.

Our method has the following signature and return type:

```
static public bool
invokeMethod( string type, string method, object[] args ){}
```

First we retrieve a `Type` object of the specified type. If it cannot be found, we return `false`:

```
Type t = Type.GetType( type );
if ( t == null )
    return false;
```

Next we retrieve the method. Again, if we can't find it, we return `false`. (I can easily imagine an argument for throwing an exception instead in these two cases. We'll consider that option at the end of this section.):

```
MethodInfo mi = t.GetMethod( method );
if ( mi == null )
    return false;
```

If the method is static, we can invoke it without further work because a static method does not require an object of the class:

```
if ( mi.IsStatic )
    mi.Invoke( null, args );
```

If the method is nonstatic, however, we have to come up with an object of the type in order to invoke the method. It turns out to be very easy to do this—for example,

```
if ( mi.IsStatic == false ){
    object o = Activator.CreateInstance( t );
    mi.Invoke( o, args );
}
```

The `Activator` class is defined within the `System` namespace. It provides a set of methods to create a local or a remote object given a `Type` object. By default, it invokes the no-argument constructor of the associated type, if defined, to initialize the object. Alternatively, we can build up an object array of argument values to be passed to the matching constructor.

The `Invoke()` method returns an object holding the return value of the method, or `null` if the method has a `void` return type. Our current implementation ignores that value, and users may complain. A more appropriate implementation of our method returns the value returned by `Invoke()`. To indicate failure, rather than returning a `false` value, we now throw an exception:

```
static public object
invokeMethod( string type, string method, object[] args )
{
    Type t = Type.GetType( type );
    if ( t == null )
        throw Exception("Unable to find type "+type);

    MethodInfo mi = t.GetMethod( method );
    if ( mi == null )
        throw Exception("Unable to find method "+method);

    if ( mi.IsStatic )
        return mi.Invoke( null, args );

    object o = Activator.CreateInstance( t );
    return mi.Invoke( o, args );
}
```

In addition to the `Invoke()` method of the `MethodInfo` class, there is a `GetValue()` and `SetValue()` pair of methods in the `FieldInfo` class that allows us to read and write the reflected field.

Invoking the get or set accessor of a property is a two-step process:

1. We retrieve a `MethodInfo` object for the *get* accessor through the `PropertyInfo` method `GetGetMethod()`. For the *set* accessor, we use `GetSetMethod()`.

2. We invoke the `Invoke()` method of the `MethodInfo` object.

8.5   Delegating the Test to Reflection

In the introduction to the `delegate` type in Section 2.12, there is a brief discussion of a `testHarness` class. `testHarness` maintains a static delegate member in which other classes register test functions they wish executed. It looks like this:

```
public delegate void Action();
public class testHarness
{
    static private Action theAction;
    static public Action Tester
        { get{ return theAction;  }
          set{ theAction = value; }}
```

```
        static private void reSet() { theAction = null; }
        static public  int  count()
            { return theAction != null
                ? theAction.GetInvocationList().Length : 0; }

        // ...
    }
```

By convention, a class wishing to register one or more member functions with `Tester` does so within the static constructor of the class—for example,

```
public class testHashtable
{
    public void test0(){ ... }
    public void test1(){ ... }

    static testHashtable()
    {
        testHarness.Tester += new testHarness.Action( test0 );
        testHarness.Tester += new testHarness.Action( test1 );
    }

    // ...
}
```

The program entry point invokes the `testHarness` static `run()` member function. `run()` tests whether the delegate addresses any functions; if it does, `run()` executes them and then resets the delegate:

```
public class EntryPoint
{
    public static void Main(){ testHarness.run(); }
    // ...
}

public class testHarness
{
    public static void run()
    {
        if ( Tester != null )
            { Tester(); reset(); }
    }

    // ...
}
```

There is one piece missing, however, in order for this to work. Our strategy depends on the invocation of the static constructor of each class wishing to register its test methods. Moreover, these constructors must be invoked before `run()` executes. Because `run()` is the first statement of the `Main()` entry point, we don't have much working space to get this done. So there are two questions we need to answer:

1. Where can we get the work done, in order to ensure that `run()` is invoked prior to the first statement of `Main()`?

2. What work, exactly, needs to be done to guarantee the invocation of the appropriate static constructors?

There is only one absolutely certain place that we can locate the work we need to get done. We are guaranteed that the `testHarness` static constructor is invoked before `run()` is evaluated within `Main()`. This is exactly the time when our work needs to be done. This is where we place it.

What does the work consist of? First we need to discover all the types within the application. These classes potentially have test methods they wish to register.

Next we need to trigger the execution of the type's static constructor. We do this by creating an instance of the type. As an optimization, we check if the type is part of the predefined .NET framework, and if so, we do not create an instance.

This will take some time, of course, but we're testing, so time is not terribly critical. Moreover, we save staff time by automating the test process.

To discover the types present in an executable, we first retrieve the assemblies associated with the application—for example,

```
AppDomain appdomain    = AppDomain.CurrentDomain;
Assembly [] assemblies = appdomain.GetAssemblies();
```

`GetAssemblies()` returns an array of `Assembly` class objects that have been loaded into the application. We can then filter out the `System` assemblies:

```
foreach ( Assembly a in assemblies )
{
     if ( isSystemAssembly( a ))
          continue;
```

The remaining assemblies may contain classes that wish to register test functions to be executed. For each assembly we invoke `GetTypes()` to retrieve an array of the `Type` objects contained within the assembly. We then iterate across and create an instance of the types:

```
Type [] t = a.GetTypes();

foreach ( Type tt in t )
        if ( tt.isClass )
                Activator.CreateInstance( tt );
}
```

The `CreateInstance()` linvocation triggers the invocation of the associated static constructor of the class, if defined, which in turn populates the `test.Tester` delegate before `test.run()` executes.

There are other design strategies, of course. We could have the class register its name, or pass in its type, or somehow make itself known to `testHarness`. I wanted to try something in which the classes themselves are passive. Their mere presence seems to magically cause instances to be created and the tests to be executed.

8.6 Attributes

Attributes serve as *meta*declarative information. C# supports several predefined (sometimes called *intrinsic*) attributes. In addition, the programmer can define new attribute types. These can be retrieved and queried at runtime through type reflection. Both the intrinsic and user-defined attributes are classes, although their syntax appears text based. Before we look at how we can define our own attribute types, let's briefly review the intrinsic attributes.

8.6.1 The Intrinsic `Conditional` Attribute

The `Conditional` attribute enables us to define class methods that are conditionally invoked on the basis of whether an associated string is defined. (We cannot, however, place a `Conditional` attribute on data members or properties.) The attribute is placed within brackets ([,]) preceding the method it modifies. For example, the methods `open_debug_output()` and `display()` are provided with the `Conditional` attribute:

```
using System.Diagnostics;
public class string_length : IComparer
{
    [Conditional( "DEBUG" )]
    private void open_debug_output()
    {
        FileStream fout =
            new FileStream("debug.txt", FileMode.Create );
        of = new StreamWriter( fout );
    }

    [Conditional( "DEBUG" )]
    public void display( string xs, string ys, int ret_val )
    {
        of.WriteLine("inside conditional function display()!");
        of.WriteLine("word #1: {0} : {1} ", xs, xs.Length);
        of.WriteLine("word #2: {0} : {1} ", ys, ys.Length);
        of.WriteLine("return value: {0} ",  ret_val);
    }

    // not allowed: conditional data member
    // [Conditional( "DEBUG" )]
    private StreamWriter of;
}
```

The string within parentheses always refers to a #define statement. For example, for the Conditional attribute to evaluate as true, we write

```
#define DEBUG
```

The use of #undef undefines a name—for example,

```
#undef DEBUG
```

Because the preprocessor commands must occur before any C# statements, we cannot nest a #undef command within our code. The methods themselves are invoked unconditionally, although they may or may not be invoked at all—for example,

```
public class string_length : IComparer
{
    public string_length(){
        // if DEBUG is defined, this executes
        open_debug_output();
    }
```

```
public int Compare( object x, object y )
{
        if (( ! ( x is string )) || ( ! ( y is string )))
            throw new ArgumentException("both must be strings");

        string xs = (string) x, ys = (string) y;
        int ret_val = 1;

        // calculate result in ret_val

        // if DEBUG is defined, this executes
        display( xs, ys, ret_val );

        return ret_val;
    }
}
```

If the `Conditional` string is not defined, invocations of the `Conditional` methods within our code are ignored.

8.6.2 The Intrinsic `Serializable` Attribute

The `Serializable` attribute indicates that a class can be serialized. *Serialization* is the persisting of an object beyond the lifetime of our executable, preserving the current state of the object for subsequent reloading. We can serialize to a particular storage device, such as a hard disk, or to a remote computer. In addition, we can specify that individual fields are to be `NonSerialized`. For example, here is a `Matrix` class defined as `Serializable`, but with its `out_stream` members marked as `NonSerialized`:

```
[ Serializable ]
class Matrix
{
    [ NonSerialized ]
    private string out_stream;

    float [,] mat;
}
```

Now that we've marked our class as `Serializable`, how do we serialize the thing? Here is an example of serializing a class object to and from a disk file—but without any error checking. This requires amazingly little work on our part.

First let's serialize the object to disk. We'll use the `BinaryFormatter` class defined within the nested `Binary` namespace. The serialization is done through `BinaryFormatter`'s `Serialize()` method:

```
using System.Runtime.Serialization.Formatters.Binary;
using System.IO;
public void ToDisk()
{
    Stream s = new File( out_stream ).Open(FileMode.Create);
    BinaryFormatter bfm = new BinaryFormatter();
    bfm.Serialize( s, this );
    s.Close();
}
```

The reverse operation, restoring a serialized object from disk, is done through the `Deserialize()` method of `BinaryFormatter`:

```
public void FromDisk( string filename )
{
    Stream s = (new File (filename)).Open(FileMode.Open);
    BinaryFormatter bfm = new BinaryFormatter();
    Matrix m = (Matrix) bfm.Deserialize(s);
    s.Close();

    mat = m.mat;
    out_stream = filename;
}
```

To work for every type, `Deserialize()` must return an `object` type. This is why we must explicitly downcast it to the `Matrix` type.

8.6.3   The Intrinsic `DllImport` Attribute

The `DllImport` attribute allows us to invoke a method that has not been built under .NET. For example, we'd like to implement a simple start/stop `Timer` class to instrument the duration of selected routines.[2] The underlying routines are unmanaged methods of the Win32 API. Here is the declaration of the two functions within the `Timer` class:

---

2. When the Counter class was removed from an earlier beta version of the .NET framework, Eric Gunnerson, author of *A Programmer's Introduction to C#* (Apress, 2000), kindly shared his own Counter class, which I dumbed down a bit for the simpler `Timer` semantics.

```
public class Timer
{
    private long    m_elapsedCount;
    private long    m_startCount;
    private string m_context;

    [System.Runtime.InteropServices.DllImport("KERNEL32")]
    private static extern bool
            QueryPerformanceCounter(ref long cnt);

    [System.Runtime.InteropServices.DllImport("KERNEL32")]
    private static extern bool
            QueryPerformanceFrequency(ref long frq);
}
```

The functions are declared `extern` because they are defined externally. We declare them, but of course we do not provide a definition. They can be private, public, or anything in between. We invoke them just as we would an ordinary member function—for example,

```
public class Timer
{
    public void start() {
            m_startCount = 0;
            QueryPerformanceCounter(ref startCount);
    }

    public void stop() {
        long stopCount = 0;
        QueryPerformanceCounter( ref stopCount );
        m_elapsedCount = ( stopCount - m_startCount );
    }

    public override string ToString()
    {
            long freq = 0;
            QueryPerformanceFrequency( ref freq );
            float seconds = m_elapsedCount
                    ? (float) m_elapsedCount / (float) freq
                    : 0.f;
            return m_context + " : " +
                    seconds.ToString() + " secs.";
    }
    // ...
}
```

In our `WordCount` program of Chapter 1, we use the `Timer` class as follows:

```
private void writeWords()
{
    Timer tt = null;³
    if ( m_spy )
    {
        tt = new Timer();
        tt.context = "Time to write file ";
        tt.start();
    }

    // ... the actual writing goes here ...

    if ( m_spy )
    {
        tt.stop();
        m_times.Add( tt.ToString() );
    }
}
```

where `m_spy` is an option the user can set on the command line, `m_times` is an `ArrayList` object into which we add the timing strings of the instrumented routines, and `context` is a public property of the `Timer` class encapsulating the `m_context` string data member.

8.7 Implementing Our Own `Attribute` Class

An attribute is actually an instance of a class. We can introduce our own attributes, provided that the class representing an attribute inherits either directly or indirectly from the `System.Attribute` class. In addition, for nonabstract classes there must be at least one public constructor, and the class must have public accessibility. Here is a simple attribute class suggested from the Microsoft documentation. It defines an `Author` attribute that allows the programmer to tag her code with metadata attributes such as the implementor's name, the code version, and comment:

---

3. Although the program logic does not require an explicit initialization of `tt`, its absence causes the compiler to flag the second `if` statement as a use of an uninitialized object. See Section 1.8 for a discussion of the static flow analysis used by the compiler.

```
[AttributeUsage( AttributeTargets.ClassMembers,
                 AllowMultiple = true )]

public class AuthorAttribute: Attribute
{
      public AuthorAttribute( string nm )
          { name = nm; version = 1.0; }

      public string name
      {
            get{ return m_name; }
            set{ m_name = value; }
      }

      public double version
      {
            get{ return m_version;  }
            set{ m_version = value; }
      }

      public string comment
      {
            get{ return m_comment;  }
            set{ m_comment = value; }
      }

      private string m_name;
      private string m_comment;
      private double m_version;
}
```

The `AttributeUsage` attribute:

```
[AttributeUsage( AttributeTargets.ClassMembers,
                 AllowMultiple = true )]
```

prescribes where an `Author` attribute can occur. The `ClassMembers` enumerator allows the attribute to be placed on any member of a `class`, `struct`, or `enum`, as well as on the type itself.

By default, only one instance of an attribute can be associated with an entity. But because code may have many authors, we need to signal that we allow multiple entries. This is what the `AllowMultiple` named parameter does.

Here's a class heavily decorated both with the `Author` attribute and the intrinsic `Serializable` attribute:

```
[Author( "Anna Lippman', comment = "new hire; first project" )]
[Serializable]
class testAttributes
{

    [Author( "Kenny Meyer", version=2.0,
            comment = "added threading support" ) ]

    [Author( "Danny Lippman", version=1.1 )]
    static public bool doit(){ return true; }

    [Author( "Kenny Meyer", version=2.0,
            comment = "extensibility for user" ) ]

    public virtual void display() { /* ... */ }
}
```

You might wonder why I didn't write out the full name of the attribute:

```
// unnecessary ...
[AuthorAttribute ( "Anna Lippman" )]
```

By convention the name of an attribute is internally suffixed with *Attribute*. So when we write `Author`, the compiler understands it as `AuthorAttribute`. It's a syntactic convenience to save us some typing.

There is little to be gained from using custom attributes unless a mechanism is in place to retrieve these attributes at runtime. And of course there is. For example, here is some sample output retrieving our `Author` attributes from the `testAttributes` type:

```
There are 1 attributes associated with testAttributes
Author Attribute: Anna Lippman :: version 1.00
        new hire; first project

There are 7 members associated with testAttributes
There are 1 attributes associated with display
Author Attribute: Kenny Meyer :: version 2.00
        extensibility for user
There are 0 attributes associated with GetHashCode
```

```
There are 0 attributes associated with Equals
There are 0 attributes associated with ToString
There are 2 attributes associated with doit
Author Attribute: Danny Lippman :: version 1.10
Author Attribute: Kenny Meyer :: version 2.00
        added threading support
There are 0 attributes associated with GetType
There are 0 attributes associated with .ctor
```

Notice that when multiple attributes are attached to the same member, they are retrieved from the bottom up under the assumption that those closest to the member are the oldest.

In the subsections that follow, let's see if we can make sense of all this.

8.7.1 Positional and Named Parameters

Positional parameters in an attribute declaration are those values required by the attribute constructor(s). In our example, only the author's name is a positional parameter. It must be present in every `Author` attribute instance.

Named parameters represent public property (or public data members) of the `Attribute` class. These may be optionally set in an attribute instance. They take the form of an assignment to the named member—for example,

```
name = expression
```

In our example there are two named parameters: `version` and `comment`. These may or may not be provided with explicit values in an `Author` attribute. If they are present, they must come after the positional parameters in a comma-separated list.

Named parameters can be listed in any order, provided that they follow the positional parameters—for example,

```
[Author( "Kenny Meyer", version = 2.0,
        comment = "added threading support" ) ]
```

Because the order in which the named parameters is listed is not significant, the following attribute is equivalent to the previous one:

```
[Author( "Kenny Meyer", comment = "added threading support",
        version = 2.0 )]
```

8.7.2 `AttributeUsage`

We use the `AttributeUsage` attribute to identify the locations where users can place an instance of our attribute. By default, the attribute can be placed anywhere.

The placement choices are defined within the `AttributeTargets` enum. These include `Parameter`, indicating that the attribute can be used to tag a method parameter; `Return`, to tag the return value of a method; `Constructor`, `Method`, `Property`, `Field`, `Event`, and `Delegate`. In addition, we can specify a `class`, `struct`, `enum`, or interface. `ALL` allows placement anywhere.

To compose an explicit set of allowed positions where the attribute can be placed, we bitwise-OR the enumerator values:

```
[AttributeUsage( AttributeTargets.Class |
                AttributeTargets.Struct )]
```

This permits the usage of this attribute only on the general `class` or `struct`. An attempt to decorate a method or field is flagged as an error.

A named parameter of `AttributeUsage` is `AllowMultiple`. When set to `true`, multiple instances of an attribute can be attached to the same location.

8.8 Runtime Discovery of Attributes Using Reflection

Now that we've decorated our classes with custom attributes, we'll want to access them during the execution of our program. There are several ways to do that. For example, we can invoke the static `GetCustomAttributes()` method of the `Attribute` class, passing it a `Type` object:

```
static public void retrieveClass1( object obj )
{
    Type tp = obj.GetType();

    Attribute [] attrs =
                Attribute.GetCustomAttributes( tp );
```

An `Attribute` array holding an instance of each custom attribute retrieved is returned. If no custom attributes are present, an empty array is returned. Note that intrinsic attributes are not retrieved. For example, the intrinsic `Serializable` attribute of our class is not returned.

The instance `GetCustomAttributes()` method of the `Type` class can also be used. This method, however, returns a more general object array:

```
static public void retrieveClass2( object obj )
{
    Type tp = obj.GetType();
    object [] attrs = tp.GetCustomAttributes();
```

Both instances of `GetCustomAttributes()` return an array of all custom attributes associated with the type. If we are looking for a specific type, such as `Author`, we can use either the `is` operator or the `as` runtime operator:

```
Attribute [] attrs = Attribute.GetCustomAttributes( tp );

foreach( Attribute attr in attrs )
    if ( attr is AuthorAttribute )
    {
            AuthorAttribute auth = (AuthorAttribute) attr;
            Console.WriteLine(
                "Author Attribute: {0} :: version {1:F}",
                auth.name, auth.version );

        if ( auth.comment != null )
                Console.WriteLine( "\t{0}", auth.comment );
    }
```

Because we're interested in only the `Author` attribute, it would be simpler to retrieve only instances of that attribute. We do that by passing in a `Type` object of the attribute that interests us. An object array is returned filled with the matching instances, if any—for example,

```
static public void retrieveMembers( object obj )
{
    Type tp = obj.GetType();
    MemberInfo [] mi = tp.GetMembers();

    // prepare to select retrieval type
    Type attrType = Type.GetType( "AuthorAttribute" );

    foreach( MemberInfo m in mi )
    {
        // retrieve only AuthorAttribute instances
        object [] attrs = m.GetCustomAttributes( attrType );
```

```
        if ( attrs.Length == 0 )
            continue;

    foreach( object o in attrs )
    {
            string msg = "Author Attribute: {0} :: version {1:F}";
            AuthorAttribute auth = (AuthorAttribute) o;
            Console.WriteLine(msg, auth.name, auth.version);
            if ( auth.comment != null )
                Console.WriteLine( "\t{0}", auth.comment );
    }
}
```

Intrinsic attributes are currently not retrievable.

8.9   The Intermediate Language

When we compile a C# program, the code generated does not execute; it is not a machine assembly language. Rather it is a machine-independent *intermediate language (IL)* representation of our program.[4]

All .NET languages are compiled into the IL. This means that at the IL level, all language code looks pretty much the same. There are two primary benefits to compiling all .NET languages into a common intermediate language. The first, of course, is real language interoperability—not only at the binary level, but at the source level as well. Not only can we combine modules written in different .NET languages, but we can make use of and inherit from classes defined within different .NET languages.

The second benefit is in having a language-neutral code base upon which to target tools. The delivery of a tool built on top of the IL should work with each .NET language through a common interface.

The one caveat is that not all languages support all the features of the IL. C#, for example, supports unsigned types. VB.NET (Visual Basic) does not. C# recognizes upper- and lowercase when distinguishing identifiers. VB.NET does not. To promote language interoperability, .NET defines a Common Language

---

4. For details of the intermediate language beyond the discussion in this section, see *The IL Assembly Language Programmers' Reference* and *The MSIL Instruction Set Specification* within the `Program Files/Microsoft.NET/FrameworkSDK/Tool Developers Guide/docs` folder.

Specification (CLS). The CLS represents the basic features common to a broad range of languages. To know if your code is CLS compliant, you can set the CLSCompliant assembly attribute to true:

```
[CLSCompliant( true )]
```

Noncompliant code triggers a compile-time error when CLSCompliant is set to true.[5]

8.9.1 Examining the Intermediate Language

As we've discussed, the primary difference between a value and a reference type is that a value type stores its data directly within its object, while the reference type is separated into a handle/object pair. The handle is allocated locally; the object is allocated on the managed heap. As an illustration of the intermediate language representation, let's look at the code generated to support the definition of a struct value type and a class reference type:

```
structDef sd = new structDef(1, 2, 3);
classDef  cd = new classDef( 1, 2, 3);
```

The intermediate language uses an evaluation stack for both load and store. Each method maintains a local stack. Upon method entry, the stack is empty.

Load instructions (ld*) copy values from memory to the evaluation stack. Store instructions (st*) copy values from the stack back to memory. Arguments passed to other methods and their return values are also pushed onto and popped from the evaluation stack.

Each method maintains an array to hold locally defined objects. It is named .locals. The struct value type sd, together with the handle portion of the cd reference type, is placed in this array:

```
.locals (
    [0] value class structDef sd,
    [1] class classDef cd,

    . . .
)
```

---

5. See the Cross-Language Interoperability section of the *.NET Framework Developer's Guide* for a discussion of the Common Language Specification and writing CLS-compliant code.

Here is the code sequence to initialize the `struct` value type `sd`. It's quite simple: `sd` is loaded onto the stack, followed by the three constant literals. Then the constructor is invoked. Because the instructions are difficult to read, I've added the source code with comments set off by three slashes (`///`):

```
/// source line: structDef sd = new structDef( 1, 2, 3 );

/// the ldloca instruction pushes the address of the local
/// object onto the stack

ldloca.s    sd

/// the ldc instruction pushes a constant number onto the
/// stack; i4 represents the type - in this case, a 4-byte
/// integer; the last digit represents the literal value
///
/// so the next three instructions push 1, 2, 3 onto the
/// stack; these represent the arguments to the constructor

ldc.i4.1
ldc.i4.2
ldc.i4.3

/// an invocation of the three-argument constructor;
/// it pulls the three arguments and the object to
/// initialize from the stack

call instance void structDef::.ctor(int32,int32,int32)
```

The reference type is more complicated to initialize because it must be allocated on the heap. The `newobj` instruction allocates memory on the heap and then calls the class constructor. `newobj` returns a reference to the object on the heap, which is stored in the local handle:

```
///  source line: classDef cd = new classDef(1,2,3);

/// load the constant literals on the stack
ldc.i4.1
ldc.i4.2
ldc.i4.3

/// the constructor to be called is specified as part of
```

```
/// the newobj instruction; the parameters accepted by the
/// constructor are pulled from the stack
newobj instance void classDef::.ctor(int32, int32, int32)

/// store the heap object reference at index 1 of .locals
stloc.1
```

This should give you something of the flavor of the intermediate language. It can be quite interesting to explore in order to discover how various constructs are implemented. To help in your navigation, Visual Studio.NET comes with the intermediate language *disassembler:* `ildasm`.

Keep in mind that the intermediate language representation is a storage mechanism. It is not interpreted when our programs run. Rather, prior to execution the IL is compiled into machine assembly for the target host. This is what is executed.

8.9.2 The `ildasm` Tool

Several tools work with the intermediate language representation. One is `ildasm`,[6] the intermediate language disassembler. As a learning tool, it allows us to disassemble and inspect the IL code and view the metadata associated with our assembly. For example, Figure 8.1 captures a portion of the `ildasm` *tree view* of the core system library assembly `mscorlib.dll`. To understand the geometric icons, refer to Figure 8.2.

The tree view provides a hierarchical view of the types within the assembly organized by namespace. All types and nested namespaces are listed for each namespace. All members of each type are listed. If we double-click on an atomic icon, such as the red triangle property icon of the `ICollection` member `Count`, a window pops up with additional information. Figure 8.3 pictures the window that displays when we double-click on `Count`. We see that it's of type `int`, that it provides only a `get` accessor, and that it is nonstatic. If we double-click on a method, the window that pops up displays the IL instructions. (I'll leave that as an exercise for the reader.)

---

6. Currently, `ildasm.exe` and the many other .NET tools are located in the directory `%windir%\Microsoft.NET\Framework\v1.0.xxxx`, where xxxx is the build number of the .NET framework you are using.

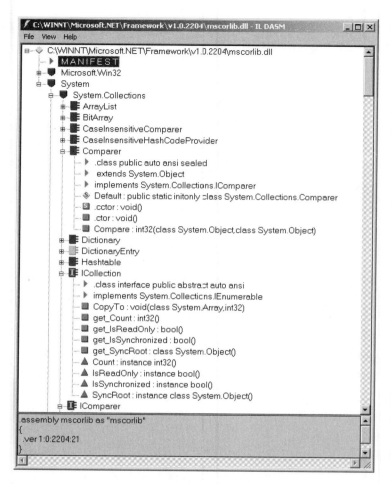

Figure 8.1 Tree View of `mscorlib.dll`

`ildasm` runs in both a default and an advanced mode. The advanced mode provides additional access to metadata information about the assembly.

The following command brings it up in default mode :

```
C:\WIN\Microsoft.NET\Framework\v1.0.2914\ildasm.exe
```

Adding `/adv` following `ildasm.exe` brings it up in advanced mode.

```
C:\WIN\Microsoft.NET\Framework\v1.0.2914\ildasm.exe /adv
```

Either command can be executed within either a *Command Prompt* window, or within the *Run* dialog box.

C# PRIMER

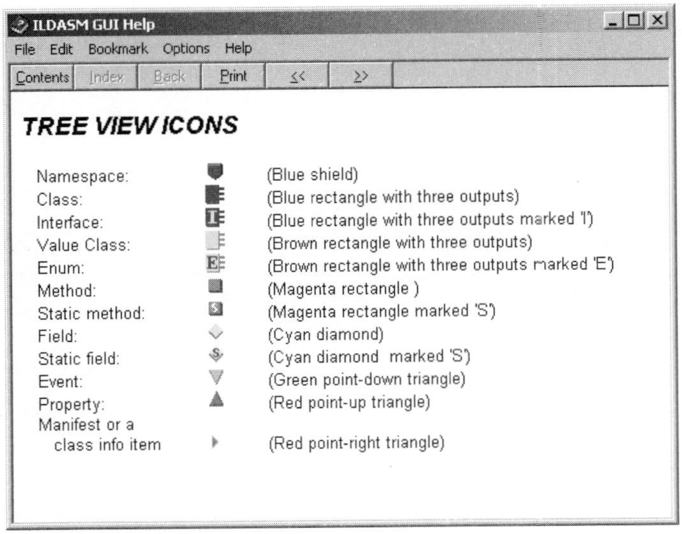

File   Edit   Bookmark   Options   Help

Contents | Index | Back | Print | << | >>

TREE VIEW ICONS

Namespace:		(Blue shield)
Class:		(Blue rectangle with three outputs)
Interface:		(Blue rectangle with three outputs marked 'I')
Value Class:		(Brown rectangle with three outputs)
Enum:		(Brown rectangle with three outputs marked 'E')
Method:		(Magenta rectangle)
Static method:		(Magenta rectangle marked 'S')
Field:		(Cyan diamond)
Static field:		(Cyan diamond marked 'S')
Event:		(Green point-down triangle)
Property:		(Red point-up triangle)
Manifest or a class info item		(Red point-right triangle)

Figure 8.2   Tree View Icon Help

The **View** menu item allows us to set various display attributes, such as the following:

- *Sort by Name:* Sort the items in tree view by name.

- *Show Public:* Show the items having public accessibility.

- *Show Private:* Show the items having private accessibility.

- *Show Assembly:* Show the items having assembly accessibility.

- *Show Source Lines:* Show the original source code along with IL.

- *Show Statistics* (advanced mode only): Show file statistics.

- *Show MetaInfo:* (advanced mode only): Show the metadata in a disassembly window.

`ildasm` is a great learning tool. It offers us the chance to peek under the hood, so to speak. I find myself going to the intermediate language when I am studying a particular language feature and wishing to confirm my understanding.

For example, while I understand the dfferent behaviors of a reference and value type when assigned to an `object` type or when initialized through a `new` expression, seeing the actual intermediate mplementation serves as icing on the cake.

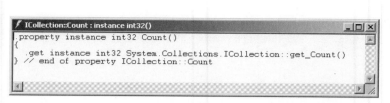

```
ICollection::Count : instance int32()                    _ □ ×
.property instance int32 Count()
{
  .get instance int32 System.Collections.ICollection::get_Count()
} // end of property ICollection::Count
```

Figure 8.3   Result of Double-Clicking on Property Member `Count`

`ildasm` provides a good way of confirming that what you think is actually happening is actually happening!

C# PRIMER

Index

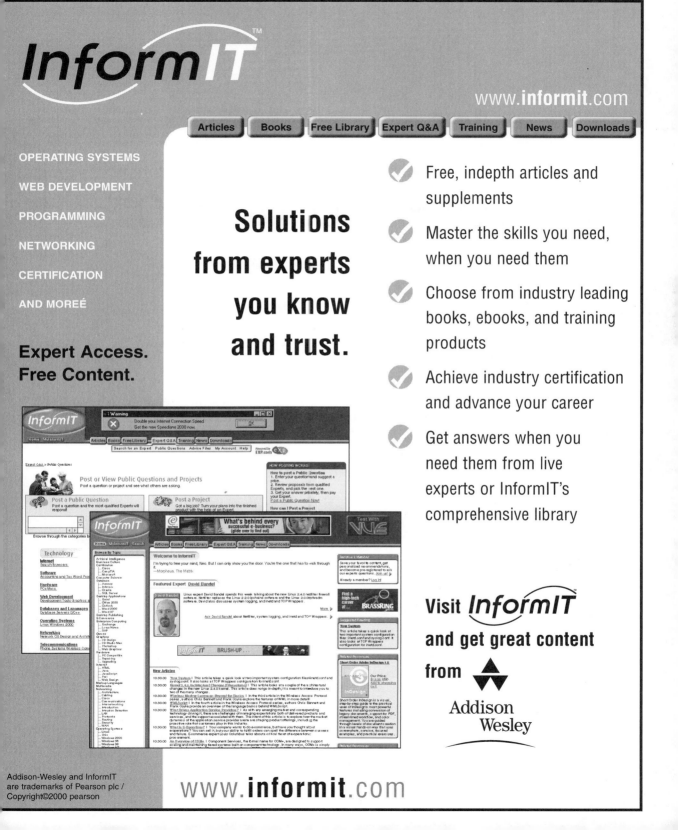